CHILD WELFARE PROFESSIONALS AND INCEST FAMILIES

WELFARE AND SOCIETY
STUDIES IN WELFARE POLICY, PRACTICE AND THEORY

Series Editors:
Matthew Colton, Kevin Haines, Tim Stainton and Anthea Symonds
School of Social Sciences and International Development,
University of Wales Swansea

Welfare and Society is an exciting series from the University of Wales Swansea, School of Social Sciences and International Development in conjunction with Ashgate, concerned with all aspects of social welfare. The series publishes works of research, theory, history and practice from a wide range of contemporary applied social studies subjects such as Criminal Justice, Child Welfare, Community Care, Race and Ethnicity, Therapeutic and Intervention Techniques, Community Development and Social Policy. The series includes extended research reports of scholarly interest as well as works aimed at both the academic and professional communities.

Child Welfare Professionals and Incest Families

A difficult encounter

INGRID K. THOMPSON-COOPER
School of Social Work
McGill University, Canada

Ashgate

Aldershot • Burlington USA • Singapore • Sydney

Published by
Ashgate Publishing Limited
Gower House
Croft Road
Aldershot
Hants GU11 3HR
England

Ashgate Publishing Company
131 Main Street
Burlington, VT 05401-5600 USA

Ashgate website: http://www.ashgate.com

British Library Cataloguing in Publication Data
Thompson-Cooper, Ingrid K.
    Child welfare professionals and incest families : a
    difficult encounter. - (Welfare & society)
    1.Child sexual abuse - England - Case studies 2.Child
    sexual abuse - Canada - Case studies 3.Family violence -
    England - Case studies 4.Family violence - Canada - Case
    studies 5.Child welfare workers - England - Case studies
    6.Child welfare workers - Canada - Case studies
    I.Title
    362.7'653'0942

Library of Congress Control Number: 00-134489

ISBN 1 85628 880 3

Printed and bound by
Antony Rowe Ltd, Chippenham, Wiltshire

Contents

Figures and Tables

Preface

The professional response to reports of sexual abuse of children by members of their family has become a topic of much public concern and controversy. A balance has to be struck between the conflicting aims of identifying and punishing the abuser, comforting and protecting the child and helping to preserve a functional family unit. After the 'discovery' of child sexual abuse in the 1970s and the development of child abuse reporting laws, there was a dramatic increase in the number of disclosed cases and child welfare professionals were forced to quickly develop policies regarding interventions in these cases. However, instead of relying on the therapeutic models of practice already developed for child physical abuse, they have tended to adopt a punitive approach, with heavy relaince on the criminal justice system. This can be traumatic for everyone including the victim and healing difficult. This more intrusive approach to child sexual abuse seems to have been reactive rather than rational and based, perhaps, on the taboo nature of the behavior. Little research has been done on the nature of the decision-making by child welfare professionals in these cases or on the impact of the different approaches on victims and their families.

The present research is a detailed study of two samples of cases of intrafamilial child sexual abuse and how they were dealt with, one in an area of England, the other in Canada. It was hoped to contribute empirical input to the issues under debate, in particular to the controversy between supporters of a primarily punitive approach utilising the criminal justice system and advocates of more informal, therapeutic interventions. The research permitted a comparison of a system which relied heavily on criminal prosecution to handle the cases (England) and a more treatment oriented system that depended primarily on child welfare and clinical services (Canada).

The present study examines the extent and nature of the incestuous abuse, how it was disclosed and the initial responses of the professionals. It then looks at how the disclosed cases are processed through the child welfare and criminal justice systems with a focus on the decisions made throughout the process and their outcome including interventions and the impact on the family. The type and length of treatment modalities as well as the nature of the social service contacts with the family is also examined. An effort was made to determine what factors influence the legal and clinical decisions that are made by the various professionals.

The research was carried out as part of doctoral studies at the Institute of Criminology at the University of Cambridge, England. I am greatly indebted to Donald West, Professor Emeritus, for his prompt and helpful criticism of the work at all stages and for his patience and encouragement. I am also grateful to Dr. Cyril Greenland for his support for the initial conception of the research and for his continued interest in the project. The study could not have been completed without access to a number of agencies and departments in Northamptonshire, England and Montreal, Canada. The senior managers and staff were consistently hospitable and helpful. I am particularly grateful to Paul Griffiths, former director of the NSPCC in Northampton, who greatly facilitated my access to the different agencies and services. I benefited, as well, from his knowledge and experience in the child welfare field. I am most grateful also to Tom Woodhouse for his assistance in processing the data by computer and to Professor Sydney Duder for providing guidance in some of the analysis of the data. My sincere thanks are offered to the staff of the Institute of Criminology, Cambridge, for their hospitality and for the intellectual stimulation they provided. I am particularly indebted to Loraine Gelsthorpe, Allison Morris, and Pam Paige for their helpful support and to Betty Arnold and Jean Taylor for their assistance in the library.

I am especially grateful to the late Peggy Quirk who started the onerous task of preparing a camera ready copy of the manuscript. A very special debt of gratitude is owed to Ann Stewart for her meticulous preparation of the manuscript on the word processor. Her patience and cheerfulness, often under very difficult personal circumstances, and expert work carried the project through to its completion. We became friends and the book became 'our book'. Finally, I am very appreciative of the love and support my family and friends have given me throughout.

Table of Statutes

List of Abbreviations

RAPSCAN	British Association for the Study and Prevention of Child Abuse and Neglect
CPJ	Comité de la Protection de la Jeunesse
CPS	Crown Prosecution Service
CYPA	Children and Young Persons Act
DHSS	Department of Health and Social Services
DPP	Director of Public Prosecutions
DYP	Department of Youth Protection
IFSA	Intrafamily Child Sexual Abuse
NCCL	National Council for Civil Liberties
NCW	Nations Council of Welfare
NSPCC	National Society for the Prevention of Cruelty to Children
PAIN	Parents Against Injustice
POSO	Place of Safety Order
USIu13	Unlawful Sexual Intercourse with a Girl Under Age 13
USIu16	Unlawful Sexual Intercourse with a Girl Under Age 16

In memory of Bruno M. Cormier

1 Development of Child Welfare Responses to Child Sexual Abuse

Introduction

The emergence of incest, and child sexual abuse in general, as a social problem warranting a range of interventions is a recent phenomenon, dating approximately from the mid to late 1970s (Gomes-Schwartz, Horowitz & Cardarelli, 1990; Vander Mey & Neff, 1986). Kempe (1978) asserted that recognition of sexual abuse would be the last stage in society's recognition of child abuse as a social problem and it has been referred to as 'the last frontier of child abuse' (Sgroi, 1975). Prior to this, because of its highly tabooed nature, incest was rarely disclosed; when it was, it was either disbelieved. or if believed, ignored or met with punitive, intrusive responses by authorities. This typical response of most communities to a disclosure of incest has been described by Giaretto (1981) as follows:

> The victim's accusations are often ignored by law enforcement officials if the evidence is weak and the parents deny the charges, thus leaving the child feeling betrayed both by her parents and by the community. On the other hand, the officials become harshly punitive if they have a court provable case. They separate the child from her mother and family and incarcerate the father, often for several years (p.179).

A similar response which is punitive of all family members (Gentry, 1978), has probably occurred in most of the Western world, including Canada and the United Kingdom. The speed, process and means by which different countries identified child abuse and later, child sexual abuse as a serious social problem varied from country to country, but it is generally acknowledged that the first major developments occurred in the United States.

A primary cause of the growth in public and professional awareness of child sexual abuse was the identification of the physical abuse of children as a social problem in the late 1950s and early 1960s, highlighted by the publication of the key work of Kempe and his associates, 'The Battered Child Syndrome' (1962). While Kempe's work was mainly directed towards medical doctors, soon child welfare workers, the media and the public defined child abuse as a major social problem (Gil, 1981). Passage of the Child Abuse Prevention and Treatment Act in 1973 was a principal step in recognition of the problem and soon most states passed statutes which defined child abuse and mandated the reporting and investigation of suspected abuse (Fraser, 1979; Gil, 1981). The inclusion of sexual abuse in the definition of child abuse occurred later - by 1979, 42 states in America included sexual molestation (Fraser, 1979).

In Canada, Quebec was the first province to include sexual abuse in its definition of child abuse in the new 1979 Youth Protection Act. Britain, which has no mandatory reporting law, was slower to respond to sexual abuse as a social problem (Mrazek, Lynch & Bentovin, 1981). In their 1980 child abuse guidelines, due to the complexity of the issue, the Department of Health and Social Services (DHSS) decided not to include sexual abuse in their definition of child abuse, a decision deplored by a British study group (Porter, 1984). A survey conducted in the UK in 1977 - 1978 showed that of the 49 Area Review Committees who responded (total in the country - 103), only 18 included sexual abuse that occurred without injury in their definition of child abuse (Mrazek et al., 1981).

After the inclusion of sexual abuse in the reporting laws, the number of known cases rose dramatically (Sgroi, 1975). For example, in the United States the number of child sexual abuse cases reported to the nation-wide data collection system increased from 1975 in 1976 to 4327 in 1977 and to 22,918 in 1982 (Finkelhor, 1984a). There was a 35 percent increase in officially reported cases of child sexual abuse in the United States from 1983 to 1984 (Associated Press, 1985, cited in Vander & Neff, 1986). A National Incidence study in the US showed that 7% of officially recorded cases of child abuse were incestuous (a projected total of 652,000 per year) (Finkelhor & Hotaling, 1984). In England the number of sexually abused children on NSPCC child abuse registers increased from 5% in 1983 to 28% in 1987 (Creighton & Noyes, 1989). In Quebec, Canada, the percentage of cases that were handled by the youth protection services rose from 7.4% in 1978 to 17.7% in 1979 and to 22.9% in 1980 (Canada, 1984, Vol.1). It is generally acknowledged by researchers and clinicians that these increased figures are a fraction of the total number of cases of child sexual abuse.

Because of the dramatic increase in the number of cases of reported child sexual abuse over a short period of time, the child welfare systems had to quickly develop procedures and policies for responding to the problem. The powerful effect of this has been well described by Summit (1986) who wrote that 'the unprecedented emergence of child sexual abuse has created the psychological equivalent of a disaster for victims, parents, and professionals alike. It is a disaster played in slow motion....a nightmare of exposure, fear, confusion, helplessness, and paralysis' (p. xi).

In America (Finkelhor et al., 1984; Tyler & Brassard, 1984), England (Porter, 1984), and Canada (Cooper & Cormier, 1985), interventions have tended to be reactive, haphazard and non-coordinated. With the exception of a few centres which developed specific programs for child sexual abuse (for example, Santa Clara in California, Giaretto, 1976, 1981, and in Denver, Colorado, Topper & Aldridge, 1981), uniform practices are rare and every area is at a different stage in developing procedures.

The professional body most involved in developing practice policies have been child welfare services and their efforts have taken place within the structures and policies of the child welfare system. *However, instead of using or relying on the already established practices for dealing with child physical abuse that had been debated and developed in the 1960s and 1970s following the enactment of child abuse reporting legislation, the child welfare professionals have generally used a coercive and overly punitive approach. Furthermore, this approach seems to have been a reactive one, based on assumptions rather than empirical data.*

Society's response to disclosed incest has been complicated by the fact that two legal systems are involved - the criminal justice system and the child protection system. Either or both courts can respond to cases, resulting in considerable differences in the impact on the family (Cooper, 1978; Fraser 1981). The choice of court (that is, criminal or juvenile court) [1] has often been arbitrary and dependent on such factors as whether the family went to the police, the professional the case was first disclosed to, his or her knowledge of resources and the policy of the professional agency aware of the case (Cooper).

Interventions in child sexual abuse have been more intrusive in two areas 1) the criminal justice system is routinely used and 2) child welfare interventions have become more intrusive. An American analysis (Finkelhor, 1983) of 6096 child sexual abuse cases officially reported in 1978 showed that criminal action was taken almost five times more often in cases of sexual abuse than in cases of physical abuse. In addition, foster placement occurred in more cases of sexual abuse than physical abuse and involved older children who disclosed their own abuse. The more recent 'Cleveland scandal' in England where 121 children were removed from home in a three month period because of a doctor's reliance on an unproven test indicating possible anal penetration illustrates well the extreme intrusiveness by child welfare professionals in these types of cases (Hobbs & Wynne, 1986; Home Office, 1988). [2]

The 'punishment vs. treatment' controversy - child physical abuse

Following the 'discovery' of child physical abuse in the early 1960s in the US, a major controversy developed in the field, i.e. whether it was necessary or desirable to use the criminal justice system. The debate on 'punishment versus treatment' was prominent during the development of services and policies for child physical abuse. Tibbits (1977) asserted that 'punishment and the difficulties it presents, seem to be at the very hub of the problem in cases of battered children. It is what it is all about' (p. 185). Doubt about whether physical abuse should be treated within the criminal law derives from the relationship between the parental abuser and the victim as 'there is usually a continuing relationship between the victim and the abuser, and the victim is usually dependent on the abuser for nurture and support' (Rosenthal, 1979, p. 144).

The fact that two different legal systems with different statutes, the criminal justice system and the child protection system, can respond to cases of child abuse, creates a number of complications. The goals and scope of the criminal statutes and the civil statutes are different - the purpose of the former to punish and deter the perpetrator, and of the latter to protect a child's short and long-term interests (Fraser, 1979). Protection of the parent-child relationship has also been cited as a purpose of child abuse legislation as the philosophy of these laws is to strengthen the family and keep the child in the home whenever possible (Chamberlain, Krell & Preis, 1976). In most states in the US (Fraser, 1981), in Canada and the UK (Porter, 1984), the jurisdiction of the youth court extends only to the child victim and not to the familial perpetrator. The civil laws grant considerable power to child welfare agencies to intervene in the family unit when it is thought a child's health, safety and welfare is at risk. Possible outcomes include the provision of protective services in the home (Chamberlain et al.), placement of children and termination of parental rights (Chamberlain et al.; Fraser, 1974). The standard of evidence required is lower than in criminal court where proof beyond a reasonable doubt is demanded (Fraser, 1981). In the criminal court system there are usually no services or treatment for the child and/or family (Cooper, 1978; Fraser, 1974; Libai, 1969). While the child protection system has a mandate to offer treatment to the family, the main focus is on the child (Fraser). In addition, the dual system may bring the rights of the child and the accused into conflict. Because the burden of proof and the penalties are greater in the criminal court, the criminal justice system strongly defends the rights of the accused. This can be traumatic for the victim who may have to face the accused in court and undergo cross-examination (Fraser, 1981; Libai, 1979).

Arguments to retain the criminal law in relation to physical abuse were based on several factors including a retributive function in that it allows 'the community to express its moral outrage with the abuse of its children' (McKenna, 1974, p.174) and serves as a symbolic affirmation that it is 'wrong, immoral and/or blameworthy' (Rosenthal, 1979, p.146). Another argument in support of its use was that it served a general and individual preventive effect (Rosenthal). These views, however, appeared to be in a minority. Pfohl (1977) observed that a survey of major law journals between 1962 and 1972 revealed that 'almost all the legal scholars endorsed treatment rather than punishment to manage abusers' (p.320).

Result of debate

The result of the debate in the United States was that eventually in most states child welfare interventions were based on a therapeutic model and efforts were made enabling parents to accept help voluntarily (Chamberlain et al., 1976). [3] This position was summarised in a report to the American Senate Subcommittee on Children and Youth (Mondiale, 1978) as follows:

> The third discovery we made was more subtle, but perhaps it was the most important. It was that our efforts to deal with child abuse must build upon the family as the first line of defense, and that means treating, and hopefully rehabilitating the abusing parent... We found that the challenge in most cases is not just to rescue the battered child from the home, but to rescue the home for the child (p.636).

This position views the abusive parents as deprived individuals, frequently with histories of excessive abuse in their own childhoods

(Blumberg, 1977; Green, 1975; Tibbits, 1977), whose abusive behaviour is not intentional but learned from their parents (Pollock & Steele, 1972).

Canada's approach to child abuse developed along lines similar to the United States. Jacobs (1978), writing on protective services in Canada stated the principle that it is better to protect the child by voluntary programmes than by the force of the court and referral to the police only occurred in severe cases of physical abuse.

Iatrogenic effects   The decision in the US and Canada to opt for a non-punitive approach in child abuse was largely due to a growing body of evidence of iatrogenic effects of using coercive measures in child abuse cases.   It was felt that 'the degree of psychic trauma is as much, or perhaps even more, dependent on the way that the problem (child victim) is treated after discovery than on the act itself' (Guttmacher, 1951, pp.117-119). There was even a reluctance to use the family court which stemmed from the belief that adversary proceedings can be psychologically damaging to the child and the child's parents (Poitrast, 1976).

Criminal prosecution was viewed as not only non-pragmatic but also counter-productive (Pollock & Steele, 1972; Silver, 1968) on the basis that such measures failed to deal with the vital problem of re-educating the parents so as to ensure that the cycle of abuse stopped (Fraser, 1974) and did not result in long-term protection of the child (Chamberlain et al., 1976). Judge Delaney (1972), who supported the use of the juvenile and family court to resolve the problem, expressed the issue well when he stated:

> The criminal prosecution of an abusive parent merits critical examination. First, we need to look at the methods by which the law exacts its toll, and the effect on those most directly concerned, the parent and the child. Second, we must assess the results obtained in terms of lasting benefits and detriments to these same parents and child. A criminal proceeding once set in motion, is formidable, impersonal and unrelenting...its aim is primarily punitive rather than therapeutic (p. 185).

The numerous concerns about the use of criminal court included the following views - fear of punishment leads to delays of request for help (Tibbits); punishment further alienates abusive families (Silver, 1968; Franklin, 1977), and may actually lead to more abuse (Besharov, 1975; Dickens, 1984; Chapman, Woodmansey & Garwood, 1985 [4] (Davoren, 1975); using civil courts helps the abusive parent avoid the persecution feeling he/she would feel in criminal court, thus making him/her more willing to co-operate with the agencies in a treatment plan; if a parent is convicted and incarcerated, it is usually for a short period of time and when released, he/she is likely to repeat the abuse as the abusive behaviour is likely unchanged (Fraser, 1974; Newberger & Bourne, 1980); and also that if an abusive parent is prosecuted and charges are dismissed, the hostility felt by the parent towards authority figures would be compounded by a feeling of justification and self-righteousness (Delaney,1973; Newberger & Bourne, 1980). It was generally concluded that the use of the criminal courts in cases of abuse satisfies our need for retribution and is neither a helpful or pragmatic solution to the problem (Fraser, 1974; Shelton, 1975).

Debate in England

A similar debate emerged in Great Britain as well which appears to have resulted in a considerably less resolution than in the United States and Canada. While arguments were put forward supporting a therapeutic model relying on civil procedures Davoren, 1975; Franklin, 1977; Tibbits, 1977, [5] it did not gain complete support. Several treatment programmes for physically abusive parents, based on the therapeutic model developed in the United States (Pollock & Steele, 1972), were developed (Baher, Hyman, Jones, Kerr & Mitchell, 1976; Pickett & Maton, 1977) but their value was questioned. [6] For example, after a study of 134 battered children and their families, Smith (1975) supported a legal approach. Evidently strong pressures were placed on psychiatrists, social workers and probation officers to take child abuse cases to either criminal or civil court (Carter, 1977).

The debate centred in part, on the role of the police in the management of child abuse and the relationship between the police and social work departments in the management of these cases has not always been one of co-operation. Prior to the mid to late 1970s, in many local authorities police were not involved. One report stated that only a third of child abuse cases were referred for police investigation (Smith, 1975). The police consistently argued for their own immediate involvement (Collie, 1975; Mounsey, 1975; House of Commons Select Committee on Violence in the Family 1977 [HCSC], 1977; Wedlake, 1977) but doctors and some social workers were apparently reluctant to involve police automatically in every case conference because of concern about the consequences if the police wanted to prosecute the parents and other members of the conference were opposed (Hallett & Stevenson, 1980). Differing views from other sources emerged - while the NSPCC (Baher et al., 1976), whose emphasis was on treatment and rehabilitation, preferred police not to be involved, the Select Committee on Violence in the Family recommended that they be involved in all case conferences. In 1976 the DHSS and Home Office (DHSS and Home Office, 1976) issued a letter containing guidelines for the role of the police at case conferences, recommending their attendance, [7] a practice reported to have been followed in most areas.

Iatrogenesis in the child welfare system

Responses to child sexual abuse have developed within the child welfare system and the structures and policies established for child physical abuse.   These policies also developed in the midst of an extensive literature on the potential for abuse of power by social workers in their interventions in child abuse cases. A major criticism of the child welfare system is that while they exercise extensive power, there is often little accountability for the mismanagement of children (Silverberg & Silverberg, 1982) by organisations such as police, medical institutions, social service departments and group homes (Gelles & Cornell, 1983). Families are seen as being broken-up without being helped; interventions are ineffective or harmful and tend to be applied unequally in that while abuse occurs in all classes, most of the interventions are with poor families (Newberger & Bourne, 1980; Silverberg & Silverberg).

There has been grave concern about the power social workers have to remove children from their home and take over parental rights (Freeman, 1983, Ch.4; Geach & Szwed, 1983; King, 1981; Mnookin & Szwed, 1983; Packman, 1983).   Aber (1980) has referred to removing children from home as 'the most powerful, least restricted form of modern state intervention into the heart of family life' (p.158). Holt (1974) described these professionals as sometimes playing God and creating helplessness in their clients. Referring to children in institutions, he wrote, 'no one is more truly helpless, more completely a victim, than he who can neither choose nor change nor escape his protector' (p.52). These remarks could apply equally as well to families suspected of child abuse. In England, the lack of rights of parents in care proceedings, their inability to attend case conferences and the fact that sometimes they are not told when a child is placed on the 'abuse' register were some of the criticisms (Freeman, 1983).   An organisation called *Parents Against Injustice* (PAIN) was formed in England in 1985 to lobby for the rights of parents accused (often unjustifiable) of child abuse (physical or sexual) (Amphlett, 1987).   Tragic cases of child abuse deaths, notably Maria

Colwell (Colwell, 1974) and others (for example, Brewer, 1977 and Mahmedagi, 1981), have resulted in major criticism of social workers' decisions not to remove children. [8] The lack of reliable criteria to validate decision making in workers relying on 'practice wisdom' (Stevenson, cited in Pickett & Maton, 1977, p.63) for major decisions was noted as well as the need for 'research into the processes of decision making and the outcome' (Pickett and Maton, p.63, 1977).

Newberger and Bourne (1978) suggest that child welfare authorities often use a coercive/punitive model of intervention because of the extreme lack of resources for other measures. The development of a set of rules and procedures to respond to child abuse, including the mandatory reporting laws, may have actually harmed children (Thomas, 1982). Reliance on a standard method of service has resulted in the breakdown of the more informal helping systems that could respond more sensitively and directly to the needs of a specific child and his/her family. Solnit (1980) has also criticised the mandatory reporting laws for child abuse, claiming that it has spread already limited resources too thin so that very few families are given adequate services.

Because of the improved abilities of the authorities to identify the problem, and the fact that the numbers of cases accumulate at the rate of 1½ to 2% more children each year, the system of treatment and intervention is seen as collapsing (Besharov, 1985; Fraser, 1979). The events in Cleveland in 1987 well illustrate how this increased identification results in a greatly diminished quality of service for children and their families (Home Office, 1988). Describing the development of child abuse legislation and services as a reactive process, Fraser (1979) recommended focusing resources on planning, co-ordination and prevention.

Legal and clinical responses to child sexual abuse

In spite of the well established, treatment oriented practices of dealing with child physical abuse and the reported damaging effects of the criminal justice system, the best known programmes for managing child sexual abuse that emerged strongly endorse using the criminal justice system in co-ordination with the child welfare system (Giaretto, 1976, 1981; Graves & Sgroi, 1982; Topper & Aldridge, 1981). Giaretto's comprehensive programme based on a humanistic philosophy of behaviour and change, and emphasizing coordination of the many systems and professionals involved once incest is disclosed (Giaretto, 1976), became the most well known programme and has been implemented in different parts of the United States and Canada. Giaretto has suggested that while he does not always agree with using the criminal courts, when he started his treatment program in 1976 he felt he had no choice but to build it around a system that was already being used (i.e. the criminal justice system). [9] This would correspond with what appears to be a basic contradiction between the punitive nature of the criminal justice system and the philosophy of the humanistic treatment model which has the goal of helping the individual achieve his/her highest potential. In contrast, other American programs strongly endorse the use of the adult courts (Berliner, 1977; Sgroi, 1982a; Topper & Aldridge, 1981).

The use of the criminal court differs - the Santa Clara program uses deferred sentencing whenever possible (Giaretto, 1981), while the Colorado program has a system of deferred prosecution for a limited number of carefully selected incest offenders (Topper & Aldridge, 1981). A similar program exists in Devon, England (Crine, 1983; Porter, 1984)) and the establishment in England of the Crown Prosecution Service replacing the Director of Public Prosecutions (DPP), may result in greater discretion in prosecution (Prosecution of Offences Act 1985).

One of the apparent results of the dissemination of the Giaretto treatment model and the adherence in the recent literature to a criminal justice model is that in areas where previously the interventions were based only on the child protection system, child welfare authorities started to routinely involve the police and potentially, the criminal justice system. For example, in Canada in the early to mid 1980s, several provinces including British Columbia, Ontario and Alberta, adopted a policy of routinely involving the police in the investigation of cases of child sexual abuse. This was contrary not only to their previous procedures with this type of case but also to the procedures they use for child physical abuse where police are rarely involved (Cooper & Cormier, 1985).

In England, as elsewhere, responses to child sexual abuse developed within the structure established for dealing with physical abuse. Recognition of the problem was slow, as reflected in the failure of the DHSS to recommend registering sexual abuse as a separate category (DHSS, 1980). However, due to the fact that in most areas police routinely attended case conferences (mainly because of guidelines from the DHSS and Home Office, 1976, discussed earlier), police were involved in the decision-making in those cases that came to the attention of social services.

One noteworthy exception to the trend to utilise the criminal justice system is the 'confidential doctor' program in the Netherlands which allows child welfare professionals to use their discretion and inform the police of cases only when treatment efforts have failed (Doek, 1978; Christopherson, 1981).

Rationale for use of criminal justice system

One of the rationales for using the criminal justice system in incest case is that it is the only way to ensure that the perpetrator engages in and maintains treatment (Conte, 1984; Summit & Kryso, 1978; Topper & Aldridge, 1981; Sgroi, 1982b). Walters (1975) has described this position as follows: 'The major motivation of a large number of abusers is directly proportionate to the legal threat to the abuser' (p. 153). However, the view that the familial incest perpetrator requires the criminal court as a leverage for treatment is not based on any empirical data. Clinical reports of the incest perpetrators' persistent denial of their actions are essentially anecdotal (see, for example, Conte, 1984 and Snowden, 1982) and there has been no effort to explain the underlying psychodynamics of the denial. This is markedly different from the work of clinicians who described the denial mechanisms of physically abusive parents in the 1970s. (See, in particular, Pickett and Maton (1977) and Steele (1976)). The latter wrote that:

> The lack of 'true confession' and pattern of not telling the 'whole truth' is often interpreted as 'lying and manipulation' on the part of the abusive parent. In a way this is true, but it is deliberately counter-productive for the worker to view the parent as a 'deliberate liar'. It is more useful to understand the parent's story as a response to fear and anxiety over discovery and punishment, and as a desperate attempt to defend against further attack and trouble (p.19).

In contrast, Sgroi (1982a), an influential sexual abuse clinician in the US, wrote that 'after disclosure of child sexual abuse, the perpetrator is going to be engaging in evasive and defensive activity *regardless of the posture of the intervenor*' (emphasis added, p.91).

It may be that the denial of the incest perpetrator is as much the result of the clinician's negative counter-transference towards the perpetrator as the perpetrator's inability to admit to his actions (Cooper & Cormier, 1985; Cooper & Cormier, 1990).

Clinicians advocating use of the criminal courts also do not seem to discriminate between intrafamilial and extrafamilial child sexual abuse (i.e. incest perpetrators and pedophiles). For example, Berliner and

Stevens (1980) write that 'it has been our experience that child molesting is often a compulsive behaviour; therefore, if the offender is not prosecuted for his crime, a series of children will undoubtedly be exposed to his abuse' (p.47).

The argument sometimes offered that sexual abuse of a child is a criminal offence while physical abuse is not, is not valid as both behaviours are prohibited by various criminal statutes of most Western countries.   It is simply that the procedures that developed after the discovery of child physical abuse in the 1960s focused on clinical interventions rather than criminal ones.

That more coercive measures seem to be taken in case where the child has been sexually rather than physically abused suggests that it is viewed as a more serious type of abuse with more severe consequences for the victim.   These different reactions are curious, especially in view of the potentially lethal nature of physical abuse. In spite of this, there has been no attempt to explain the essentially different approach to the two types of abuse which suggests that the reasons are emotional rather than rational. Lempp (1978), one of the few authors to have commented on the 'absurdity' of the different social response to sexual abuse, wrote that:

> ... For many years crimes of violence in our penal code (slight and grievous bodily harm, ill-treatment, etc.), have been less harshly judged than sexual offences. This differing assessment between crimes of violence and sexual offences, which on closer examination appears to a certain extent absurd has its roots in a system of values which no longer operates in our current society.

A re-evaluation of standards, with a decrease in moral indignation towards sexual offences, would be favourable with regard to the positive education of children and advantageous for the mutual relations in a community... It would be desirable if the social harmfulness of isolated and aberrant forms of sexuality were clearly distinguished from the social harmfulness of violent physical aggression against other people and if society's system of values and sanctions supported this distinction (p.245).

While sexual abuse of children has been distinguished from physical abuse on etiological and dynamic grounds (Avery-Clark, O'Neil & Laws, 1981; Gil, 1970; Steele, 1970), there have been few empirical studies comparing consequences.   Furthermore, the difficulty in determining consequences of sexual abuse (Constantine, 1981; Schultz, 1980b; Steele & Alexander,1981) as well as the necessity for more research on both the long and short-term effects have been acknowledged (Mrazek & Mrazek,1981). Schultz (1980b), commenting on the poor quality of research on the effects of incest wrote that 'many of the studies confuse moral damage with psychological damage. Such finality is indefensible to the open-minded. The literature does not support a causal relationship between incest and any single piece of pre-or post-incest behaviour, yet policy and practice assume such a relationship' (p.95).

Lack of debate

It is interesting that the speedy acceptance by child welfare professionals of a criminal justice model for cases of child sexual abuse occurred with little or no debate. Their uncritical acceptance of a criminal justice model was evident in the shift of focus in the International Meeting on Child Abuse and Neglect shortly following the 'discovery' of child sexual abuse. At the third meeting of this organisation in Amsterdam in 1981 the potential harmful effects of state intervention was identified as a major problem for all countries (Besharov, 1981). However at the next meeting in 1984 in Montreal, only one of the 200 papers that were presented questioned the use of criminal court (Cooper, 1984) while the rest seemed to automatically accept the idea.

At the time when the child welfare professionals were developing policies for responding to child sexual abuse, a considerable body of literature on iatrogenesis specifically related to child sexual abuse was emerging which was essentially ignored. A number of researchers and clinicians had concluded that while it is difficult to separate the 'environmental' and 'legal process trauma' (Gibbens & Prince, 1963) from the negative effects of incest (Libai, 1969), there was real cause for concern (Besharov, 1981; Cooper, 1978; Gibbens & Prince; Libai; Schultz, 1980b; Tyler & Brassard, 1984; Walters, 1975). It is interesting that with a few exceptions, most of the criticism of using criminal court in such cases came from the legal literature.

Similar to the conclusions of the earlier studies of the effects of using the criminal court in cases of child physical abuse, this criticism was based on the principle that the interests of the family are better served by clinical and social interventions than by the criminal justice system. Fraser (1981), noting the victimisation of the child by both the criminal and civil legal systems, concluded that there is no sure way of knowing which legal route works best. Doek (1981), in his review of European statutes related to child sexual abuse, observed the absence of 'clear or thoughtful policies concerning child sexual abuse' (p.80) and also that there was no debate on whether prosecution is desirable or necessary in terms of both the victim and the perpetrator. His opinion was that 'when criminal justice is directed only at avenging or opposing the general welfare of society and can yield no reasonable advantage to a particular child, criminal prosecution should not be the first option... whenever the perpetrator is someone in the family, criminal prosecution may not be the best course' (p.82). This view is similar to that taken by a major study of sexual offences in England (Howard League, 1985) which supports a policy of avoiding prosecution when the incest perpetrator acknowledges responsibility and co-operates in treatment. An equally decisive stand was taken by the Law Reform Commission of Canada (1978) which recommended that cases of child sexual abuse where the perpetrator is a family member should be handled only in a family court.

Clinicians writing about the use of criminal court include Walters (1975), who recommended that ways other than criminal court be found to engage the family perpetrator in treatment and stressed the importance of treating the child and parent a unit in need of help and Cooper (1978) who suggested the use of a three tier system in incest cases, whereby the majority of cases would be handled in voluntary settings and through the child welfare system, reserving the criminal court for the few very difficult cases.

Similar to the studies on the effects of court procedures in cases of child physical abuse, sources of trauma for the sexually abused child arising from the criminal court process were identified as repeated interrogations and cross examinations, causing the child to relive the experience (Fraser, 1981; Katz & Mazur, 1979; MacFarlane & Bulkley, 1982; Parker, 1982), or feel they have done something wrong (Lempp), numerous court appearances (de Francis, 1969, [10] facing the accused in court (Fraser, 1981; Gibbens & Prince, 1963), particularly a parent or someone in a close relationship (Lusk & Waterman, 1986), long delays in any action (Porter, 1984; Fraser, 1981), the awesome atmosphere and ritual in court, the acquittal of the accused (Libai, 1969), the conviction of the accused who is the child's parent or relative (Chamberlain et al., 1976; Kaufman et al., 1954) and imprisonment of a familial perpetrator (British Association for the Study and Prevention of Child Abuse and Neglect [Baspcan], 1982; Cooper, 1978; Gentry, 1978; Marvesti,1985; Tyler & Brassard, 1984).

The combination of incarceration of a father and placement of the victim in foster care was described as disrupting the family's equilibrium (Furniss, 1983) and frequently precipitating a crisis (Westermeyer, 1978). Imprisoning a father perpetrator was reported as adversely affecting the victim who may feel guilty that her disclosure resulted in the punishment of a relative she may still care for (Cooper & Cormier, 1990; Gentry, 1978). Such feelings are often reinforced by the negative reactions of other family members (Cooper, 1978; Paulsen, 1978). Reports that many sexually abused children who utilize Childline (a telephone help line for sexually abused children in London England) request anonymity for themselves and their perpetrators support this view. [11] Incarceration of a family breadwinner may bring considerable financial hardship (Chamberlain et al., 1976; Cooper; Tyler & Brassard, 1984; Paulsen) and sometimes disintegration of the family if the remaining parent is unable to cope alone (Baspcan, 1981; Cooper & Cormier). Besides the obvious impact of incarceration on the familial perpetrator (usually a father) of loss of employment (Tyler & Brassard), loss of freedom and abuse from other inmates who learn of his offense (West, 1987), one study comparing recidivism rates of incarcerated perpetrators and perpetrators who were given sentences of probation concluded that as far as the researchers were able to determine, [12] none of those under probation supervision recidivated. While those in prison may have been more serious offenders, a policy change had occurred which resulted in more incest cases being prosecuted in juvenile court than in adult court (Cormier, Kennedy & Sangowicz, 1962).

It had been observed that the source of iatrogenesis was not confined to the criminal justice system. 'While both psychiatrists and social workers have criticised law enforcement and the law profession, for inducing legal process trauma, they have not critically examined their own interventions for possible victimogenesis, traumatogenesis or iatrogenesis' (Schultz, 1981, p.29). The harmful effect on sexual abuse victims of highly negative reactions of adults to the abuse had been documented in a number of studies (Brunold, 1964; Chaneles. 1967; Ingram, 1979; Landis, 1956; Peters, 1976; Tormes, 1968; Tsai, Feldman-Summers & Edgar, 1979). For example, Walters (1975), a clinician working specifically with sexual abuse, suggested that most of the psychological damage 'stems not from the abuse but from the interpretation of the abuse and the handling of the situation by parents, medical personnel, law enforcement and school officials, and social workers' (p.113). These iatrogenic effects have been described as causing a double victimisation of the victim (Cormier & Cooper, 1982). For example, the Cleveland Inquiry (Home Office, 1988) referred to the 'plight of the double victim' (p.7).

Studies on the effects of child welfare interventions on sexually abused children reported similar findings to those earlier reports on the effects on physically abused children. For example, short or long-term placement of the victim (Cooper,1978; Tyler & Brassard,1984) and/or the victim's siblings (Tyler & Brassard) were found to be stressful for the victims and their families. The former can cause considerable stress to the victim who, often feeling guilty for the occurrence of incest and then its disclosure, interprets his/her removal from home as punishment.

The over-all quality of care for sexually abused children removed from their homes has received much criticism (Rabb & Rindfleisch, 1984; Shaughnessy, 1984). One consequence can be exposure of the child to both physical and/or sexual abuse by peers or by their adult 'care-takers' (Green, 1988b; Smith, 1987; Fisher, 1979; Duncan, 1979). Publicity from the media can result in considerable shame and humiliation for the victim (Howard League, 1985; Tyler & Brassard). Medical examinations, initiated by child protection services or police have also been seen as a potential source of stress (Gentry, 1978; Lesnik-Oberstein, 1982; West, 1987).

The literature on the iatrogenic consequences seems to have influenced movement towards mitigating the effects of the court while retaining its use (Berliner, 1977). For example in the United States. a range of innovative uses of videotapes involving child victims have been proposed and enacted (Rogers 1982). However, because of concerns that their use will result in a lengthy appeal process or in the making of bad case law, many of them have never been used in court (MacFarlane & Krebs, 1986). Legislation has been passed in Canada (Canada Evidence Act 1985; Bill C-15 1986) and England (Criminal Justice Act 1988), which allows non-corroborative evidence as sufficient proof in cases of child sexual abuse and the use of closed-circuit television to enable the child to testify without appearing in court. [13] Also, treatment programmes have been initiated which attempt to help victims undergo the ordeal of court.

Emotional reactions to child sexual abuse

The late 1970s and early 1980s represent a period when a greatly increased social awareness of the problem of child sexual abuse forced child welfare professionals to develop policies and practices within a short period of time. However, instead of using the already well established responses to child physical abuse based on a treatment model and ignoring numerous studies on iatrogenic effects, the child welfare services opted for a more punitive approach to child sexual abuse. Whereas before the decision to use criminal court was frequently arbitrary (Cooper, 1978), it became deliberate and, as Finkelhor's research indicated, interventions within the child welfare system became more intrusive (1983). The state of social flux and change was noted by Soothill (1980) who, remarking on the work of the 1980 English Criminal Law Revision Committee who were examining sexual offences wrote that 'there is clearly a revival of interest in the crime of incest; the range of opinion already expressed to this committee rather suggests that incest may be an area where the boundaries of social response have been changing or at least will be in a state of negotiation for some time yet' (p.173).

The question must be asked as to the basis of the more punitive and intrusive response to sexual abuse. In all probability a major contributing factor is the strong emotional reactions the behaviour evokes, even at an unconscious level. The result of this is that many professional interventions are based on an emotional rather than a rational analysis of the case, and on the needs of the interveners rather than the clients. The problem of professional counter-transference has been described in the area of child physical abuse (for example, Krell & Okin, 1984) and, given that intrafamily child sexual abuse involves the breaking of a strong societal taboo, it is probably a much greater feature in this type of child abuse.

The powerful feelings evoked by the breaking of the taboo of incest, sometimes called an 'incest dread', have been described for many years in non-clinical literature on the topic, particularly in anthropological and sociological articles. Schultz (1980c), commenting on the historical records of children and sexuality wrote that the 'evolution of childhood and sexuality is characterised by superstition, unreasonable fears, folklore, religious fanaticism, medical sadism, and fundamental ignorance' (p.3).

Increased knowledge does not appear to have greatly diminished the strong emotions the behaviour arouses and Constantine (1981b), referring to incest, writes 'no topic seems more capable of disabling the rational faculties of the most intelligent adult than the subject of incest' (p.261). Summit (1986) claims that 'here in the midst of the flowering of twentieth-century reason and scientific enlightenment is a neglected relic of mythic and superstitious issues almost untouched by mainstream adult consciousness' (p. xi). The strong public and professional reaction to the 'Cleveland scandal' which resulted in a lengthy and intense inquiry (Home Office, 1988) illustrates well the emotional essence of the taboo. The events themselves were referred to as 'this particular bit of human wickedness' (Whitehorn, 1988, p.35) and a reporter commented that 'polarization and hysteria have been the hallmarks of the Cleveland controversy' (Philips, 1988).

Similar feelings have even been evident in the legislative responses to incest. For example, in the parliamentary debates that took place prior to the passage of the Incest Act in England in 1908, the behaviour was referred to as having 'the most appalling nature', 'this exceedingly unpleasant subject', 'a most abominable thing', and 'not a pleasant topic or one which any member of your Lord's House would wish to discuss at length' (Hansard, 1908).

Current clinical literature acknowledges that until recently, the frightening nature of the taboo resulted in ignoring of the problem by society in general and by professionals in particular (Finkelhor, 1984; Vander Mey & Neff, 1986). Thus families found it very difficult to disclose the problem and if they did, they tended not to be believed (Gentry, 1978). The 'horror of incest' (Ayalon, 1984) has also been cited as inhibiting researchers' objectivity in looking at data (Gentry; Herman & Hirshman, 1977). Professionals are not immune to the extreme reactions and examples of their over reactions abound. For example, the zealousness with which the professionals in Cleveland pursued the diagnosis of sexual abuse and their sense of moral rightness in their later defense of their actions betray the emotional and non-rational basis of their interventions (Cooper, 1990; Home Office, 1988). The language used by some of the professionals involved in that situation indicates their strong emotions about the behaviour. For example, after the publication of the Cleveland Report the Director of Cleveland Social Services referred to the sexual abuse of young children as 'the most disgusting of social evils' ('Child Sexual Abuse Scandal, 1988, p.2) and later at a conference described the perpetrators as often 'the best liars in the country' (Ballantyne, 1988, p.20). The emotional difficulties encountered by professionals working with sexual abuse for the first time have been noted by some authors who describe reactions of revulsion, hatred and fear (Barry & Johnson, 1958; Gentry, 1978; Shelton, 1975; Giaretto, 1976). One of the ways these feelings can impede the treatment of the child was described earlier by Walters (1975) who wrote that the child, sensing the professional's unexpressed anger against the parent, becomes protective of the parent and draws away from the therapist. While some authors emphasize the importance of dealing with their negative feelings before working with an incest family (for example, Davis, 1981; Sgroi Porter & Blick, 1982), overall, there is a paucity of clinical literature on the subject and no research into the effects that the severe discomfort experienced by professionals can have on their interventions.

The early clinical writings on the subject caused Libai (1969) to conclude that 'the fact agreed upon by psychiatrists that a child may be affected not only by the events subsequent to the offense (which itself did not affect him), or that the ill-effects of the offense may be aggravated by those reactions, calls for further inspection of the relations between the child and the authorities' (p.195). This is beginning to happen only now with movements in the United States, England and Canada to mitigate some of the adverse effects of adult court on the victim (MacFarlane & Krebs, 1986; Spencer, 1987). However, this does not constitute an examination of what Finkelhor and his colleagues (1984) identified as the major debate preoccupying the professional community in the management of child sexual abuse, namely prosecution of the abuser. The need for this type of research had been identified even earlier by Hallett & Stevenson (1980) who described the need for further study on the effects of prosecution in cases of child abuse, on the parent or parents prosecuted, on the injured child and other siblings, and perhaps on the parent who is 'left behind' if only one is prosecute... in its absence the temptation is for us all to harbour prejudices (p.42).

Finkelhor (1984) also identified the urgent need to evaluate the effects of the different types of interventions, observing that

communities around the country are currently struggling to set up programs to respond to the challenge of sexual abuse. A variety of long-standing programs offer themselves as models, but policy makers have little objective evidence to guide them in decisions about what are the relative advantages and disadvantages of different models. Such outcome research will greatly advance the welfare of sexual abuse victims (p.231).

This need has been identified even more recently by McFarlane (1992) who writes that 'one of the greatest gaps in this field at the present time is the lack of available data on the effects of intervention and the outcomes of various types of treatment methods and approaches' (p. 77).

Notes

[1]   In some jurisdictions child protection cases are handled by a family court rather than a juvenile court. However, both courts are civil courts.

[2]   The professionals' interventions created such a furore that there was an extensive public inquiry into the events resulting in a landmark report, *The Cleveland Inquiry* (Home Office, 1988) which was highly critical of the professionals' actions, particularly those of the doctors and social workers. Prior to the publication of the report, most of the children, including a few who had in fact been sexually abused, were returned to their homes by a high

court judge, mainly because of the trauma they had experienced at the hands of the professionals.

[3] For a fuller description of the two positions, see chapter 2 in Gill (1970) where he presents the therapeutic model as described by Steele and Pollock (1968) and in contrast, a legal model prepared by Polansky and Polansky (1968). These latter authors stated that interventions should be 'authoritative, intrusive and insistent' (Polansky and Polansky cited in Gil, 1970, p.43).

[4] These authors claim that several of the child abuse death inquiries in Britain have illustrated this point, as do their own cases described in their appendix (pp.12 & 13).

[5] Tibbits (1977) identified three phases in child welfare practice in England re the resolution of the punishment issue. First, in the 'pre-Kempe' phase the primary goal was to protect the child. While there was a basic distrust of punishment, courts were sometimes used so that conflicts could be recognised and dealt with. In the 'post-Kempe' stage, theory and research evolved so that the emphasis was on treatment which appeared to show results. The third phase, the 'post-Maria Colwell' period, is marked by over-burdened social service departments attempting to deal with an increasing number of identified cases, child abuse registers and a defensiveness against criticism. The issue of whether punishment is necessary in these cases is still unanswered.

[6] See, for example, Dale and Davies (1984) who claim that 'reparenting therapy' (p.12) neglects limit-setting and control.

[7] The guidelines were very low key and clearly suggested that the duty of the police to investigate is not absolute and that they have discretion both to investigate and prosecute (Hallet & Stevenson, 1980). In the guidelines it was stated that 'the Departments hope that where a case conference has been held chief officers of police (whilst retaining the capacity to take independent action) will take into account any views expressed by the conference about the effect of an investigation on the welfare of the child' (DHSS & Home Office, 1976, p.3).

[8] In England, the 1989 Children Act, described as a 'radical reforming statute' (Allen, 1990, p.6), has addressed some of these issues, in particular the right of natural parents vis-a-vis social service departments and the importance of preserving links between children and their families (Allen). The Act was implemented in part in 1991.

[9] While this has not been described in any of his writings, Giaretto expressed this view in response to a query at a workshop in Montreal, October, 1987.

[10] In the 173 cases of DeFrancis' study that were prosecuted, more than 1,000 court appearances were required, causing added stress, resentment and tension for the children and their parents (1969). A study surveying judges showed that 84% of the judges thought that children who testified in court were emotionally traumatised (Bohmer, 1974).

[11] Paul Griffiths (member of Childline team), personal communication, July, 1988.

[12] The researchers were fairly confident of this finding as the likelihood of a father who recidivated after completing his probation being referred back to their clinical service was high.

[13] For a discussion of these issues in the English and Canadian systems, see Spencer and Flin (1989) and Hallett (1991) respectively.

2 The Research

Summary of issues

The following issues shaped the research:

1. Prior to the recent social discovery of intrafamily child sexual abuse and the dramatic increase in the number of cases child welfare services are required to respond to, cases tended to be either ignored by professionals or responded to by punishing the familial perpetrator and/or removing the victim from the home, often for a lengthy time;
2. The increase in disclosed cases forced child welfare services to develop procedures and policies quickly and with the exception of a few comprehensive and coordinated programs of intervention, most areas respond in a haphazard and ill-planned way;
3. In spite of a small but consistent body of literature on the iatrogenic effects of interventions which criticizes the use of criminal courts for the problem and the intrusiveness of child protection agencies, the programs that have developed emphasize the use of the more coercive legal system; also, social services tend to be too intrusive in the family, for example frequently removing the victim and sometimes the siblings. This observation which gave rise to the study in 1982 has been further reinforced by the events in Cleveland, England (Home Office, 1988) and more recently, for example, in Orkney (Black, 1992).
4. There is no research that looks directly at the interventions that are made in terms of how much coercion is used and their impact on the family.

There is a series of decision making in both systems (child welfare and criminal justice) that determine subsequent interventions:

1. In the criminal process there are different levels of discretionary decision making in the legal hierarchy which determine (i) whether the police will refer the case to the Department of Public Prosecutions (DPP) for consideration of laying a charge of incest, lay a lesser charge or lay no charges, (ii) whether the DPP lays a charge, (iii) if the offender is charged and found guilty or pleads guilty, what the sentence is and (iv) if the decision is incarceration, the decision of the release date by the Parole Board.

2. In the child care system there are decisions about referring to the police, referral to psychiatrists, removal of the child and/or siblings from home and type of placement and applying for parental rights.

Focus of research

The research focused on professional interventions in cases of intrafamily child sexual abuse and looked at the following points:

1. The process of disclosure (how sexual abuse is disclosed to professionals, to what type of professionals are the allegations of abuse made);

2. The nature of the decision-making (who makes the decisions, how are decisions make);

3. The type of interventions (by the child welfare and criminal justice systems) and their observable impact on the victim and family;

4. Which legal channel is the least traumatic for the victim and family, at the same time providing protection of the victim and other children in to disclosed cases of incest; and

5. Whether criminal procedures are desirable or necessary in responding to incest cases.

The writer approached the problem with several concerns:

1. Coercion should be kept to the minimum necessary to secure cessation of offending;

2. The less amount of coercion that is used in a family, the better their chances of a positive recovery;

3. Professionals tend to over-react to child sexual abuse in general and incest in particular, making unnecessary intrusive interventions that

are damaging to the victim, perpetrator, other family members and the family as a whole; and

4. The decisions and interventions that are made are often based on the emotional responses to the fact that incest has occurred rather than a rational response to the needs of the victim and his/her family.

The study examined the way disclosed incest cases are processed through the criminal court system and the child welfare system in two countries, England and Canada, with a focus on the decisions made throughout this process, and their outcome in terms of referral to other systems and direct interventions with the family. However, as the study was a file study, this question could not be answered in terms of personal reactions of the family members to the interventions but were determined by the more obvious consequences or sequelae such as loss of employment, the identity and number of persons removed from the home and marital and family break-up.

Analysis included an examination of the treatment modalities used with the family members and the duration and frequency of treatment and social service contacts with the family. Some effort was made to determine what factors (for example, age of the victim, type of incestuous abuse) influence the legal and clinical decisions that are made.

The data is from two samples, one in Canada and one in England, and at the time of the study, the two areas had a major difference in policy in responding to child sexual abuse. In the period covered by the research (1979 to 1984), unlike the policy in England, the policy of the Canadian child welfare system that was studied was for the social workers *not* to involve the police when cases of incest were disclosed to them. (Except in cases of severe violence, this policy also existed for cases of child physical abuse). Thus the two samples allowed a comparison of a child welfare system where the criminal justice system was routinely involved (England) and one where criminal procedures were rarely involved (Canada).

Methodology

Sample

The British sample, obtained in Northamptonshire county, comprised all of the cases of intrafamily child sexual abuse (IFSA hereafter) referred to the National Society for the Protection of Children (NSPCC), the monitoring agency for all cases of child sexual abuse, and/or the social service department, between January 1979 and July 1984 (Total - 96 cases). Where available files from the NSPCC, social services, police and probation service were consulted. Ninety-three NSPCC and 33 social services files were examined. In 31 cases both were looked at. In addition 50 police files and 37 probation files were studied, both sources being used in 28 cases.

The Canadian sample consisted of all of the cases of IFSA referred to the Department of Youth Protection (DYP) in Montreal, Quebec, in the area serviced by the Ville Marie Social Service (VMSSC) during the same period, January 1979 to July 1984. Ninety-five files from the DYP were examined and psychiatric files of 27 of these cases were also consulted. In five cases probation records were also seen. Permission to obtain access to police files was very difficult, but since very few of the cases were seen by the police, this was not considered to be a serious omission.

Data

In order to determine what information was available in case record in England, I arranged access to files of sexual abuse victims in a psychiatric clinic in Cambridge where I studied the last 20 cases referred by the social service department. In Canada I had worked for several years in a forensic psychiatry clinic which routinely dealt with incestuous families referred by the criminal court or the child welfare authorities. Using the impressions formed in these two experiences, a comprehensive schedule was designed for abstracting as much as possible of the information the different records contained. The items were pre-coded to ensure that the information obtained from the various files was recorded consistently in all the cases.

The schedule contained 585 variables and covered the following topics:

1. Sexual abuse (34 variables):
    (1) Details of the alleged sexual abuse which initiated the current referral;
    (2) Details of previous sexual acts between the perpetrator and victim including nature of acts, their frequency and duration,[1] victim's age at onset, and violence;

(3) Victim, perpetrator, victim's mother and family (135 variables).

2. Victim, perpetrator, victim's mother and family (135 variables):
   (1) Information on the victim including age at referral, behavioural problems, previous sexual abuse by other perpetrators, physical abuse, previous statutory contact with social services (for example, placement out of home, care proceedings);
   (2) Perpetrator's age, alcohol use, medical/psychiatric history, delinquent/criminal history, employment status;
   (3) Victim's mother's use of alcohol, medical and psychiatric history;
   (4) Family information (size, legal relationship of functional parents, violence, other sexual abuse in family, and current employment of parents.

3. Previous contact with professionals (18 variables):
   (1) Previous contact of victim and/or family with professionals for reasons other than sexual abuse;
   (2) Prior attempted disclosure of victim's sexual abuse with current perpetrator, or abuse of other children in the family to professionals;
   (3) Response of professionals to attempted disclosure.

4. Current referral for alleged sexual abuse (52 variables):
   (1) Identity of person the victim first disclosed to (mother, friend, etc.);
   (2) Identity of first professional service abuse disclosed to; their intervention (who they interviewed);
   (3) Who informed the police and child protection authorities.

5. The decision-making process (121 variables):
   (1) Number of case conferences (In Canada, the number of reports);
   (2) Identity of professionals attending case conference (England).
   (3) Length of time case opened at child protection service;
   (4) The reports that contributed to the various decisions.

6. Professional decisions about interventions following referral (172 variables):
   (1) The nature of the decisions including assessment of family members (who was interviewed, by whom), removal of victim

and/or siblings from the home, applying for parental rights, conducting a medical examination, prosecuting and sentencing the perpetrator, returning victim and/or siblings home and treatment (who, by whom and for how long).

7. Follow-up (53 variables):
    (1) Follow-up of victim (behavioural symptoms, pregnancy, further sexual abuse, completion of school, employment and living situation).
    (2) Marital status of victim's functional parents.
    (3) Follow-up of perpetrator (recidivism, suicide attempts, employment status).

Analysis

A goal of the study was to determine what features in a case affected the professional decisions by social workers, police and the courts and the impact of the different decisions on the families. The major decisions were identified as well as the variables that were thought might have influenced the various decisions. These included such items as the victim's age at referral and at the onset of the sexual abuse, the nature and frequency of the sexual acts, and the perpetrator's history of convictions. In each sample the decisions were cross tabulated by the chosen variables and values of chi-square calculated. To facilitate analysis, composite variables were also calculated and a path diagram was used. These are described later when this data is presented (Ch. 8).

Presentation of data

To facilitate the presentation of the extensive amount of data, it was decided to organize the material in the following way. Some of the descriptive data from the two countries are presented together (for example, a description of the samples and follow-up). Data concerning police, court and social service decisions are presented separately, followed by a presentation of the path analysis. A discussion comparing the decision and interventions of the professionals in the two countries concluded the work.

Limitations of study

The generaliseability of the findings are limited by the fact that the study was conducted in one area in each country and covered a specific time period. At the time of the study, however each area was reputed to be advanced in its response to child sexual abuse. Northhamptonshire had evolved a multi-disciplinary approach and, in spite of the failure of the DHSS to specify sexual abuse as warranting attention in their 1980 guidelines (DHSS, 1980), the Northampton authorities had identified it in their own guidelines in 1978 (Crine, 1983). [2] The social service centres in Montreal, Canada, had access to one of the foremost psychiatric/medical centres for children in North America, the Montreal Children's Hospital, which had evolved a sophisticated and comprehensive system of response to child physical abuse. They also had access to the McGill Clinic in Forensic Psychiatry, a pioneer in the research and treatment of incestuous offenders and their families (Cormier et al., 1962; Kennedy & Cormier, 1969; Cormier & Cooper, 1984). Moreover, the child welfare workers had a recently developed structure (the Department of Youth Protection) and new, innovative child protection legislation which specifically identified child sexual abuse as warranting intervention (Youth Protection Act, 1977).

While the findings of the study would not be representative of practices in other areas which were likely less advanced, they would represent the most developed types of interventions in child sexual abuse for the period of the study (1979-1984) and the findings may be helpful to other child protection authorities in the development of policy and procedures. The issues explored in the study are still relevant, especially since the debate of the efficacy of using the criminal justice system to respond to incest families has yet to be resolved and it is still unclear what interventions are the most helpful.

The sources of the data were the official records of the different organisations and while such records are often used as a valid source of data, it is important to be aware of the social processes involved in the construction of these case records. Wheeler (1969) has observed that what is in the record in the first place and what is drawn from the record in decision-making are both determined to an important degree by the values, tastes, ideologies, and biases of hose who contribute to and draw from the record system (p. 13). [3]

Furthermore, as Garfinkel (1967) notes, the choice of material that is in a case record may be frequently there "in the interests of justifying an actual or potential course of action between clinic persons and patients" (p. 191). Needless to say, this partial representation of the facts raises questions about the reliability and validity of the data (Belson & Hood, 1967; Madge, 1965; Walter, 1977; Wheeler, 1969).

In order to respond to this difficulty and enhance the validity of the data, where available, the writer consulted other files besides the information which she had abstracted from these main files. As already noted, these were records from police, social services, psychiatric clinics and probation departments. At the very least the writer hoped that the professional's decisions about proposed interventions and the actual interventions would be recorded in the majority of cases and in fact, this proved to be the case.

In both samples details of the abuse was particularly scarce in the social service files, which is of some concern, given that interventions and treatment are primarily carried out by these agencies. Data on the perpetrator was obtained primarily from the police files in the UK sample and from psychiatric reports in the Canadian group.

Notes

[1]   'Duration' refers to the period of time from the onset of the sexual behaviour until it was terminated, usually at disclosure.

[2]   In an examination of the level of services to sexually abused children in England in 1983, Northamptonshire was heralded as "one of the authorities most organised in dealing with incest." (Crine, 1983, p. 17).

[3]   See for example, David Sudnow (1973), *Normal Crimes*.

3 Child Welfare System - England and Canada

As in America (Fraser, 1981) and most European countries (Doek, 1981), Canada and England have two sets of statutes that relate to child sexual abuse - civil statutes concerned with child protection and criminal statutes. While some cooperation and integration may occur between the adult court system and the child welfare system in some areas of the two countries, essentially they are separate entities, operating with their own mandate, polices and procedures. Only one system may be applied, or both, either concurrently or in either sequence (Dickens, 1984). The definitions of incest and related sexual offences and penalties, described in the criminal codes of the two countries, differ in some respects and are described below. As well, there are variations in the Canadian and British child protection legislation and in the systems that implement the laws, which will be apparent in the following discussion. The information describes what existed during the period of the study (1979-1984).

Child protection system in England

Child protection services: organisational structures and policy

The body which has the main statutory responsibility for the protection of children is the local authority and its agents, namely the local authority social workers. [1] In April 1974, the Department of Health and Social Services (DHSS) recommended a two tier system of management: first, the Area Review Committee whose main function was to act as a policy making body in the area of child protection and second, the case conference (LASSL(74)13). The recommendation was officially accepted and in 1974, 102 Area Review Committees were set up in England and Wales (Smith, 1979). While the DHSS issued general guidelines for the management of child abuse, the responsibility for developing and stating procedures for case management rested with each Area Review Committee. Issues for the committee to address included the membership of the committee, the establishment of 'at risk' registers, confidentiality, arrangements when a family moves, case conferences and liaison with the police (DHSS, 1976; LASSl (76)). This new administrative structure was primarily in response to the tragic death of Maria Colwell who had been in the care of a local authority (Colwell, 1974). The subsequent inquiry had concluded that the major problem had been a failure of the system and massive breakdown in communication between departments and individuals in the case.

The committee had a multi-disciplinary structure - all had police and probation representatives and most had general practitioners, and representatives from education, and Housing Departments and National Society for the Prevention of Cruelty to Children (NSPCC) social workers. Other members included police surgeons, Family Service Units, Community Relations Officers and the legal or administrative departments of local authorities. The DHSS further recommended that representatives from social service departments with statutory duties relating to non-accidental injury be increased and not confined solely to the director of the department (DHSS, LASSL(76)).

A major issue for the committees was the establishment and maintenance of the 'at risk' registers [2] and by July 1975, 83 of the 102 area review committees had established central registers, eight had taken the decision to do so and the others were actively considering the matter (DHSS & Home Office, LASSL (76)). At the time of the study all of the areas had a register although there was considerable disparity in the criteria for both entry on and removal from the register, and information provided to the register.

It was further recommended that one of the participants in the case conference take the role of 'key worker'. This is the professional responsible for the actual management of the case through whom information is channeled and who is responsible for ensuring that it reach all other participants (DHSS & Home Office, LASSL(76), para.29).

As already discussed in Chapter I, the liaison between police and social services in child abuse cases was a major issue. Social workers feared that police presence at case conferences and their prosecuting powers would inhibit discussion and interfere with therapeutic endeavours (HCSC, 1977, p.248). Police argued strongly for their right to attend and the 1976 circular issued jointly by the DHSS and the Home

Office (DHSS & Home Office, 1976) recommended that they be invited to all case conferences. [3] While the circular recognized that the police should retain the capacity to take action independently of the case conference, Dingwall and Eekelaar (1982) have observed that they do have discretion whether or not to prosecute and are under no statutory or informal duty to prosecute in a case where there is insufficient evidence.

In 1980 the DHSS decided to extend the definition from physical injury and neglect to include 'failure to thrive' and 'emotional abuse' but decided against including sexual abuse.

When the Department sought comments on a draft circular in December 1978, a number of the responses suggested that the sexual abuse of children should be included in the definition of child abuse and should be dealt with under the child abuse procedures. The Department, along with other Government departments, is examining this suggestion, which raises complex issues. Meanwhile the attached memorandum does not recommend that sexual abuse be included as a separate category, though some aspects of sexual abuse will fall within the criteria set out in paragraph 2.2 ('physical injury'). (LASSL(80)4; HN(80)20)

Several reasons for the exclusion that were suggested included difficulties of definitions and where the boundary might be set, fears of 'overloading' the system and concern about applying the same procedures to sexual abuse as used in physical abuse. [4] Some Area Review Committees, including the Northamptonshire committee, decided on their own to include a category of sexual abuse. It was not until 1988 that the DHSS provided clear guidelines for responding to child sexual abuse (1988), a delay deplored by David Jones, general secretary of the British Association of Social Workers (Morris, 1988). [5]

Civil statutes and procedures

The protection of children is achieved through civil proceedings in juvenile court, a specialized form of magistrates' court. [6,7] The duties of this court in relation to the protection of children were first described in the 1933 Children and Young Persons Act (CYPA) as 'in a proper case take steps for removing him from undesirable surroundings and for securing that proper provision is made for his education and training' (CYPA, 1933, s.44). When it is felt that a child is in need of protection from his caretakers there are two alternatives: (1) wardship in High Court or (2) care proceedings in juvenile court. Both measures, if successful, result in a transfer of responsibility for the child, including parental rights, from the child's parents to a local authority, to the court, or to some other person, and with that, the right to remove the child from his or her parents or guardians on a temporary or permanent basis. (Wilford, McBain, Angell & Tarlin, 1979, p. 315).

In care proceedings, transfer is made to the local authority while in wardship, the child becomes a ward of the court (Dingwall & Eekelaar, 1982).

Care proceedings   Care proceedings, which involve taking children into care involuntarily, can be initiated by the local authority, the police or the NSPCC (CYPA, 1969, s.1). The principle that these measures are a last resort for the local authority was first articulated in the Children and Young Persons Act, 1963:

> It shall be the duty of every local authority to make available such advice, guidance and assistance as may promote the welfare of children by diminishing the need to receive children into or keep them in care under this Act or to bring children before a juvenile court; and any provisions made by a local authority under this subsection may, if the local authority think fit, include provision for giving assistance in kind or, in exceptional circumstances, in cash.

This measure was welcomed by the local authorities who had been doing preventative work with families since the late 1940s and early '50s, but without legal sanction. While the earlier 1948 Children's Act had provided a new direction in dealing with deprived children and a new administrative structure, it had not addressed the issue of prevention. However, this act created specialist services for children (Children's Departments) which developed a range of preventative strategies, in particular, intensive family casework (Packman, 1981). By the time the 1963 Act was passed, the idea of the importance to the child of his own family was well established in child welfare practice and policy.

Under the CYPA legislation 'child' means a person under 14 and 'young person', a person between 14 and 17 (Smith, 1979). While the local authority does not have to seek children out, if it receives information about a suspected case of child abuse or neglect it must investigate unless it feels it is unnecessary (CYPA, 1969, s.2 (1). The act states that where it appears there are grounds for a care order the local authority is under a duty to commence proceedings. However, it has the discretion not to initiate proceedings if it is satisfied that proceedings would not be in the interests of the child or the public or if some other body is about to take care or criminal proceedings (CYPA, 1969, s.2(1) & (2)).

Care proceedings may be brought under seven primary conditions (CYPA, 1969, s.1(2) as amended by the Children's Act 1975), four of which are relevant in cases of intrafamily sexual abuse. These are

a) (the child's) proper development is being avoidably prevented or neglected, or his health is being avoidably impaired or neglected, or he is being ill-treated;
b)i) It is probable that condition (a) will be satisfied because a court has previously so found in the case of another child who is or was a member of the same household;
  ii) It is probable that condition (a) will be satisfied having regard to the fact that a person who has been convicted of an offence under Schedule 1 to the CYPA 1933, is, or may become, a member of the same household as the child; [8]
c) he is exposed to moral danger.

Conditions (a) and (c) are the ones used most frequently in cases of incest and incestuous behaviour, the choice depending on the policy of the particular area review committee. In Northamptonshire because the moral danger condition is easier to prove than the ill-treatment condition, the policy in 1978 was to use the moral danger condition if there was to be no prosecution or if prosecution had not yet occurred. Moral danger was also used in cases where, for example, a convicted father returns to the home after a period of incarceration. In cases where the adult perpetrator was convicted, the ill-treatment condition was used.

When there are criminal proceedings for the same act that initiated the care proceedings, as may happen in cases of incestuous abuse, the civil hearing is usually postponed until the criminal hearing is completed. The usual practice is to use a series of interim care orders until the criminal prosecution is completed, at which time full care measures are sought. If a parent is convicted, the conviction proves the care proceedings. Alternatively, if the parent is acquitted, the issue may be tried again in juvenile court where the burden of proof is less strict (Smith, 1979).

Wardship Any person with a legitimate interest in the child may initiate these proceedings and if issued, the High Court has immediate power over the child. There is considerably more judicial discretion in wardship proceedings as compared to care proceedings and the judge has a wide discretion in the conduct of the hearing. Their immediacy and less stringent requirements of proof results in them being the preferred course of action in some situations (Smith, 1979).

The courts tend to be conservative in allowing the use of these proceedings, but although they still remain relatively uncommon, there has been an increase in wardship applications as an alternative to care proceedings (Dingwall & Eekelaar, 1982). If wardship is granted, while the High Court has legal custody of the child, it assigns the actual care to whoever seems suitable who, in many cases is the local authority. The local authority, however, has less power over the child than if he/she was committed into its care through a care order (Dingwall & Eekelaar).

Place of safety order When it is assessed that there is a need for immediate removal of the child from the home, an application may be made to the magistrate for a place of safety order (CYPA, 1969, s.28). If granted, the order authorises the detention of the child in a place of safety for 28 days or in some situations, for a specified shorter period. [9]

In terms of parental rights, the parents are not represented before the magistrate and do not have to be notified of the intent of the applicant. While they have to be told about the procedure and the reasons for it as soon after the decision as possible, they do not have the right either to know where the child is or to appeal the order (CYPA, 1969, s. 28 (3); Wilford et al., 1979).

The court hearing and dispositions In child care proceedings where only the local authority and the child are parties to the action, the parent, not a true party to the action, [10] can only respond to allegations by calling witnesses, giving evidence at the end of the child's case and before the final speeches (R. 14B of the 1970 Magistrates' Courts Rules) and cannot question or cross-examine witnesses (Smith, 1979). In addition, the parent has no right of appeal against any order that may be made. The child, on the other hand, may appeal the decision to the Crown Court (Booth, 1979).

If a case of abuse or neglect is proved, there are a range of dispositions the court may make.

a) an interim care order. Either the police or the local authority can apply for an interim care order which can be given for a maximum period of 28 days (CYPA, 1969, s.2(10)). The applicant does not have to prove his entire case for the order to be granted and there is no limit on the number of interim care orders that may be granted. These applications are usually made in order to obtain medical and/or psychiatric reports on a child prior to a final disposition of the case and when the case is being heard in criminal court (Smith, 1979). Care orders and supervision orders are the most common disposals (Dingwall & Eekelaar, 1982).

b) a supervision order (CYPA, 1969, Ss.11-19). This order lasts for a specified period of time up to a maximum of three years. If it is made as a result of care proceedings or when a care order is discharged, it terminates on the juvenile's eighteenth birthday (CYPA, 1969, s.17). Originally intended as an intermediate treatment programme for juvenile offenders, the supervision order simply puts the authority under a duty to 'advise, assists and befriend' the child. There is little power in the order (for example, the supervisor is not able to enter premises or remove or detain the child) and some of the requirements may be residence with a specified individual who agrees and treatment for a 'mental condition' (CYPA, 1969, s.12, as amended by s.37 of the Criminal Law Act 1977). The advantage of the order is that if the local authority wants to change it into a care order, it may return to court and do so without having to prove the preliminary grounds again (Dingwall & Eekelaar, 1982).

c) a full care order (CYPA, 1969, ss.20-24). A care order transfers all the powers and duties of the child's parents to the local authority whose power is only limited by the requirement to continue the child's upbringing in the same religion and not to arrange the child's adoption. They are expected to inform the parents about their plans for the child and discuss parental access. Unless there is clear evidence about serious mishandling of the case, the local authority's decisions about a child cannot be challenged in court (Dingwall & Eekelaar, 1982).

The local authority has an obligation to review the cases of all children in care every six months to consider whether the order can or should be discharged (Child Care Act 1980, s.20). At the time of the research there were no regulations governing the review procedures and each local authority decided the form these should take (Smith, 1979). Parents are rarely invited to case review conferences where decisions about care are made (Hall & Mitchell, 1982).

The placement options include a community home, a voluntary home and a foster home. Although the law allows the child to live at home (Children's Act, 1948, s.13; Child Care Act, 1980, s.21 (2)), there is a common assumption that keeping a child at home does not correspond to the purpose of a care order (Dingwall & Eekelaar, 1982). Less than a sixth of the children in care are allowed to live with their parents and approximately a third are placed outside the home (Smith, 1979).

Child protection system in Quebec, Canada

New Youth Protection Act and its history

Each province in Canada has its own child welfare legislation and with the passage of a new Youth Protection Act in 1977, Quebec emerged as a leader in developing innovative child protection legislation and policy. [11] The new act, the result of a lengthy debate in the province on the question of youth protection (Quebec, 1980a), was commended because, for the first time, it provided a separate and distinct basis for the rights of children (Smith, 1979), and as well, an improved system for decision-making and review and appeal procedures for children in care (National Council of Welfare [NCW], 1979). An earlier law on child protection, passed in 1950, that the new act replaced, established a separate court, the Social Welfare Court, for handling of these cases. This law defined a child in need of protection as one who was particularly exposed to moral or physical danger, because of his environment or other special circumstances (Youth Protection Act 1950). In 1971 Quebec passed the Health and Social Services Act which established a legal framework allowing the establishment of Social Service Centres which would render services previously assumed by private corporations (Quebec, 1980a). An amendment to the Youth Protection Act in 1974 created a provincial Youth Protection Committee which was to investigate each reported case of a mistreated child.

This act, as well as the new Youth Protection Act (1977), was responding in part to what had been identified as a serious deficit in the child welfare system by a federal government inquiry into the Canadian child welfare system, namely the over-use of substitute care for children rather than prevention and support services for families (NCW, 1979). The report stated the principle that 'there is universal agreement that social services should be more family-oriented to reflect what should be the overriding objective of the system: to support families and help them cope with their problems at an early stage, when those problems can be checked or at least kept at a manageable level' (p.24). This concern corresponds to one of the principles of the United Nations Charter of the Rights of Children which states that '... he shall, wherever possible, grow up in the care, and under the responsibility of his parents...' United Nations, 1983, p.129). Adherence to this principle was reflected in part of the functions of the new committee which was to 'preserve to the degree possible the family life of the child' (The Law on Children Subject to Mistreatment 1974) and received further legislative support in the 1977 act which states that 'decisions must contemplate the child's remaining in his natural environment' (Youth Protection Act, Art.4). This aspect of the new legislation was seen as having profound implications for social work practice and Smith (1979) observed that

It means that we are obliged to provide all our skills and energies to preserve the child's family for him, that severing the child from his family is major social surgery, only to be undertaken under extreme circumstances and with utmost care.

The new act also addressed the problem of the rights of children and their parents. The federal study (NCW, 1979) recommended that, because decisions taken by child welfare authorities can affect a child's life so profoundly, both his rights and those of his parents should be better recognised and protected. This would involve separate legal counsel for the child and his parents as well as stricter, more detailed regulations and guidelines for removal of a child from home, length of placement and frequency of review. This issue was taken up in Quebec in 1975 by a major committee which studied the rehabilitation of children and adolescents placed in reception centres (Batshaw Committee, 1976). This report, which specified the importance of children's rights, had considerable influence on the adoption of the Youth Protection Act (Quebec, 1984a).

The Youth Protection Act, adopted in 1977, came into force in January, 1979. Contrary to England, mandatory reporting by all persons, including professionals, which had been part of the 1974 act (The Law on Children Subject to Mistreatment), was clearly detailed in the new act

(Youth Protection Act 1977, Art.39). The act describes the professionals' obligation to report as:

> every professional who, by the very nature of his profession, provides care or any other form of assistance to children and who, in the discharge of his duties, has reasonable cause to believe that the security or development of a child is in danger within (specific articles of the act)...

and refers specifically to teachers, policemen and employees of an establishment. The only professional exempted from the obligation to report is an attorney whose client is implicated in a case of possible abuse (s.39). There is a provision in the law for a penalty of $200 to $500, in addition to costs, for persons who fail to report a case of suspected child abuse (s.134). Publicity of a case is punishable by a fine of $500 to $1,000 (s.135).

Unlike previous legislation, the act specifically identifies sexual abuse as an indicator that a child is in need of protection (Art.38, s.f) as follows '... the security or development of a child is considered to be in danger where, in particular, he is the victim of sexual assault or he is subject to physical ill-treatment through violence or neglect'. The act further specifies that this does not apply if the child is the victim of sexual abuse from any person other than his parents and the latter take the measures necessary to remedy the situation. 'Child' refers to a person under 18 years of age (s.1).

The act also effected other changes including the replacement of the Social Welfare Court with the Youth Court, alteration of the role of the Youth Protection Committee to that of an ombudsman for the rights of children, and creation of the post of director of youth protection in each of the 14 social service centres in Quebec (Quebec, 1984a).

Implementation of the 1977 Youth Protection Act

The system of protection functions in the following manner. All referrals of a suspicion of abuse go through a central intake unit where there are two steps in the decision making. Firstly, the referral, or '*signalement*' is briefly assessed, usually on the phone, to determine if it is 'retainable' or 'non-retainable' on the basis of whether the information provided describes a situation that comes under the terms of the law (Comite de la Protection de la Jeunesse [CPJ], 1981, s.2.6.3). After determining if the child or family is known at any provincial social service centre, the 'receivable signalement' is verified to determine if it is 'retainable' or 'non-retainable' on the basis of the credibility of the declaration, the facts as they are reported and the possible risk to the child (CPJ, s.2.6.5). If judged 'retainable' at this point, the case is referred to an agency within the area of service for a more thorough assessment.

The director of youth protection has the responsibility and authority to assess and make decisions on every signalement that is received (Youth Protection Act, Art.45). This authority is delegated to a social worker in two ways - a worker may have a functional delegation, i.e. a blanket delegation applicable to any case which, unless revoked, is in force for a maximum of one year, (CPJ, 1981, s.3.1.3), or a specific delegation which relates to a specific child only and is time limited to the period required to carry out the assessment phase (CPJ, S.3.1.4.1). The youth protection delegate, representing the director of youth protection, has the authority and responsibility to assess the case and decide on the treatment plan. In emergency situations, and after trying to obtain parental consent, the delegate can remove the child from its home without the consent of either the child or the parents. [12] The law specifies that the child must be consulted about the application of 'urgent measures' and his parents must also be consulted whenever possible. 'Urgent measures' are not allowed for more than 24 hours without an order of the court and the court can only permit urgent measures for five working days (Youth Protection Act 1977, s.47). [13]

The assessment of the child and his/her family, which is expected to be completed within two months, is thorough and involves obtaining information from such persons as school personnel, paediatrician, declarant and relations, visiting the family and interviewing each member to obtain their version and determine the precipitating factors and also to obtain pertinent historical background to aid diagnosis (CPJ, 1981, s.3.5).

If the assessment determines that the child is not in need of protection, the assessor either closes the case or refers the case to voluntary services (Chapter 48 services) (CPJ, 1981, s.3.6.1). Alternately, if the assessment confirms that the child needs protection, two main options are available: i) 'voluntary measures' or ii) 'seizing the court'.

Voluntary measures A principal innovation of the act was the provision of an intervention option called 'voluntary measures'. This is a contract which the worker negotiates and concludes with the child and his/her parents which contains specific activities which the worker has assessed will help remedy the child's situation and it must be signed by the parents and the child if he/she is 14 or older (Youth Protection Act 1977, Arts.51, 52, 53, 54, 60). The spirit of the law requires that 'voluntary measures' be applied whenever possible as it eliminates the necessity of going to court to force measures on the family or child. The measures envisioned by the law are outlined in general terms in article 54 of the act to serve as a guide (see Appendix 3) but the social worker and family can negotiate measures specific to the situation. These measures, which should include the goals the worker hopes to obtain in concrete terms, are also supposed to be designed so that they (1) adapt to the personalities of the parents and child (2) are within their capacity to carry them out and (3) are in proportion to the identified problems. In addition, the worker must be prepared to offer support to the child and family to apply the measures (CPJ, 1981, s.3.7.3). After six months if the worker feels that the child is still in need of protection, the measures are renewed for another six months, with any necessary alterations.

'Seizing the court'   'Seizing the court' refers to applying to the Youth Court when voluntary measures have not been able to be worked out with the child and family. While the court may be 'seized' during each of the stages of assessment and treatment, only certain persons may seize the court. Besides the youth protection delegate, acting on behalf of the director of youth protection, the child or his/her parents may also 'seize' the court if they are in disagreement with any of the decisions regarding the child taken by the Department of Youth Protection, including the initial decision that the child is in need of protection (Quebec, 1980b). The Youth Court is obliged not only to inform the child and his parents of their right to be represented by an advocate, but must also ensure that an advocate is assigned to defend the child when his interests are different from those of his parents (Youth Protection Act, 1977, ss.78 and 80). If the court concludes that the security or development of a child is in danger, it may make a variety of orders including an order that one or several measures proved for in section 54 (i.e. voluntary measures) be applied, an order withdrawing the exercise of certain rights of parental authority from the parents, a recommendation that a tutor be appointed to the child, or any recommendation it considers to be in the interests of the child. Appeal of the court's decisions may be made to the Quebec Superior Court and the Court of Appeal by the child, the parents or the social service agency (Quebec, 1980b). [14]

Once a 'voluntary measures' agreement is signed or a court order has been issued, the director of youth protection is said to 'take charge' or have a *'prise en charge'* of the child (Youth Protection Act 1977, Art.33d). This *'prise en charge'* is delegated to the social worker to whom the client is assigned and the delegation form contains the date the *'prise en charge'* begins as well as the required due date for the case review.

Every decision that is made in a case of suspected abuse from the time the 'signalment' is received until the case is closed, including decisions about referrals, 'voluntary measures', 'seizing the court' and placement, are reviewed by a group of professional social workers called 'review analysts' at the Department of Youth Protection (DYP), whose only job is to review the decisions of the workers working directly with the clients. This is done through a series of special forms sent between the worker and the analyst and include as well, the comprehensive psychosocial assessment that is done in the initial assessment.

At the time of the research, unlike in England, police were not routinely involved in the social work management of child abuse and if they (the police) became aware of a case, it was usually because they had been informed from another source. The draft of a policy statement regarding criminal charges recommended that the less closely related the abuser is to the child, the more the option of criminal charges should be considered (Comité de la Protection de la Jeunesse [CPJ], 1981). The recommendations were as follows: when the abuser is a parent or sibling, a 'psycho-social approach with the aggressor is the preferred approach' (CPJ, p.2). In cases where the abuser is an adult of the extended family and the parents do not seem able to protect the child and do not agree to voluntary measures, the parents should be encouraged either to press charges, or to 'seize' the Youth Court or, alternately, the director of youth protection can 'seize' the Court. Another option was for the DYP, with the authorisation of the committee of youth protection, to press criminal charges. This happened very rarely. The adoption of a policy in 1985 of referring cases to the police represented a drastic change for the youth protection services and the implications are discussed in the final chapter.

Article 33, Juvenile Delinquents Act   Until April 1984 when the Juvenile Delinquents Act (1970) was repealed and replaced by the Young Offenders Act, article 33, 'contributing to juvenile delinquency', provided an alternative in the youth court system to the youth protection acts for the protection of abused children. Under this article the sexually abusive adult could be charged with contributing to the delinquency of a minor and given a sentence ranging from a fine to probation, to two years of incarceration. This was used quite extensively in Quebec and seen as a valuable alternative to the youth protection court (before 1977, the social welfare court), as it allowed the legislative focus to be on the abuser rather than the child, and at the same time, avoided the punitive and disruptive consequences of criminal court (Cooper, 1978). This provision was not replaced and the child protection authorities must rely on the options cited above which are focused on the child.

In summary, at the time of the research (1979-1984) there were several differences in the two youth protection systems in England and Canada. These include the availability of a non-coercive (non-court mandated) means of engaging with the family in the Canadian system, the rights of parents, the dispositions available to the youth court, and the involvement of the police in the management of child abuse. The ability to prosecute the offending parent in the Canadian youth court also represents an important difference.

Criminal justice system

Statutes related to child sexual abuse - England and Canada

Sexual acts between adults and children are prohibited in a variety of statutes, the choice of which depends on the age and sex of the child, the nature of the acts and sometimes, the relationship of the two persons. [15]

In both England and Canada incest is a specific offence which prohibits sexual intercourse between parent and child, grandparent and grandchild, and brother and sister. Half-siblings are also included in the legislation. The British law makes a distinction between the age of the child - if the victim is a girl under 13 and the offender is a man, the maximum sentence is life imprisonment, otherwise it is seven years imprisonment. The maximum penalty in Canada is 14 years imprisonment.

Other statutes are applied for intercourse between minors and adults in non-blood relationships, for example, between an uncle and niece, step-father and step-daughter and mother's cohabitee and daughter. In England these are rape (punishable by life imprisonment), attempted rape (maximum sentence seven years imprisonment) and unlawful sexual intercourse (punishable by life imprisonment if the girl is under 13 and by a prison sentence not exceeding two years if the girl is under 16). In Canada there is a specific offence prohibiting intercourse with a step-daughter. Offences of sexual intercourse with a female under 14 (punishable by life imprisonment) and sexual intercourse with a female 14 or 15 (punishable by five years' imprisonment) can also be applied. Until 4 July, 1983 when a number of amendments to the *Criminal Code* sexual offences were proclaimed (Canada, 1984), a charge of rape could be used. This has been replaced by the offence of sexual assault with maximum penalties of ten years' imprisonment or six months' imprisonment. [16] 'Sexual assault' can include everything from a threatened sexual advance to 'unwanted sexual intercourse unaccompanied by incest threats or the use or threatened use of a weapon' (Canada, vol.1, p.308).

The offence of buggery (prohibited anal intercourse) exists in both countries but with different maximum sentences - in England, life imprisonment (or 10 years if the victim is a non-consenting male), in Canada, 14 years' imprisonment.

Incestuous acts (fondling, touching, masturbation and oral-genital contact) are covered by a variety of statutes. In England, until the 1985 Sexual Offences Act, indecent assault against a girl under 13 had a maximum sentence of five years' imprisonment; against a girl aged 14 to 16, two years' imprisonment and against a male, ten years' imprisonment. The amendments in the 1985 act provide a maximum penalty of 10 years' imprisonment for females. Indecency with or towards a child under 14, which does not require that the victim be actually touched ('assaulted'), is punishable by a maximum sentence of two years and on summary conviction, by a maximum of six months' imprisonment and/or a fine of up to £100. [17] In Canada, the offence of assault on a female, punishable by a maximum sentence of five years' imprisonment, was repealed in January, 1983 and replaced by the above mentioned sexual assault offences. Similarly, indecent assault on a male was also repealed and replaced by sexual assault offences. The offence of gross indecency with a maximum custodial sentence of five years, can also be applied. However, it has never been defined and 'although originally limited to homosexual male behaviour, it now refers to an ill-defined range of homosexual and heterosexual behaviours variously involving adults, adolescents or children, depending on the circumstances' (Canada, 1984, Vol.1, p.323).

Police investigation and laying of charges - England

Access to information about procedures and policies followed by the police in cases of alleged sexual abuse in Canada was difficult. Because only a few are investigated by the police (as data subsequently showed) this was not considered to be a serious lack. Thus information in this section focuses only on England.

Police   Once the police have been informed of a case of suspected incest or incestuous behaviour, they commence their investigations. If they arrest the alleged perpetrator without a warrant and charge him with a criminal offence, he may either be released on bail or held in custody to appear before a magistrates' court on a specified date. When the police arrest a person on a warrant that has been endorsed for bail the police must release him on bail (Home Office Criminal Statistics, 1981, p.181). During the police investigation of a case of alleged father-daughter incest it is a common practice to remove the father from home. He is usually granted bail on the condition that he has no further contact with this wife and daughter before the case is heard. In more rare instances, for example, if there is a danger of repetition of the alleged incest, the father is remanded in custody (Manchester, 1979; Howard League, 1976). Once their investigation is complete, the police have the option to discharge the case because of lack of evidence, issue a caution, lay a charge that is less than incest or attempted incest or refer to the Director of Public Prosecutions (DPP).

Since 1985, after the period for this research, the role of the DPP was taken over by the Crown Prosecution Service (Prosecution of Offences Act 1985). However, until this change, in cases where it appeared that there was sufficient evidence to form the basis for a charge of incest or attempted incest, the police had to report to the DPP. 'A prosecution may not be commenced except by or with the consent of the Director of Public Prosecutions' (Sexual Offences Act, 1956, s.37, Sched.2, paras.14 and 15, as amended by the Criminal Law Act, 1977). A charge of buggery was also subject to the approval of the DPP (Sexual Offences Act 1967, s.8).

When a case of suspected incest had been referred to the DPP for consideration of prosecution, in some areas it appeared to have been the practice for the police to lay a lesser charge such as indecent assault. This could be changed later to a charge of incest if the DPP decided to prosecute. [18]

One of the options of the police as an alternative to prosecution is to issue a police caution. This is a formal warning given to an offender that his conduct was a criminal offence which could have led to his being prosecuted. A caution, usually given orally by a senior police officer at a police station, can only be applied if the accused admits to the offence or, alternatively, is found guilty by the courts (Home Office, 1981a, p.76).

Director of public prosecutions   The DPP had 55 professional officers grouped into eight divisions drawn up primarily on geographical lines. When a case of alleged incest or attempted incest was referred to them for consideration, they first ensured that there was no defect in the file that the police submitted, for example, lack of jurisdiction, then considered whether there was enough evidence to support a reasonable chance of conviction and finally made a decision as to whether it is in the public interest to institute proceedings. Factors influencing this decision have been cited as the age of the case, age, infirmity, mental illness and instability of the accused and public expense (Barnes, 1975 cited in Manchester, 1978, p.494). Evidence of previous convictions or findings of guilt could conceivably influence the DPP's decision to prosecute. However, Soothill's analysis of the criminal statistics failed to give a clear indication of this as 57% of his 1961 cases of alleged incest offenders appearing in court and 56% of the 1976 series, had no previous criminal convictions (Soothill, 1980).

Notes

[1]   Local authorities are set up in metropolitan districts, non-metropolitan counties, London boroughs and in the Common Council of the City of London. Among other things, the local authority is responsible for social services. It appoints a director of social services and establishes social services committees which have statutory responsibility for children, the aged and disabled persons (Smith, 1979). This followed the recommendations of the Seebohm Report (1968) which, in 1971, resulted in the end of the children's departments which were integrated into the newly formed social service departments (Packer, 1981, Ch.8).

[2]   The UK, unlike Canada and the United States, have no mandatory reporting laws. Thus, while social workers have a statutory responsibility to investigate cases of abuse, they are not legally obliged to report cases either to the police or to the register. This leaves the register and the case conference format the principal means of monitoring cases of child abuse.

3   See Appendix 1 for a copy of this circular which describes the roles of the various professionals in the management of child abuse.

4   Personal communication, Margaret Clough, Social Work Service Officer, DHSS, February 1983.

5   Jones stated 'I don't feel the DHSS has served workers as well as it might have done. It left us for six years (since 1982 when the DHSS minister said they would take action) without guidance about questions which had been raised.' (Morris, 1988, p.5).

6   The magistrates' court, which is at the bottom of the criminal hierarchy of courts, is staffed by justices of the peace or magistrates. Most of the magistrates are lay magistrates and unpaid. Full-time paid magistrates, or 'stipendiaries', who are lawyers, are appointed when there is a large work load. Stipendiaries usually sit on their own while lay benches usually comprise three magistrates. Since lay magistrates are not trained lawyers, a legally qualified clerk who advises on law and procedure is attached to the court (Smith, 1979).

7   The following description of the laws and procedures involved in child protection are of those existing at the time of this research, prior to the 1989 Children Act which had yet to be implemented. The new act was created in response to widespread dissatisfaction with the child case law. Allen (1990) observed that if there is one outstanding feature of legal development in the child care field in recent years it is the sheer bulk and frequency of legislation passed by Parliament, legislation which by virtue of its complexity has made this branch of the law virtually impenetrable to those without full legal training (p.1).

8   Schedule 1 of the Children and Young Persons Act 1933 lists various assaults and sexual offences where children are the victim (amended by the Sexual Offences Act 1956). The wording of the Act does not allow a rubber-stamping because of a previous conviction and requires establishing a probability of harm under the appropriate development condition (Dingwall & Eekelaar, 1982).

9   This has been altered in the 1989 Children Act and will be discussed in the last chapter. See footnote 7.

10 This has been altered by the 1989 Children Act. See footnote 14.

11 Unlike in England where there is a wealth of literature on child welfare law and practice, there is a lack of material in Canada. Thus, for this section, the researcher had to rely on the statutes, procedure manuals and a few journal articles.

12 This is referred to as 'urgent measures' and can also be done at the initial intake point after a brief assessment.

13 This is in contrast to the 28 days allowed for the maintenance of place of safety orders in the British system.

[14] At the time of the data collection (1979-1984) there were major contrasts concerning the rights of parents in the British and Canadian civil courts. Parents in England were not parties to the action and had no right to a lawyer. Neither they nor, in most cases, the local authority social workers, had the right to appeal the court decisions. The resolution of these issues by the new Children Act has yet to be seen. Section 93 of the Act merely states that 'rules of court *may* make provision as to the persons entitled to participate in proceedings under this Act' (Allen, 1990, p.115, emphasis added). Government spokesmen during the parliamentary debate said only that persons with parental responsibility for the child will normally be parties (Allen).

[15] The relevant statutes in each country that are discussed, are as follows: in England - Sexual Offences Act 1956, ss.10, 11, 1, 5, 6, 14, 12; Sexual Offences Act 1985, s.3; Indecency with Children Act 1969, ss.1, 14; in Canada -Criminal Code (s.150, 155, 143, 153(1)(a), 146(1)2), 149(1), 156, 157, 246.1).

[16] This offence is 'procedurally "hybrid"': the Crown has a discretion to proceed either by indictment or summarily, hence, can directly influence the maximum punishment to which a person convicted of this offence will be liable' (Canada, 1984, vol.1, p.307).

[17] This offence includes masturbating before the child and having the child touch the offender.

[18] Personal communication, Inspector Ralph Ellam, Juvenile Liaison Officer, Cambridge Police Department, November 1982.

4 Description of Samples - England and Canada

In the following, data on the victim, the perpetrator, and the family, as well as on the nature of the sexual abuse, are presented. The data on the two samples from England and Canada are presented separately. To better appreciate the findings, comparisons are made with findings from other studies. While such comparisons were relatively easy for some of the material (for example, age of the victim at referral, size of family, family problems), there was a striking scarcity of data in the literature in other areas. For example, information on the nature of the abuse, age of onset (of victim and perpetrator) and frequency was often lacking.

In the study, 'incest' or 'intrafamily child sexual abuse' (IFSA), is broadly defined and refers to sexual activities with a young person by one of the family circle, including parents, siblings, grandparents, uncles, aunts, step-parents' and parents' cohabitees. '*Sexual activities*'refer to both non-contact and contact sexual behaviours, including voyeurism, exhibitionism, fondling, masturbation (of self and/or other), oral-genital contact, vaginal intercourse, anal penetration, and 'deviant' acts, such as flagellation and urination.

'Victim' refers to the child or young person who is the object of the sexual activities of the perpetrator. The term is used with some reluctance because of certain meanings attached to it, in particular, the idea that the consequences are always negative.[1] However, because the term is commonly used in the current literature and its usage facilitates discussion, it is employed throughout this study. Throughout the text, the terms 'British' and 'English' are used interchangeably.

General description of the samples

The victims

The British sample consisted of 96 victims, 86 females and ten males, who were referred because of disclosure of suspected sexual abuse by 81 different perpetrators within the family. (Note: unless stated otherwise, all of the statistics which follow are based on victims; thus, some perpetrators are counted more than once.) Only one victim in the study is described as involved with more than one perpetrator. This was a girl, whose two brothers had sexual play with her simultaneously. [2,3] The 96 victims were from 82 different families, 69 being the only victim from their family, 12 families contributing two victims each and one family having three victims.

The Canadian sample consisted of 95 victims, 83 females and 12 males, referred because of suspicion of sexual abuse by 76 different familial perpetrators. The 95 victims were from 77 different families, 60 being the only victim in the family, (two of the victims were cousins abused by the same perpetrator), 13 families contributing two victims each (two victims in one of these families were abused by different perpetrators), and three families with three victims each (two victims in one of these families were abused by different perpetrators), and three families with three victims each.   As in most surveys (Gordon & O'Keefe, 1984; Herman & Hirschman, 1977; Maisch, 1972; Weinberg, 1955; Vander Mey & Neff, 1986), over 80% of victims were females (85.5% English, 87.4% Canadian). While estimations vary, recent literature suggests that more males are sexually abused than are reported (Finkelhor & Baron, 1986; Kempe & Kempe, 1984; Swift, 1977; Wood & Dean, 1984). However, unlike girls, the sexual abuse of boys is more likely to come from outside the family (American Humane Association, 1981; Finkelhor, 1984).

With the exception of one unusual case with a 20-year-old victim, [4] the victims' ages at the referral ranged from one year to 17, with 45.8% being between nine and 13 years of age.

Table 4.1   Age of victim at referral - England and Canada

	Victims			
	England		Canada	
Age	N=96	%	N=95	%
1- 3	4		2	
4- 6	8	24	10	18.8
7- 8	11		6	
9-10	10	45.8	11	
11	5		7	38.5
12	14		9	
13	15		9	
14	11		15	
15	9	30.2	16	42.7
16-17	8		10	
20	1			

As can be seen from Table 4.1, the ages of the Canadian victims were rather similarly distributed except that there were fewer in the younger age group and more in their later teens.

In both samples, the boys were younger, their average age was 8.3 (England) and 9.6 (Canada), compared to 12.1 (England) and 16.6 (Canada) for the girls. The age distribution of the victims generally corresponds to the findings reported in the literature, which suggests that victims tend to disclose in the early teen years (Finklhor & Baron, 1986: Vander Mey & Neff, 1986). For example, the American National Incidence Study of Child Abuse and Neglect (National Center on Child Abuse and Neglect [NCCAN], 1981) reported that 60% of the sexually abused children were twelve or older.

The majority of surveys do not distinguish between intrafamilial and extrafamilial abuse. However, two studies that do, one by Julian and Mohr (1979) on a national survey of father-daughter incest in the United States (N=102) and the other by Burgess, Holmstrom and McCausland (1977) reporting on a survey of 44 incest victims seen at a hospital clinic, report ages of victims at disclosure respectively older (63% at 14 to 17 in the Julian and Mohr survey) and younger (52% under 9 in the Burgess survey) than in the present English and Canadian samples. While it is not possible to fully explain these discrepancies, two contributing factors may be: 1) the current research had a considerably larger sample than both studies and 2) unlike the Julian and Mohr study, which only examined father-daughter cases (the identity of the incest perpetrators were not defined in the Burgess sample), this survey included all types of intrafamilial relationships. It could be thought that girls victimised by their father have more difficulty disclosing the abuse and are more able to at an older age. However, a statistical analysis of the samples (the current one and the two in the literature) did not reveal a significant relationship between type of perpetrator and age at disclosure.

The perpetrators

As shown in Table 4.2, the large majority of perpetrators in both samples were male, a finding reported in all the studies. (See for example, Berliner, 1977; Burgess et al. 1977; Finkelhor & Hotaling, 1983; Giaretto, 1976; Maisch, 1972). In the Canadian population survey (Canada, 1984), only 2.8% of offenders were female. Some researchers suggest, however, that more females sexually abuse children than are reported (Sgroi, 1982; Schetky & Green, 1988; West, 1987). Explanations for the low reporting include such factors as the likelihood that boys tend to complain less about sexual abuse, women's child caring role, which allows them to sexually fondle a child without being observed and cultural biases, which prevent people from interpreting the sexual behaviour of adult women with children as abusive. [5]

While there were slightly more biological fathers as perpetrators in the English sample, Table 4.2 demonstrates that the relationships of perpetrators to victims were similar in both samples with some four-fifths being fathers, step-fathers, or male cohabitees. There was no obvious difference in the distribution of relationships between the penetration and non-penetration cases.

Table 4.2   **Relationship of perpetrator and victim - England and Canada**

Perpetrator	England No. of victims N=96	%	Canada No. of victims N=95	%
father	40	41.7	54	56.8
step-father	22	22.7	17	17.9
male cohabitee	11	11.5	5	5.3
mother	1	1.0	3	3.2
brother	10	10.4	7	7.4
grandfather	4	4.2	2	2.1
other*	8	8.3	7	7.4

* uncle, brother-in-law

Similar to this survey, most reports in the literature cite biological fathers as the most common familial perpetrator of sexual abuse (Finkelhor, 1979; Julian, Mohr & Lapp, 1980; Machotka, Pittman & Flomenhaft, 1967; Meiselman, 1978). Similar to the English sample in this study, Creighton's report (1985) on the NSPCC cases described natural fathers and father substitutes (step-fathers and male cohabitees) as being implicated almost equally (1985). Some recent studies, however, have suggested that molestation by step-fathers may be proportionally more frequent (Frude, 1982; Russell, 1984). This is supported by Sagarin (1977), who cites Maisch's data (1972), which showed almost as many step-fathers as fathers as perpetrators. Various studies (de Young, 1982; Gruber & Jones, 1983; Russell, 1984) found that having a step-father actually increases the risk of sexual victimisation. Finkelhor (1984a) in his retrospective study of 796 college students, found that a step-father was five times more likely to sexually abuse a daughter than was a natural father. The ages of the perpetrators ranged from 12 to 70.

Sexual behaviour

General description of samples

There were two distinctive types of sexual behaviour: penetrative acts of sexual intercourse or buggery and sexual touching without penetration (fondling, touching, kissing, oral-genital contact and masturbation), [6] and the sample was divided into the two main groups: 'penetrative and non-penetrative'. A majority of victims, greater in the Canadian than in the British sample (79% against 61.5%), were in the non-penetrative group (see Table 4.3). This coincides with most of the surveys which report that the most common type of sexual activity is non-genital or genital fondling. The estimations vary as follows: Kinsey (1955), 58%; Finkelhor (1979), 40%; Pierce and Pierce (1985), 59%. Some studies, like the present one, which focus exclusively on intrafamilial sexual abuse, report a higher incidence of sexual intercourse; in the survey by Gebhard and his associates (1965), 49% and in Maisch's (1972), 55%. Both these figures are higher than what was found in this study, even though anal intercourse was not included.

Consistent with the results in other studies (see, for example, Gebhard, Gagnon, Pomeroy & Christenson, 1965: Meiselman, 1978), for the majority of victims the sexual relationship was initiated with some form of physical contact. A small number of victims (five in Canada) had no physical contact with the perpetrator, who committed such acts as exhibiting himself, watching the victim bathe, and showing the victim pornographic pictures after giving her drugs. [7]

Data was collected on the age of onset of the different types of sexual behaviours, the frequency with which they occurred and their duration. The sexual relationship was initiated with the victims as young as one year of age and the oldest age of onset was sixteen and one half. While sexual activity began for a larger number of victims in the British sample when the child was eight or older (76.9%), it began at a younger age for a larger proportion of the Canadian victims (36.0% versus 23.1%) (Table 4.4). The distribution is similar to other samples which report incestuous activity for most victims beginning between eight and 12 years of age (De Young, 1982; Goodwin, McCarthy & Divesto, 1981; Herman, 1981). However, Maisch (1972) found a larger proportion, 67%, aged nine to 15, as compared with 54% of the English and 39% of the Canadian sample.

**Table 4.3   Type of sexual acts between perpetrator and victim -
England and Canada**

Sexual behaviour non-penetration/ penetration	No. of victims				No. of penetrators	
	England (N=96)		Canada (N=95)		England (N=81)	Canada (N=76)
	No.	%	No.	%	No.	No.
sexual fondling, etc. with no penetration	59	61.5	75	79.0	51[a]	58[b]
vaginal/anal intercourse	37	38.5	20	21.0	33[a]	20[b]
Other sexual behaviour[c]						
oral/genital contact (perpetrator on victim)	12	12.5	10	10.5	12	9
oral/genital contact (victim on perpetrator)	14	14.6	12	12.6	14	10
deviant acts	8	8.3	5	5.3	5	5

[a]　3 perpetrators are in both groups
[b]　2 perpetrators are in both groups
[c]　Categories are not mutually exclusive

Table 4.4   Age of onset of sexual manipulation with present perpetrator - England and Canada

Age in years	England (N=78)		Canada (N=75)	
	No.	%	No.	%
1	1		4	
2	1		0	
3	0	23.1	0	36.0
4	1		4	
5	4		5	
6	2		8	
7	9		6	
8	6		9	
9	4		6	
10	10	50.0	7	40.0
11	6		7	
12	13		1	
13	10		8	
14	7	26.9	7	24.0
15	2		1	
16	2		2	
not known	18		20	

Table 4.5   **Frequency of sexual manipulation with present**
perpetrator - England and Canada

Frequency	England (N=52)		Canada (N=45)	
	No.	%	No.	%
once	6		3	
2 - 5 times	16	42.3	12	33.3
6 - 10 times	4	7.7	3	6.7
11 - 20 times	5	9.6	2	4.4
21 - 30 times	5	9.6	0	0
31 - 60 times	3	5.8	3	6.7
61 -100 times	2	3.8	4	8.9
more than 100 times	11	21.2	18	40.0
not known	44		50	
total	96		95	

As Table 4.5 shows, frequency ranged widely in both samples, with nine victims having experienced only one incident and 29 known to have experienced over 100. Approximately twice the number of Canadian victims than British experienced this high rate of incidents. In the British sample, the length of the sexual relationship varied from less than six months (29.3%) to four years or more (14.7%). A somewhat similar distribution is seen in the Canadian sample except that almost three times the number of victims (34.7%) had a relationship which lasted four years or more (Table 4.6). These findings generally correspond to those reported in the literature. Few studies report on the actual frequency of the abuse except to state that more incestuous relationships involve more than one incident (Frude, 1982; Finkelhor, 1980). Maisch (1972) reported that 29% of his sample had experienced only isolated acts or ones lasting less than six months. Meiselman (1978) described 25% of her sample (N=58) as having experienced one incident. The average length of relationships lasting over one year has been reported as 3.1 years (Maisch), 3.3 years (Tamm, 1965, cited in Maisch), and 3.5 years (Meiselman).

Table 4.6   **Duration[a] of sexual relationship from age of onset to age at referral leading to professional action - England and Canada**

Duration	No. of victims			
	England (N=82)		Canada (N=72)	
	No.	%	No.	%
once or > 3 mths.	22	26.8	11	15.3
3 mths. - 11 mths.	18	21.9	14	9.4
1 yr. - 23 mths.	17	20.8	9	12.5
2 yrs. - 35 mths.	11	13.4	9	12.5
3 yrs. - 47 mths.	3	3.7	4	5.6
4 yrs. or more	11	13.4	25	34.7
not known[b]	14		23	
total	96		95	

[a]   Period between age of onset and age at referral leading to action
[b]   As far as could be determined, these victims had experienced more than one incident or incidents continuing three months or more

Some victims also experienced other types of sexual acts, including oral/genital contact (perpetrator on the victim or vice versa) and deviant acts which ranged in severity from being shown pornographic pictures while being given drugs, and watching parents have intercourse, to tying up, flagellation, and urination. Oral/genital contact was more common than other deviant behaviour, to which only eight English and five Canadian victims were subjected. This corresponds to other studies which report deviant or 'perverse' type acts as rare (Frude, 1982) but oral/genital contact as more common. The studies, however, which give various figures for oral/genital acts (Gebhard et al., 1965 - 30%; Meiselman, 1978 - 22%) do not differentiate between the types of oral/genital contact. There was considerable variation in the age of onset, frequency, and duration of these sexual acts. Considering the possibility of increased trauma for the victims experiencing these behaviours, particularly oral sex by the victim on the perpetrator, it is disturbing to observe that as many as nine English and ten Canadian children under 9 years of age were subjected to one or another type of oral/genital contact. (Two in each sample were under the age of 6 when they performed oral sex on the abuser). This is in keeping, however, with the finding of Gebhard and his associates, which showed that those daughters in the study who had had oral/genital contact with their father were under 12. Meiselman suggests that these techniques are a substitute for intercourse in this young age group.

Non-penetration group

It is convenient to consider separately the substantial part of the sample who experienced a variety of sexual acts but never penetration. In the British sample, there were 59 such victims, five of them boys, (61.5%,). [8]

In the Canadian sample, 75 victims (79%), 11 of them boys, were subjected to some form of sexual contact without penetration by 58 perpetrators. Most of these were fathers (44) or father-substitutes (11); there were two mothers and the remainder were siblings, grandfathers and uncles.

As indicated in Table 4.7, it appears that in terms of the severity of the non-penetrative abuse (using the number of incidents of sexual contact and duration of the relationship), Canadian victims experienced more serious sexual abuse than British victims. In those cases where the frequency was revealed, over a third of Canadian victims (13/35), but under a tenth of the British victims (3/32) experienced 100 or more incidents. Assuming that the victims known to have had a sexual relationship lasting three years or more were subjected to more than 30 incidents of sexual abuse (five in the British sample, nine in Canadian), it would appear that 70% of the Canadian victims, compared to 21.2% of the English victims, are known to have experienced more than 30 incidents of sexual contact.

Penetration group

Although it is probably the most serious cases which come to the attention of the social services, it was a minority of children in both samples (in England, 37 out of 96; 38.5%; in Canada 20 out of 95; 21.1%) who experienced sexual penetration of anus or vagina. In England, these 37 included five boys, who had been submitted to anal intercourse (buggery), three girls who had had anal as well as vaginal intercourse, and two girls who had only had anal intercourse. In four other cases, intercourse was alleged to have occurred but there were only the girls' statements, which were vague and changeable, and on medical examination they were found to be virgo intacta. [9, 10]

Table 4.7   Frequency or duration of sexual contact* (non-penetration group) - England and Canada

No. of incidents	Victims			
	England (N=47)		Canada (N=58)	
or duration	No.	%	No.	%
1	6	12.8	3	5.2
2- 5	12	25.5	10	17.2
6-10	3	6.4	2	3.5
1-20	4	8.5	1	1.7
21-30	2	4.3	0	0
31-60	1	2.1	2	3.5
61-99	1	2.1	4	6.9
100 or more	3	6.4	13	22.4
1 month or less	0	0.2	0	3.5
2- 6 months	2	4.3	4	6.9
7-11 months	4	8.5	1	1.7
12-23 months	3	6.4	5	8.6
24-35 months	1	2.1	2	3.5
36-47 months or more	5	10.6	9	15.5
both frequency and duration not known	12		17	
total	59		75	

*   Duration is given when frequency is not known

The 20 Canadian children who had been sexually penetrated included one boy, who had allegedly experienced anal intercourse [No.88C], and nineteen girls, two of whom had had anal as well as vaginal intercourse with the perpetrator. In the Canadian sample, the perpetrators were all fathers or step-fathers.

Vaginal intercourse   The age intercourse began was recorded in 27 of the 30 British cases and ranged from 11 and 12 (eight cases) to 15 or 16 (four cases) with a majority (16 cases) at 13 or 14. This corresponds to most of the studies which report the average age of onset of intercourse as ranging from 12.3 (Maisch, 1972), 12.9 (Tamm, 1965) and 13 (Gebhard et al.,

1965) to 15.3 (Weinberg, 1955). Gorry (1986) reported that most of his sample were between 13 and 15. [11] It is suggested that intercourse occurs when the girl has reached a stage of sexual maturity that allows for such a behaviour (Maisch, 1972; Meiselman, 1978). The age of onset of intercourse in the Canadian sample tended to be younger. Only six of the 15 where information was available had their first experience at 13 and intercourse began at 12 or younger for eight victims, of whom five were between 8 and 10. One of these girls [No.87] whose case is somewhat difficult to understand in terms of the evidence of the nature of the abuse, was 5 when intercourse occurred. [12] Others have reported very young girls being subjected to intercourse by a family member. Gebhard and his colleagues (1965) found that only 9% of their sample of incarcerated fathers had had sexual intercourse with daughters under the age of 12; five of Meiselman's sample had done so and one girl in Maisch's sample had been 6 years of age.

For most of the Canadian victims (12 out of 19) and some of the English victims (11 out of 30) intercourse had occurred at or shortly after the onset of the sexual relationship but for others, (seven English, four Canadian) 1½ to 4½ years passed before intercourse was initiated.

Table 4.8   Duration* and frequency of sexual intercourse - England and Canada

Duration	Canada (N=19)	England (N=30)
less than 12 months	5	15
12 months and longer	10	14
not known	4	1
Frequency	**Canada (N=19)**	**England (N=30)**
1-20 times	5	19
21 or more times	4	8
not known	10	3

*   Duration is the length of time the sexual relationship involved sexual intercourse

As Table 4.8 indicates, while there was a wide range of number of incidents of intercourse and duration of the behaviours in both groups, the data suggest that when it occurred, the penetrative behaviour was more serious in the Canadian sample. Two-thirds of the 15 Canadian victims where the information was available, compared with approximately a half of the 29 English victims, had experienced sexual intercourse for 12 months or longer. A similar breakdown of the available figures for the frequency of sexual intercourse shows a similar trend - almost half of the Canadian victims (four out of nine) compared with approximately a third of the English victims (eight out of 27) were subjected to the behaviour on 21 or more occasions.

While it appears that in some cases the period of time in which the incidents occurred corresponded to the number of incidents, i.e. the longer the duration the more incidents. (For example, [No.77C] where intercourse took place 61 to 100 times over a period of three to four years, and [#76C] where intercourse took place well over 100 times for six-and-a-half years), this was not always the case. For example, in case [#82C] there were only six incidents within two years, whereas in case [#79C], intercourse occurred approximately forty times in six months. For a few girls (five Canadian, five English), the number of incidents of both sexual fondling and intercourse was high, with episodes of sexual fondling only, occurring on over 100 occasions.

Buggery   There is little comment in the literature on incestuous relations on the incidence of buggery. Gligor (1966), however, who included anal intercourse as well as oral/genital contact and sexual activity with two or more partners simultaneously in his definition of 'deviant sex activity', found that 20% of his sample of incestuous daughters (N=57) had been subjected to such behaviours by their fathers. Buggery occurred with ten of the British victims (five girls and five boys) and three of the Canadian victims (two girls and one boy). While the girls experienced it with a father or a father substitute, with two exceptions the boys experienced it with a more distant type relative - two with a male co-habitee, two with an uncle, one with a half-brother, and only one with a father. Although very small, the figures are consistent with the assumption that, among children exposed to buggery, boys less often than girls are victims of their own fathers.

The age of onset of buggery was less than three years for three of the 13 victims, all of them boys. The very young age of some male victims of anal penetration by perpetrators within the home has been commented on by Hobbs and Wynne (1986). Girl victims of buggery were exposed to that experience less often than girls were subjected to sexual intercourse. One girl experienced buggery on one occasion, four on two occasions (two cases not known). Six of these seven girls had fairly long sexual relationships with their perpetrators (two for 6½ years), and five of these had also experienced intercourse as part as the relationship. The infrequent occurrence of buggery in the course of an extended sexual relationship suggests that the incidents occurred as part of a developing sexual relationship, was not the perpetrator' main goal, and was not motivated by a desire to avoid insemination. The potential discomfort for the victim of anal penetration and her probable resistance might also have contributed to the low frequency of this behaviour. With one exception [#93], the frequency of buggery with the five male British victims was similarly low and the sexual relationship brief. In the exceptional case involving an adolescent with his 10½-year old brother, the buggery was of much greater duration and frequency, at least 20 times in a 2½-year period [#93].

Other characteristics of the sexual relationship

Information was collected on the amount of access the perpetrator had to the victim, the direct involvement of other adults and/or children in the sexual acts, violence by the perpetrator towards the child during the sexual contact, and whether or not the penetrator was under the influence of alcohol during any of the sexual episodes. Findings were remarkably similar for both samples. The majority of victims were living with the perpetrator at the time of referral (70 British, 71 Canadian). Only a minority of the victims, (11 of the British victims, and six of the Canadian) had known their perpetrator for less than two years, and for five of these the contact had been less than three months.

Absence of the mother due to desertion, illness or death has been identified as a risk factor in incestuous abuse (Henderson, 1972; Maisch, 1972; Meiselman, 1978; Weinberg, 1955). Finkelhor (1979) reported that girls living without a mother in the home were three times more likely to be sexually abused than girls living with their mother. In approximately one third of the cases, the perpetrator was able to be regularly alone with the victim, and in 12 British and ten Canadian cases, the abuser, a father or father-substitute, had total access as there was no spouse or co-habitee in the home. Due to the mother working, going out with friends, or visiting, private access was still occasionally available in 22 cases (26 Canadian) and rare in only six (four Canadian); (26 British and seven Canadian cases are not known).

There have been some reports of adults other than the perpetrator participating in the sexual acts (see, in particular, Gligor, 1966 and Maisch, 1972), as well as some accounts of the participation of children other than the victim (Porter, 1984). In four cases of each sample, adults other than the perpetrator took part in some of the sexual acts with the perpetrator and victim. These included adult family members (for example a mother and an older sister) and friends of the perpetrator. In 15 British and eight Canadian cases other children, both from the family and outside the family, occasionally were included in the sexual acts.

Contrary to other studies which report rates of alcohol use ranging from 25% (Gebhard et al., 1965), 33% (Cavallin, 1966) and 49% (Rada, 1976), to as high as 73% (Kaufman, Peck & Tagiuri, 1954) and 77.3% (Virkkunen, 1974), alcohol was a factor in only a few cases. [13] Seven perpetrators in each sample claimed they were under the influence of alcohol when they approached the victim. In another six British and four Canadian cases, both the perpetrator and another family member, usually the victim, stated that the perpetrator was inebriated during one or more of the sexual acts. These findings correspond to those of Maisch (1972), who claimed that the direct effects of alcohol have been over-emphasized. Although 20% of the perpetrators in his study had been drinking before the first incestuous act, only 3% were highly intoxicated. Also, Flanzer and Sturkie (1983) in a small study of ten, found no relationship between parental drinking and sexual abuse.

As described by others (Gebhard et al., 1965; Maisch, 1972; Meiselman, 1978; Weinberg, 1955), violence during the sexual act was unusual. In 66 of the 76 British cases (where information was available) and 70 of the 73 Canadian cases, the perpetrators were never violent with the victim during the sexual abuse. This is similar to Gorry's study (1986), where 78% of the cases reported no violence. The minority of perpetrators who behaved aggressively did so on only one or two occasions. Alcohol was a factor in some but not all of the incidents of aggression. Threats of violence were more common than actual violence and reportedly occurred more often in the Canadian sample (12 out of 67 known cases) than in the British (seven out of 75 known children). This corresponds to other studies which report that while threats of violence are more common than actual violence, they still do not occur in the majority of cases (see, for example, Meiselman).

Characteristics of the victim's family

While 96 British victims came from 82 households, the 95 Canadian victims were from 77 households.[14] As shown in Table 4.9, which describes the major characteristics of the victims' families at the time of referral, the family composition in terms of the birth rank of the victim and the number of children living in the households were similar for both samples. At least half the households had three or more other children living in the home; only a small number of victims (ten British and 17 Canadian) were the only children at home. These findings are in line with other studies which report that incestuous families tend to be larger than non-incestuous families. Tormes (1968) found a median number of 4.7 children in his sample, Lukianowicz (1972) - seven, Cavallin - 5.1, and Julian and Mohr (1980) describe 36.3% of their incestuous families as having four or more children.

Table 4.9   Characteristics of victim's family - England and Canada

Characteristic	England (N=96)		Canada (N=95)	
	No.	%	No.	%
eldest in family	33	34.4	26	27.4
only child in household	5	5.2	17	17.9
3 or more children in household	47	49.0	55	57.9
living with natural parents	38	39.2	34	35.8
living with single mother	11	11.5	24	25.3
living with single father	12	12.5	10	10.5
living with mother/step-father	18	18.9	19	20.0
living with mother/male co-habitee	8	8.3	2	2.1
living with father/step-mother	3	3.1	2	2.1
livingh with other parent figure(s)	6	6.2	4	4.2
head of household unemployed	45	46.9	21	22.1
parental instability	45	46.9	23	24.2
spousal abuse by perpetrator	26	27.1	10	10.5
conviction for juvenile delinquency of victim's sibling	13	13.5	5	5.3
family seen by social agency prior to present referral	69	71.9	54	56.8

Only a minority of the children in both samples were living in an intact family with their biological mother and father (39.2% British, 35.8% Canadian). This is slightly smaller than the number reported in other studies. Creighton (1985) described 45% of the sexual abuse victims as living with their natural parents; Pierce and Pierce (1985) found 48% doing so (N=205). The increased risk for children living without their mother has already been noted. As many as ten Canadian and 12 British were victims living alone with their father who, with one exception in the Canadian sample, was the perpetrator. Creighton reported a similarly high rate in her sample - seven out of 101.

Surveys have indicated that child sexual abuse is over-represented in the lower socio-economic strata (see, for example, Julian et al., 1980 and Finkelhor, 1979). This, however, is usually attributed to the higher vulnerability of lower income groups to being reported (Finkelhor & Baron, 1984; Gomes-Schwartz et al., 1990; Julian & Mohr, 1979), although it is unclear whether this fully accounts for the difference. The findings in this research were similar. The rate of unemployment in the heads of the households where the victims lived was much higher than the population at large, especially in the British sample (46.9% of the victims). This corresponds to the findings of another British survey which covered approximately the same time period as the current study (1977-1982) and which found that the number of unemployed male caretakers of the abused children [15] increased from 35% in 1977 to 58.2% in 1982 (Creighton, 1985). Where the occupation of the head of the household was recorded, it was more often manual in the British sample (60 out of 67) than in the Canadian sample (41 out of 62).

Various studies have reported a high level of family problems in sexually abusive families (see for example, Creighton, 1985; Julian & Mohr, 1979; Server & Janzen, 1982; Vander Mey & Neff, 1986). This study produced similar findings - over half the families in both samples (57 of 82 British, accounting for 69 victims, and 41 of 77 Canadian, 54 victims) had been seen by a social service agency for problems prior to the referral for sexual abuse. Of these, 36 British families (of 45 victims) and 26 Canadian families (of 34 victims) had been followed for a period of time for a range of difficulties including delinquency, child physical abuse, financial problems and marital and family breakdowns.

Spousal abuse and physical abuse of children have been described by some authors as existing in sexually abusive families (Julian et al., 1980; Renvoize, 1978; Tormes, 1978; Weinberg, 1955; Vander Mey & Neff,

1986). Finkelhor (1983), however, has observed that while there are suggestions that there is a high correlation between spousal abuse and child physical abuse (by the same perpetrator), 'the connection between sexual abuse and physical abuse or spouse abuse... is less well established' (p.22). The findings in this study suggest a correlation. The most evident problem in both samples was family violence with over half of the British victims (59 out of 96) and almost half of the Canadian victims (46 out of 95) living in households where violence occurred. They either witnessed marital violence or violence against other children in the family or were themselves victims of physical assault. In the British sample, the mother was the family member most likely to be physically abused, but with that exception, it was the child victim of sexual abuse who was most likely to be the one physically abused. A substantial proportion of child victims were physically assaulted by the perpetrators, usually fathers or step-fathers in situations other than the commission of sexual abuse (21 of 63 British cases where information was available, 18 out of 60 Canadian cases). Fifteen of the British victims and eight of the Canadian had been physically assaulted by their mother.

Consistent with the findings in other sexual abuse studies (Finkelhor, 1984; Fromuth, 1983, cited in Finkelhor & Baron, 1986; Gorry, 1986; Gruber & Jones,1983; Landis, 1956; Peters, 1984), the marital relationships (of the victim's functional parents) were unstable for between one-quarter and one-half of the victims and marked with excessive fighting (physical and verbal) and separations.

Data was collected on other sexual abuse in the family, including abuse of the victim's siblings and earlier abuse of the victim's parents (Table 4.10). The transmission of incestuous behaviour from one generation to the next through parents who themselves experienced sexual abuse in their family has been described (Cooper & Cormier, 1982; Meiselman, 1978). As professionals probably very rarely questioned the parents about their history of sexual abuse, data was scarce but suggestive of unusually high prevalence. This corresponds to the findings of other studies. Server and Janzen (1982) reported that 33% of the parents in their sample of sexually abusive families (mother or father) (N=48) had a history of sexual abuse. Finally, Goodwin and her associates (1982) reported that the mothers whose children were physically or sexually abused were eight times more likely to have had previous incestuous experiences than were women in a control group.

As described by some (Chaneles, 1967; Nakashima & Zakus, 1977), the significant degree of family problems in both samples suggests that sexual abuse often occurs in the context of generalised family disorder, and is perhaps a symptom of much wider disturbance. Thus, as several studies linking the exhibition of symptoms to impoverished, multi-problem families have suggested (Lukianowicz, 1972; Westermeir, 1978), some of the victims' troubles may not be due to sexual abuse alone.

Table 4.10   Other sexual abuse in the family - England and Canada

Victim's family of origin	England (N=14)	Canada (N=25)
mother by her father	5	9
mother by her sibling	4	7
father [a] by his sibling	1	2
father [a] by his uncle	3	4
father's [a] sister by their father	1	3
Siblings [b] by	**England (N=23)**	**Canada (N=29)**
sibling	2	1
functional father	14	15
non-functional father	3	7
mother	1	2
grandparent	1	1
uncle	2	3

[a]   father-perpetrator
[b]   does not include victim's siblings in study

The most common pattern of multiple victims of incestuous abuse is that of a father who has sexual relations with more than one daughter (Cooper & Cormier, 1982; Meiselman, 1978). Another type involves male siblings abusing sisters (Bluglass, 1979; Justice & Justice, 1979). Incestuous relations in the current family seem extensive. Excluding the 35 Canadian victims from families in which more than one child was included in the study as a result of reported sex abuse, 53 of the 60 remaining victims had siblings of whom 29 had experienced sexual abuse (54.7%). The corresponding figures for the British sample were 23 out of 61 siblings not in the study (37.7%). This is similar to the Server and Janzen survey

(1982), which found that in 61% of the twenty-three cases where there was more than one daughter in the family, more than one daughter was sexually abused, but higher than Herman's survey (1981) which reported a rate of 27.5%. Rates quoted by other studies are difficult to assess as the number of cases where there were no female siblings, are not identified (Gligor, 1966, 31%; Meiselman, 19%).

Victim characteristics

Data was collected on the victims' medical history, behavioral problems, school performance, delinquency, and previous statutory involvement with social services. In both samples, most were in good health at the time of referral, and none had medical problems related to the abuse. Contrary to some studies which suggest that some victims have unusual physical characteristics (such as physical abnormalities) (Browning & Boatman, 1977; Davies, 1979), none of the victims did so. More of the British than the Canadian victims were of low intelligence (ten as compared to five), four had IQs of 70-80, five had IQs of 60-70, and one was assessed as severely impaired (IQ under 60). The five Canadian victims had mild retardation (60-70) and four others had been diagnosed as dyslexic.

At the time of referral, approximately half of the British and Canadian victims (50 and 43 respectively) exhibited one or more symptoms that could be interpreted as indicative of emotional disturbance (Table 4.11). However, only a small number of victims (19 Canadian, 18 English) exhibited several symptoms simultaneously (19 victims from both samples showed three to five of the listed disturbances).

Twenty-four Canadian and 32 English victims had only one symptom, of which the most common was absconding. In most cases this only occurred once or twice and was not chronic. This is much lower than that found by Herman (1981), who reported 33% as running away and Meiselman (1978) who reported a rate of 50%. The most common combination of symptoms was disruptive behaviour in school and a decline in performance or poor performance. [16]

Table 4.11   Victims' problems at time of referral[a] - England and Canada

Problem	England (N=50)	Canada (N=43)
enuresis	5	1
absconding	4	10
truanting from school	11	7
disruptive conduct at school	12	14
chronic poor performance in school	16	9
decline in school performance	9	8
mood change	3	3
mild drug use	2	6
alcohol abuse	0	1
suicide attempt	1	2
delinquency	4[b]	2[c]
total number of problems	75	64

Note: Victims may appear in more than one category
         Information was not available for all categories

[a]   Within 2 years prior to disclosure
[b]   All received a caution
[c]   2 of these received a caution; 1 was convicted

Contrary to much of the literature which stresses the serious short-term effects of sexual abuse (for an overview, see Browne & Finkelhor, 1986 and Mrazek & Mrazek, 1981), [17] the findings in this study suggest that many have no major symptoms.   This would concur with the findings of other studies (Bender & Blau, 1937; Burton, 1968; Gibbons & Prince, 1963; Lukianowicz, 1972; Tsai et al., 1979; Yorukoglu & Kemph, 1966). In a review of surveys on effects, Constantine (1980, 1983) reported that two-thirds of the studies identified some children who were unimpaired by their experience in any observable way. Symptoms found in this survey are similar to those described in other studies and include drug and alcohol abuse (Server & Janzen, 1982), absconding (Browning & Boatman, 1977; Kaufman et al., 1954; Reich & Gutierres, 1979), and truancy (Peters, 1976). However, only very few had the serious problems of delinquency, suicide attempts or drug abuse and, as the table shows, academic performance, poor behaviour at school, and truanting (English sample) emerge as the most frequent problems.   Sudden drops in school performance were also noted by DeFrancis (1969) and Goodwin and her associates (1982) and a study by Rosenfeld, Nadelson, Kreiger and Backman (1979) described poor school performance as a short term consequence of sexual abuse.   Green (1988a) has suggested that the sexually abused child might have problems concentrating in school because of preoccupation with the incest.

The difficulty in determining the sources of trauma in sexual abuse has been identified by a number of researchers (Browne and Finkelhor, 1986; Meiselman, 1978; Steele & Alexander, 1981). Smilarly, it was difficult to conclude from the data what factors contributed to the negative sequelae, for example, whether the type of sexual abuse affected the victim (six of the 20 Canadian victims who had experienced penetration exhibited some symptoms of disturbance). [18] While symptoms may be linked directly to the sexual abuse (Browne & Finkelhor; Steele & Alexander), it is likely that some, at least, were due to other causes. For example, four of the Canadian victims who had consistently performed poorly in school were dyslexic and one child with enuresis (described in some studies as associated with sexual abuse [Brant & Tisza, 1977; Mannarino & Cohen, 1986]) was a dyslexic five-year-old boy from a family fraught with marital conflict due to the father's mental illness [#88C]. A number of victims in both samples exhibiting problems came from such problematic families, which, as discussed above, may be a major factor in the creation of victim symptomatology.

A minority of victims (13 in the British and five in the Canadian samples), were known to have had sexual intercourse with a partner outside the family and the majority of these were with partners under 21. All of these 18 victims had experienced either sexual intercourse with the perpetrator or abuse extending six years or more.   While there was insufficient data to determine what factors might contribute to this, the data suggest that these more serious forms of sexual abuse may provoke precocious sexual behaviour outside the home.

Five of the British and three of the Canadian victims became pregnant as a result of intercourse with the family perpetrator. This corresponds to Meiselman's sample where 1.7% were impregnated by their perpetrator (1978). This low rate compared to earlier studies, which reported a higher incidence of pregnancy (11% - DeFrancis [1965], 20% - Maisch [1972] and Weinberg [1955]), has been explained by the recent increased sophistication in the use of contraceptives and in sex education in the school (Meiselman; Roybal & Goodwin, 1982). It may also be due to the trend towards earlier reporting. The British perpetrators were fathers or step-fathers [19] while the Canadian perpetrators were siblings - one of the latter impregnated his sister twice [#92C]. Except for three of the British girls who gave birth and kept their babies, all had therapeutic abortions. Roybal and Goodwin suggest that abortion is almost never sought when the pregnancy occurs in a patriarchal or chaotic family - in the former because the pregnancy is wanted and in the latter because the pregnancy is either unnoticed or unlikely to provoke an adaptive response.

As observed earlier, a substantial number of victims were physically abused (England 34%, Canada 26%), most often by the perpetrator, less often by their mothers, and sometimes by both. This corresponds to the findings of Vander Mey and Neff (1986), who report 30% of their sample as physically abused. Higher rates ranging from 45% to 56% are cited by other researchers (Herman, 1981; Julian & Mohr, 1979; Server & Janzen, 1982). For some victims, the physical abuse occurred only once or twice while for others the abuse was frequent.

As many as 40 victims (21 English and 19 Canadian) experienced sexual abuse by persons other than the current perpetrator. This is consistent with the findings of the Server & Janzen study (1982) where 23% had been sexually abused by more than one perpetrator, but is a smaller number than that reported by de Young (1982), who found that 23 of her sample of 60 incest victims were also sexually abused by someone other than the perpetrator. The higher rate, however, may be due to the fact that incidents which occurred within two years of the disclosure of the incest were included. The abusers included family members (parents and siblings) and adults and youths outside the family. Some of the incidence of sexual abuse by persons outside the family may reflect the poor supervision or neglect that occurs in chaotic families. A small number (five Canadian, seven English) were multiple victims in that they were both sexually abused by someone other than the perpetrator and physically abused.

Approximately one-quarter of the victims in both samples had been referred to a statutory social service agency prior to the present disclosure; most for physical abuse or neglect and some for family breakdown. This is similar to the findings of Pierce and Pierce (1985), who reported a slightly larger percentage of their sample of sexually abused children (one-third) as having had prior social service contact. Some of the current sample were still being followed at disclosure (14 British, 11 Canadian) and had been in placement; most in foster homes and a few in a community or group home.

Characteristics of victim's mother

The literature describes that a feature in some incest families is the unavailability of the mother due to ill health or emotional or psychiatric problems (Browning & Boatman, 1977; Finkelhor, 1984; Herman & Hirschman, 1981; Maisch, 1972; Meiselman, 1978). This was evident in a considerable number of cases in the samples. At the time of referral, 84 and 81 Canadian victims were living with a mother or mother-substitute. Twenty-nine English victims (34.5%) and 24 Canadian victims (29.6%) had a mother with serious health problems, either emotional or physical. A number had psychiatric problems at disclosure (13 and 15 respectively) and the most common diagnosis, as in other studies (Browning & Boatman, 1977; Herman, 1981; Justice & Justice, 1979), was reactive depression. In addition, the mothers of three of the British victims were mentally handicapped. Finkelhor (1979) identified maternal alcoholism as a risk factor for incest. Some in this study had drinking problems; in two of the British and four of the Canadian cases, serious enough to have required psychiatric treatment.

Characteristics of the perpetrator

All but one of the 81 British and two of the 76 Canadian perpetrators were male. The ages of the perpetrators at disclosure ranged from 12 to 70 and, as Table 4.12 shows, the Canadian fathers, step-fathers and male cohabitees tended to be older. In both samples, however, the average age of the father was higher than that found by Langevan, Handy, Day and Russon (1985), who reported the average age to be 37, but lower than that reported in other studies. Maisch (1972) reports that fathers and step-fathers are 'on average in their fifth decade, in between 40 and 49' (p. 103) at the start of the incest relationship.

**Table 4.12   Age range and average age of fathers, step-fathers and
male co-habitees - England and Canada**

Type of perpetrator	No.	Min. age	England Max. age	Average	Not known	Total
father	33	26	56	39.4	5	37
step-father	18	21	50	32.7	0	18
male co-habitee	4	28	54	39.5	5	9
Type of perpetrator	No.	Min. age	Canada Max. age	Average	Not known	Total
father	33	29	61	43.9	13	46
step-father	10	22	54	36.4	3	13
male co-habitee	1	60	60	60	2	3

As observed in other studies (see, in particular, Maisch, 1972, who found that at least 50% of his sample were socially and psychiatrically normal [N=67]), many were unremarkable characters free from serious pathology. Forty-four in the Canadian sample and 31 in the British had no known distinguishing features. Similar to other reports (Herman, 1981; Browning & Boatman, 1977; Lukianowicz, 1972; Maisch, 1972; Szabo, 1958; Weinberg, 1955; Meiselman, 1978), one of the most common characteristics was physical violence. Twenty-nine Canadian perpetrators and 33 British had been physically abusive to spouse, victim or to other children in the family.

Alcohol abuse is cited by many studies as particularly characteristic of incest offenders with reported percentages ranging from relatively low rates of 24% and 33% (Cavallin, 1966) and 37% (Herman, 1981) to as high as 48.9% (Virkkunen, 1974) and 73% (Kaufman et al., 1954). Two reviews of relevant studies concluded that incest offenders are the most alcohol involved of all sex abusers (Aarens, Cameron, Roizen, Room, Schnerberk & Wingard, 1978; Morgan, 1982). While the number of Canadian perpetrators known to have abused alcohol (23 compared to 13 British perpetrators) falls into the lower range reported in other studies, the smaller number of British perpetrators may be due to the larger number of cases where the information was not available (62 British versus 46 Canadian).

The small number who had received psychiatric treatment (six Canadian, 12 British) is consistent with the findings in other studies, which report little (Maisch, 1972; Gebhard et al., 1965) or no psychiatric history (Cavallin, 1966; Cormier et al., 1962; Lukianowicz, 1972; Weiner, 1964).

Considerably more of the British perpetrators were unemployed - only 14 Canadian perpetrators were not working (18.4%) while 35 of the British were unemployed (43.2%). The British rate is only slightly higher than the 32.2% reported in another British study (Gorry, 1986). This variation is consistent with the results of other surveys, some of which report unemployment or unstable work history (Kaufman et al., 1954; Lukianowicz, 1972; Weinberg, 1955), while others describe the perpetrators as good workers with regular employment (Cavallin, 1966: Cormier et al., 1962; Herman, 1982; Meiselman, 1978; Weiner, 1964). As has been suggested by Green (1988), the different results may be due to socio-economic differences among the different study populations. The community which provided the British data was seen by the social workers as having recently undergone a greatly increased rate of unemployment due to the closing down of a number of factories. This was not the case in Montreal, where the Canadian data was collected.

More of the British perpetrators had health problems [20] (12 compared to no Canadian). This may have been related to the apparent better socio-economic conditions of the Canadian sample. A minority of perpetrators had a history of previous convictions for offences either as a juvenile or adult (24 English, seven Canadian). While this is contrary to the findings of Cormier and his associates (1962), who found no criminal or delinquent history, it corresponds to other studies which describe incest offenders as having some, albeit a low, disposition to crime. (See, in particular, Gebhard et al., 1965; Server and Janzen, 1982 and Maisch, 1972). However, it is interesting to note Creighton's finding in her British study (1985) of abused children that fathers with criminal records were more likely to have been implicated than those without a record.

While it appears that the English sample was more delinquent, this may, in fact, not be true as this data was largely missing in the Canadian sample. With the exception of four of the British cases where the perpetrator had been convicted for burglary, most of the convictions for non-sexual offences had been for minor thefts and assaults, mostly on family members, and most of the offences occurred some years prior to the present disclosure. Thirteen of the British and three of the Canadian perpetrators had received custodial sentences for these offences.

More relevantly, thirteen British and three Canadian perpetrators had been convicted, either as a juvenile or as an adult, for a sex offence, five of them on more than one occasion (four twice, one at least five times). This is significantly higher than the rate of conviction for sexual offences in the normal population.   In both samples, a further number of men had definitely committed sexual offences but had not been investigated by the police (two in the British sample, 13 in the Canadian). The larger number in the Canadian sample may have been partly due to the social service policy of not routinely referring cases to the police. With a few exceptions, the majority of the offences had been against children. Five of the British perpetrators, most of whom were in their early twenties some time prior to their present referral for sexual abuse, had sexually assaulted a woman. A mother/perpetrator in the Canadian sample had been charged for soliciting. Ten British and 12 Canadian perpetrators with prior sex offences against children involved a total of 27 and 23 children respectively, most of whom were family members. While none of the convicted Canadian perpetrators received custodial sentences, six of the British offenders did. [21] It is evident that being convicted did not prevent recidivism. The sex crime histories are interesting and suggest that (1) some offenders are sex aggressors and (2) some are paedophiles.

Notes

[1]   'Victimology' refers to 'the person suffering, injured or destroyed by the action of another which may be due to some uncontrollable quality in himself - in pursuit of an object or purpose, in gratification of a passion, or as a result of events or circumstances' (Drapkin, 1975, p. xiii). Schultz and Jones (1983) have suggested that 'labelling the child a sex victim, or assuming a symptom complex may have self-fulfilling potential when coming from persons of expertise or authority' (p. 104). Also, regarding male victims as potential future sex offenders is pejorative.

[2]   Three other victims were involved with their older sister and her husband; however, as professionals did not view her as a perpetrator, only her husband was counted as the perpetrator in the study [#44][#45][#95].

[3]   are given in Appendices 3 (English sample) and 4 (Canadian sample), which also show the charge, plea, court findings and sentence for each perpetrator charged with an offence or offences relating to his sexual behaviour and the statutory decisions regarding the victim made by the child abuse team. To avoid confusion, the numbers of the Canadian cases are followed by "C", for

example [#1C]. Cases involving only non-penetrative behaviour are listed first, (Appendix 3 - [#1] to [#59], Appendix 4 - [#1C] to [#75C] followed by cases of penetrative behaviour (intercourse and/or buggery) (Appendix 3 - [#60] to [#96], Appendix 4 - [#76C] to [#95C]). The cases are listed in descending order of frequency of sexual activity. In some, only the duration of the sexual relationship is known, while in others, neither the frequency nor the duration are known. These cases are listed at the end of each group. The reference number of each victim is the same as is used in square brackets in citations in the text.

4   The twenty-year-old was retained for the study as she had younger siblings not in the study, but suspected of being abused; and she herself had attempted disclosure when she was younger.

5   Indications of the latter were found in both samples in professionals' responses to women who had allegedly sexually molested their children. For example, the older sister of three victims described in footnote 2, was not viewed as a perpetrator, even though she participated in most of the sexual incidents with her husband. In a Canadian case, after taking one-and-a-half years to assess allegations that a mother had molested her twelve-year-old son and, despite knowledge that the two had shared a bed since the boy's early years, social workers decided no abuse had occurred. A similar response was evident in an English case [#49] described on page 163.

6   'Masturbation' refers to "the touching of the victim's genitals by the penetrator or vice versa."

7   To facilitate analysis, these cases are counted as having experienced physical contact.

8   There were only 51 different perpetrators because two fathers and three step-fathers were involved with two daughters and two step-daughters, and one male co-habitee and a brother-in-law were each involved with two children. In addition, one victim was sexually molested by two male siblings simultaneously.

9   These were counted in the non-penetration group.

10   There were only 33 different English perpetrators because one father and one brother were each involved with two daughters or two sisters. One male co-habitee was involved with his partner's two sons, and one father had sexual relations with his nephew as well as with his daughter.

11   Gorry's sample consisted of all the cases of alleged incest reported to the London Metropolitan police in the period 1980-1985 (N=171). Gorry used parts of the questionnaire that had been created by the author for the current study, so his results provide an interesting comparison for those reported here.

12   While medical examination did not show penetration had occurred, at age 7 the girl vividly described the penetrative experience with her father, saying

she enjoyed it when he "put his inside in her inside." The child protection authorities accepted that she had been penetrated.

13   Most studies reporting on alcohol use by perpetrators describe their general consumption rather than their alcohol intake at the time of the sexual acts. The perpetrator's general consumption is described later. Unless otherwise stated, most of the references are to victims rather than families.

14   Unless otherwise stated, most of the references are to victims rather than families.

15   This included physically abused and sexually abused children.

16   Some of these had other symptoms as well.

17   For example, one study (Anderson, Bach & Griffith, 1981) reported externalised sequelae such as school problems and running away occurring in 66% of victims of intrafamilial sexual abuse.

18   Chi-square tests showed no significant association between symptoms and any of the factors tested (type of abuse, age of child, multi-problem family).

19   Paternity was uncertain in one case as the girl had also engaged in intercourse with a boyfriend and professionals did not inquire about the child's paternity [#72]. It appeared highly unlikely that the father was her father.

20   With the exception of a grandfather, all were fathers or step-fathers.

21   One British perpetrator had been convicted and put on probation at fourteen for examining the private parts of his five-year-old niece, despite the testimony of two psychiatrists who stated he had acted out of sexual curiosity. A similar sentence of probation had been awarded one of the Canadian perpetrators when he had been convicted of incest as an adult.

5 Disclosure of Sexual Abuse and Initial Professional Responses

A variety of professionals became involved with the family after sexual abuse was disclosed. 'Professional' refers to a person holding a position with defined responsibilities and functions in a particular system. These positions require specialised training specific to the position. The professionals in the study are social workers, medical doctors, psychiatrists, nurses, teachers, health workers, police offices, probation officers and parole supervisors.

Professional involvement with the families prior to present disclosure of sexual abuse

It is significant to note that over half the victims in both samples, (69 children from 57 different British families and 54 children from 41 Canadian families) had been followed by the Social Service Department prior to the disclosure of the sexual abuse, most of them within the previous 18 months. These figures are higher than those reported in another two studies of sexually abused children - Pierce and Pierce (1985) reported one-third of the cases as having been open previously in the social service agency and a Canadian survey (Corsini-Munt, 1982) cited 45%.

These children had been interviewed for a variety of reasons and many were under some type of statutory procedure - some in voluntary care because of family breakdown and others because they had been assessed to be at risk because of physical abuse or neglect. In many of these cases the sexual abuse must have been occurring while the victims were under the observation of social services (for example in the Canadian sample - five where sexual incidents had been happening for four years and three where it had occurred for seven to nine years). A number had been in placement (17 Canadian, 13 British) and allowed to return home after a full assessment by a social worker. While some of the victims had made vague complaints about problems at home, others had exhibited symptoms strongly suggestive of sexual abuse which had been ignored. For example, a 15-year-old Canadian girl, [#92C] with a history of absconding and impregnated twice by her brother, received two therapeutic abortions. In spite of an 'intensive' assessment at the second abortion, disclosure did not occur. In a British case, a 15-year-old, pregnant by her father, approached social services on several occasions for financial and emotional help. Although the agency was aware that her father had returned home from imprisonment for incest with an older daughter, they did not question the girl about the baby's paternity. After the birth and several more visits to the social agency, the girl finally disclosed the incest to the police. [#60] At the time of the current referral for sexual abuse, 14 of the British and 11 of the Canadian victims were being seen by the social service department.

Disclosure of present perpetrator's sexual abuse of victim and initial professional responses

Disclosure refers to the process by which abuse was revealed either within the family or to persons outside, such as friends, neighbours, and ultimately a responsible professional. The duration of the sexual relationship, which varied from under three months to over four years, reflects the different patterns of disclosure. In spite of barriers to successful disclosure, Table 4.6 shows that it tended to occur after a shorter duration of abuse in the English sample (57 of 82 under two years compared with 33 of 71; chi square = 8.33, p < .01). Over twice as many in the English sample (22 against 10) disclosed after only one incident or within three months.

While some victims revealed the abuse in response to the direct questions of someone suspicious that abuse was occurring, most victims initiated the disclosure.

Previous unsuccessful attempts to disclose sexual abuse by present perpetrator

Eighty-four Canadian and 74 British victims had experienced more than one sexual incident or incidents continuing three months or more (see

Table 4.6). Of these as many as 34 Canadian and 29 English victims 5.1). Among the victims who had attempted to disclose, six Canadians had siblings in the study. When these are combined with victims whose siblings not in the study also disclosed sexual abuse, one finds a total of 59 Canadian and 42 British victims from families where disclosure of sexual abuse of one or more of the children had taken place. Gorry (1986) reports a similarly high rate of unsuccessful previous disclosure attempts (62.6%).

Considering the number of cases discussed earlier which had previous contact with a social worker, it is interesting that only three disclosures in each sample occurred because of questioning by a social worker. The rather large number of mothers in the Canadian group who asked the victim about possible abuse runs contrary to the view that mothers tend to deny the possibility of sexual abuse occurring in the family; but it is noteworthy that, as would be expected from the literature (see, for example, Cormier et al., 1962; Finkelhor, 1979; Herman, 1981; Lukianowicz, 1972; Meiselman, 1978), of the mothers who were informed, (12 English, 26 Canadian), only a few, particularly in the Canadian sample, took any action (7 English, 5 Canadian). An example of a mother's cover-up of abuse is a British case [#78], where the mother of a 15-year-old pregnant girl, on learning of the pregnancy, forced her daughter to have an abortion. Her only action at that time was to make them promise not to resume the sexual relationship. However, one month later she went to the police when her husband hit her in a fight over the girl. The girl was removed from home because of her mother's attitude which was that 'without her she would have more chance of making a successful relationship with her husband' Later the mother informed her son that he should think of his sister as 'dead.' The GP who performed the abortion was suspicious of the baby's paternity but seemingly took no action. This case well illustrates the frequent marked hostility of the mother towards her abused daughter described in the literature (Kaufman et al., 1954; Maisch, 1972; Meiselman, 1978). The subject will be discussed later in this report.

Table 5.1 **Previous unsuccessful attempts to disclose the present perpetrator's sexual abuse of victim and victim's siblings (not in study) - England and Canada**

Victim told	Eng. (N=29)	Can. (N=34[a])	Victim's siblings (not in study) told	Eng.	Can.
mother	7	12	mother	3	1
mother and social worker	0	1	mother and professional	3	9
mother and social worker when asked [b]	2	1	professional	7	9
other family member or friend	4	1			
school professional	3	2			
social worker	2	2			
medical doctor	1	1			
mother when asked	3	11			
social worker when asked	1	2			
mother and psychiatrist when asked	0	1			
school professional when asked	3	0			
medical doctor or health visitor when asked	3	0			

[a] 6 of these had siblings in the study who were being sexually abused
[b] These victims told mother and subsequently a social worker who questioned them

When all the categories of attempted disclosure to professionals are considered (victim, and victim's siblings, Table 5.1), and action of mother, it is apparent that professionals had been aware of allegations of sexual abuse in 31 of the English cases and 32 of the Canadian cases before the current disclosure. This number (higher than that reported by Gorry, 1986), is surprising, given the heightened awareness of child sexual abuse in the period prior to and during the study (1978-1984), but it tends to confirm the view that professionals are often reluctant to acknowledge the tabooed behaviour.

Canadian professionals investigated [1] the allegations in only eight of 14 cases where they had been informed of the victim's sexual abuse. [2] Even so, this is considerably more than in an American study (Rosenfeld et al., 1979) where the victim was interviewed in only the cases referred for sexual abuse. Of the eight Canadian cases investigated, five were immediately closed and three victims received counselling for problems other than sexual abuse. Nevertheless, when finally dealt with, at least 11 of these 14 cases could be termed 'serious' - four involved intercourse (one girl was impregnated twice), four eventually experienced the abuse (sexual fondling) for between six to nine and half years, one was subsequently subjected to approximately 80 episodes of sexual fondling and two were young (3½ and 7).

In some of these cases social workers had more than one opportunity to pick up on symptoms of sexual abuse. An example of this in the Canadian sample, a case of a 7-year-old girl who disclosed a two-year sexual relationship consisting of partial penetration and fellatio with her father [#87C], is also an interesting example of pedophilic behaviour outside the family. One year previously, her father had exposed himself on the school bus where he was a monitor, and asked a young girl to touch him. Except for losing his position as a bus monitor, no action was taken. Although aware that he had sole custody of his young daughter, the Department of Youth Protection (DYP) refused to deal with the case because it was 'third party abuse' which, according to their policy, did not necessitate their involvement. [3] A year and a half prior to this, social workers ignored father's symptoms of 'pre-incestuous' behaviour. Doctors treating the girl for a medical condition, referred the family to the hospital social services department because of 'the hostility of the parents and the child's reaction to her father (undefined) who was 'over-solicitous and had a great need to do things for her'. History taken at that time revealed that the father had been very pre-occupied with his daughter's well-being since she was born and was physically abusive towards his wife when he felt she did not take proper care of her.

In another case of a 12-year-old girl who finally successfully disclosed a 7-year sexual relationship with her father to police, had discussed the abuse a year earlier in some detail with a teacher but then denied the story when interviewed by the social workers. [#5C]. While it is understandable that the social worker (who believed abuse had occurred) could take no protective action given that the girl retracted and her father denied, more understanding of the girl's position (she lived alone with her father and had never known her mother) and better interviewing of the father might have produced an admission. In the later disclosure father admitted the abuse to the investigating worker who was persistent in her approach to him. In contrast, the first worker only saw the father once and in the presence of his daughter.

In yet another example, a potential risk was not picked up. Three years prior to the disclosure of sexual molestation of a 9-year-old girl by her maternal grandfather, her mother had been followed extensively by social services for drinking and physically abusing her daughter. At that time the mother revealed that she could not forget her experience of sexual abuse by her father, and that she still saw him frequently. (He had also sexually abused her twin sister). Workers apparently did not perceive the danger of this man repeating the behaviour with his granddaughter, a phenomenon described in the literature (Cooper and Cormier, 1982).

Professional responses in the British sample were equally inadequate. Professionals investigated 16 of the 21 cases where they had been told of the victim's abuse; of these 10 were immediately closed and five were counselled for problems unrelated to sexual abuse. In the remaining case, disclosure had resulted in some action by a psychiatric service, but was insufficient to bring the abuse to an end. In fact, the case was subsequently used in clinical conferences as an example of professional failure in treating sexual abuse. The consequences were severe for at least nine victims. In eight cases, the sexual abuse continued for between one and 3½ years; in another, six years passed [#64]. Furthermore, in six of these cases the sexual abuse progressed from fondling to either intercourse or buggery.

The case of two sisters in the study, [#84, #87], illustrates how several professionals had repeatedly ignored signs of sexual abuse in one of the girls. Two years prior to the current disclosure and shortly after his wife had died of a drug and alcohol overdose, the father admitted to the police and social services that he had given 'love bites' to his 6-year-old daughter. The case was closed. A year and half later the father was interviewed by the NSPCC because of physical abuse of a son. Even though he repeated the story of the 'love bites' and the girl involved had suffered considerable weight loss (known to the NSPCC), there was no investigation of the allegations. These were only explained six months later when all five children were removed from their home because of more physical violence. It was revealed that the girl, now 8, had continued to be molested; in addition, her older sister had been subjected to intercourse by her father and had been molested by a brother.

Current disclosure of present perpetrator's sexual abuse of victim and initial responses by professionals [4]

Full information about the final process of disclosure leading to referral to a professional service was available for 65 English and 74 Canadian cases. Table 5.2 reveals that, as one would expect (Corsini-Munt, 1982; Maisch, 1972; Shetky & Green, 1988), more disclosures were made to people in the victim's intimate circle than to professionals (49 compared to 32 - Canadian sample; 46 to 24 - English sample). As described by others (Meiselman, 1978; Weinberg, 1955), mothers were the most likely persons to be told (without prompting) by the victim about the sexual abuse (19 cases in each sample). Only one of the 14 Canadian victims and none of the English victims who had voluntarily told their mother previously about the abuse attempted to tell her again.

School personnel were involved in almost as many (in the Canadian sample) or slightly more (in the British sample) disclosures as social workers. This concurs with the disclosure pattern described by Julian and Mohr (1979) in their study of 102 incest cases where 13.7 of the disclosures were made to a school professional compared with 10.8% to a social worker. As in the Julian and Mohr survey, in both samples the medical doctor was the least likely professional to be told of sexual abuse by the victim. More English victims informed the police than did Canadian victims.

There was a difference between the two samples in the responses of the mothers when informed of the sexual abuse (Table 5.3). While most of the English mothers informed a professional person about the abuse, less than half of the Canadian mothers did so. In both samples, however, when mothers did report the abuse, they mostly did so to the police.

The child protection service (NSPCC in England, DYP in Canada) and the police are the two professional bodies with the most responsibility in cases of alleged sexual abuse and it is interesting to note their sources of referrals in the sample (Table 5.4). A few victims and parents in the Canadian sample approached the child protection service, but none did so in the English sample where they all went to the police. [5] The lack of a defined role for the police in child protection services in Canada is evident from the data which shows only one professional referral to them, compared to the 49 referrals made to police by professionals in the English sample.

Table 5.2   Present disclosure of sexual abuse of victim - England and Canada

Victim tells spontaneously or when asked by or is witnessed by [a]

	Eng. (N=57)	Can. (N=61)	Eng. (N=8)	Can. (N=23)	Eng. (N=65)	Can. (N=74)
	Tell		*Asked/witnessed*		*Total*	
mother	17	12	2	6	19	18
other family member	11	9	2	3	13	12
friend	9	6	0	1	9	7
school professional	5	9	1	1	6	10
social worker	4	8	0	1	4	9
medical doctor	0	2	1	1	1	3
police	5	1	2	0	7	1
mother and social worker	0	1	0	0	0	1
mother and other family member	0	3	0	0	0	3
mother and friend	0	1	0	0	0	1
mother and school	0	1	0	0	0	1
mother and police	2	1	0	0	2	1
family member and friend	0	1	0	0	0	1
family member and social worker	1	2	0	0	1	2
friend and school professional	2	1	0	0	2	1
friend and social worker	0	1	0	0	0	1
school and social worker	1	2	0	0	1	2
mother informed by others [b]	-	-	19	10	19	10

[a]   Categories of 'mother and 'other member' include some who witnessed abuse

[b]   This represents the number of mothers not already informed of the sexual abuse (by victim or by asking victim) who were later informed by others to whom the victim disclosed

Table 5.3   Type of professional told by mother when informed of victim's sexual abuse in present disclosure - England and Canada

Mother told:	England (N=40)	Canada (N=35)
social worker	7	3
medical doctor	4	1
medical doctor and police	1	1
medical doctor, social worker and police	0	1
police	17	8
police and social worker	2	0
police and medical doctor	1	0
no professional	8	21

Table 5.4   Referral sources for cases of IFSA referred to NSPCC (England), DYP (Canada) and police - England and Canada

	England		Canada	
	NSPCC (N=90)	Police (N=89)	DYP (N=95)	Police (N=19)
victim	0	4	4	1
perpetrator	1	0	0	0
victim's parent (non-perpetrator)	0	19	11	12
agency social worker	35	27	67	1
NSPCC or DYP	-	16	-	0
police	28	-	1	-
medical doctor	1	1	0	0
other professional*	19	4	2	0
other non-professional	0	18	10	5
not known	6	0	0	0

*   psychiatrist, probation officer, health visitor

While the source of referrals to the police in the English sample is similar to some of the findings in another British survey (Mrazek et al., 1981), there are some major differences. The number of referrals from the victim are similar, 11.4% Mrazek et al., 8.9% this survey. However, while the British study reports 76% of the referrals coming from the victim's parent, the corresponding number in the current study is only 28%. Similarly the number of referrals from other professionals, including social workers is markedly different - British survey 7%, present survey 55%. One explanation for the difference, particularly in the professional referrals, may be the source of the data. Mrazek and her colleagues surveyed cases from all the area review authorities and it may be that there were different policies about referring child abuse cases to the police in the areas. In Northampton, however, there was a clear policy for the child welfare professionals to refer cases to the police (Porter, 1984).

The first professional to learn of allegations of sexual abuse has a vital role as his/her responses determine whether action is taken to protect the child. The professional person most likely to be the first to whom the disclosure was made in the English sample was the police (44 cases), and in the Canadian sample, a social worker (45 cases).

The initial interventions in terms of interviews with family members, taken by the professionals who first learned of the allegations are shown in Table 5.5. The literature emphasises the importance of these initial actions as at this point the family is in a serious state of crisis and their ability to deal with the disclosure is highly influenced by the preliminary responses of the professionals (Cooper & Cormier, 1990; Goodwin, 1982a; Sgroi, 1982; Topper & Aldridge, 1981). In approximately one-quarter of the Canadian cases (21%), and 14.7% of the English cases, only brief contact (i.e. short, superficial conversation) was made with a family member, usually the victim, who, however, was the person most likely to be interviewed. In both samples, slightly less than half of the parent perpetrators were seen at this stage of intervention and in the Canadian sample, proportionately fewer of the non-parent perpetrators were seen than parent perpetrators (Table 5.5).

A full initial inquiry (i.e. interviews with the victim, perpetrator and the other parent in cases of parent-child abuse and with both parents in other types of abuse) occurred in less than half the cases overall. Only in cases of non-parent perpetrators in the English system was a full inquiry usual.

Records of the Canadian sample showed 57 perpetrators were interviewed in the period immediately after disclosure, 46 by a social worker, two by a psychologist, and nine by a police officer (five not recorded). Fourteen were not. Eventually 56 perpetrators were interviewed by a non-legal professional in allegations involving 71 victims. Surprisingly, considering the high denial rate of incest perpetrators cited in the literature (Graves & Sgroi, 1982; Herman, 1981; Kubo, 1959; Ortiz y Pino & Goodwin, 1982; Sgroi et al., 1982), [6] 28 of these admitted to the abuse and another six neither denied nor admitted the allegations. Only 17 perpetrators outrightly denied their alleged abuse of 22 victims (no information in five cases.). In only 33 cases were the perpetrators seen by a non-legal authority in the English sample during the disclosure period. Sixteen admitted the sexual abuse to these professionals, usually a social worker, and eight did not (nine not known). As seen in the following section, the denials may have been due more to the way the interviews were conducted than to the perpetrator's resistance.

Table 5.5   Initial actions taken with family by first professional sexual abuse disclosed to - England and Canada

Persons interviewed by professional	Parent perpetrator group				Non-parent perpetrator group	
	England (N=75)		Canada (N=81)		England (N=21)	Canada (N=14)
	No.	%	No.	%	No.	No.
brief contact only*	11	14.7	17	21.0	1	4
victim only	12	16	10	12.3	0	0
perpetrator only	2	2.7	1	1.2	1	1
other parent only	1	1.3	1	1.2	0	0
victim and other parent	9	12	11	13.6	0	0
victim and perpetrator	6	8	5	6.2	0	0
victim, perpetrator and other parent	22	29.3	33	40.7	-	-
perpetrator and victim's other parent	6	8	0	0	-	-
both parents (non-penetrator)	-	-	-	-	3	1
victim, perpetrator and victim's parents	-	-	-	-	14	3
perpetrator and victim's parents	-	-	-	-	1	1
not known	6	8	3	3.7	1	4

*   brief, superficial conversation with victim or other family member

Assessment interviews   While several means of conducting the initial assessment are possible, most authors suggest that the victim and perpetrator be interviewed separately and without other family members being present. (See, for example, Cooper, 1978; Goodwin, 1982a; Sgroi, 1982b.) This allows them to disclose more fully and with less emotional discomfort and trauma. However, only the police, probation and psychiatric services conducted their interviews in this manner.   Most perpetrators in both samples interviewed by social workers were seen with other family members, often the victim and in cases of father/child abuse, his spouse. (In one Canadian case of denial, the father was interviewed in front of his mother.)   Only the Canadian and British social services sometimes interviewed victim, perpetrator and other family members all together.   At psychiatric clinics perpetrators were seen apart from their victims in all but two cases, both British. This may explain in part why frequently the social worker did not appear to have obtained details of the sexual abuse. [7]

According to the literature it is important to listen to the victim in order to let the child know they are believed. (See, in particular, Burgess, Holmstrom & McCausland, 1978, Herman, 1981, and Topper & Aldridge, 1981).   In some cases in both samples, however, when the perpetrator denied the abuse and the family rejected the victim, no attempt was made to establish the facts.   It seems that workers did not push for full disclosure if a solution presented that provided for the child's safety.   For example, when a 16½-year-old girl living with her aunt and uncle alleged that her uncle had sexually molested her, the couple accused her of lying and sent her back to the West Indies to live with a grandmother.   The social worker seemed to accept the family's version and agreed with the decision to send her away, even though she asked to be placed in a group home [#32C].

Police and medical investigation

In the majority of cases in both samples the police started their investigation before the first child abuse conference.   The police were involved in many more cases in the English sample where they investigated 89 of the 96 cases. Although aware of the allegations in the remaining seven cases (six perpetrators) the police did not initiate an investigation, usually because they felt there was insufficient evidence. This is curious given that the evidence in these cases was no less concrete than the evidence in many of the cases they did investigate. For example, in the case of an 8-year-old girl with a urinary tract infection, whose emotional decline in the past year was of concern to both her teachers and the health visitor and who had said to three different professionals 'Daddy is a wicked man when he touches me', the decision of the case conference which police attended was that 'while her behaviour could be linked to some of the presenting factors of somebody suffering sexual abuse, there was no evidence at this stage to substantiate these concerns' [#59]. [8] This case is illustrative of how the British professionals relied on police intervention to substantiate allegations of abuse. If this was not forthcoming they seemed to feel that except for 'watching', they were helpless to intervene. The recommendation at the conference was that 'all members will keep a surveillance on the possibility of confirming whether there is any sexual abuse of "...." The alleged perpetrator was never interviewed by any professional.

In another case of a man who allegedly sexually abused his two step-daughters, although a family member reported witnessing a sexual incident with one of the girls, the police felt there was insufficient evidence. An investigation resulting in charges of assault did proceed four months later when the step-father blackened an eye of one of the girls [#53]. Reasons not to investigate were clearer in the case of a victim suffering from severe neglect where the police stated that an investigation and medical exam would be too traumatic [#58].

In the Canadian sample, the police are known to have investigated or at least made some inquiries, in only 16 of the 95 cases (15 perpetrators). (No information in four cases.) Six admitted the allegations and six denied. (No information for three.) The admission rate was higher in the English sample where 48 of 75 perpetrators interviewed by the police admitted the sexual abuse (60 victims). Nineteen did not. (No information for eight.) While these rates of denial (Canada 40%, and British 25%) generally correspond to those reported in other studies (33% Gebhard et al., 1965, 39.8%, Gorry, 1986), they are considerably lower than in Maisch's survey (1972) which reported over 80% denying the allegations during the criminal process.

Most of those who admitted to the abuse confessed readily and seemed to welcome the opportunity to discuss it. Some cried while expressing remorse and shame about their acts. The nature of the act did not appear to influence the perpetrator to deny the allegations. Only three of the 19 British perpetrators who consistently denied their offences to police were alleged to have committed penetration.

**Table 5.6   Characteristics of police interviews with victim -
England and Canada**

Characteristics	England (N=84)*			Canada (N=16)		
	Yes	No	N/K	Yes	No	N/K
alone	3	66	15	2	0	14
with family member	54	15	15	1	2	13
with social worker	12	57	15	0	15	1
interviewed once	40	11	3	3	0	13
police person of different sex	12	50	24	9	1	6
at police station	50	13	21	2	1	13
at school or home	13	50	21	1	2	13
overt distress	7	9	68	1	1	14

*   5 of the 89 victims whose cases the police investigated were not interviewed

As shown in Table 5.6, much more data on the police interviews with the victims was available in the English sample due to the researcher's access to police records in England. Considering the impact that police interventions can have on the victim and the family (Cooper, 1978; Herman, 1981; Justice & Justice, 1979; Maisch, 1972; Tyler & Brassard, 1984), the paucity of information in the Canadian youth protection files regarding police intervention is unfortunate. The most striking feature of the available Canadian data is that generally, as in the British sample, social workers were not present during the interview, as is customary in some of the new programmes (Graves & Sgroi, 1982). Contrary to recommended practice that children who are alleged to have been sexually abused by a family member should not be interviewed in the presence of another family member who may influence the child (Graves & Sgroi, 1982; Sgroi et al., 1982; Topper & Aldridge, 1981), the majority of the English victims were interviewed with a family member. Gorry (1986) reported a slightly smaller number (38%) interviewed with a family member.

The fact that the majority of police interviewers in the English sample were the same sex as the victim (mostly female), compared to the Canadian police interviewers, is not surprising considering the much higher percentage of female officers in the British police force. In the English sample, the pressure that the interviews must have placed on the victim can be imagined, when it is realised that most took place in the police station and were two to three hours long. Sometimes siblings as young as three were also interviewed.

Medical

Many more of the English victims (84) received a medical examination, usually soon after disclosure to a professional. These were generally requested by the police and conducted by a police surgeon. Only two victims were examined by a gynaecologist and one child [#86] was examined by three different doctors. The majority of doctors were of a different sex from the victim. Even if there was no allegation of penetration, most English female victims had a vaginal examination to determine if sexual intercourse had occurred. Furthermore, 26 of the 84 victims seen by a doctor are known to have been examined for evidence of buggery. [9] It was noted in the files of 12 of the 84 victims that the child experienced overt distress at being examined and one was so upset that the examination was discontinued.

Medical evidence was described as conclusive in only 12 cases, two cases of sexual manipulation, nine of sexual intercourse and one case of buggery. [10] While both inconclusive and conclusive evidence was presented in court, conclusive evidence did not necessarily result in prosecution - three of the nine cases with conclusive evidence of intercourse were not prosecuted. For example, in one of these [#68], while the police believed the victim, her step-father denied the allegations and the police judged the medical evidence of penetration (said to be conclusive by the doctor) to be insufficient for a successful prosecution.

In the Canadian sample medical examinations were given to only 19 victims, 17 of whom were examined for evidence of intercourse and buggery. Only one produced conclusive evidence of intercourse. Unlike in the British sample, most of the examining doctors were gynaecologists. Thus, many victims were subjected to potentially traumatic procedures for the sake of a quite small yield of clear evidence.

Notes

[1] 'Investigation' refers to interviewing the victim and at least one other family member about the alleged abuse.

2   Information on professional action is available only for those cases where the victim's abuse was disclosed to professionals - 21 English and 14 Canadian cases.

3   At the time policy regarding 'third party abuse' (abuse by someone outside the family) was vague - some cases were dealt with while others were not. Later, DYP policy declared such cases were their responsibility.

4   The main type of analysis of the data was the use of multiple regression and the creation of a path diagram. This is presented following the description of the decisions and interventions by the professionals in chapter 8. In addition, chi-square tests were done on all the factors that were thought might have influenced the major decisions by police (investigating, laying charges), the courts and the child protection workers (for example, removing the victim from home, applying for a care order). Any significant results (of which there were few) are presented with the relevant data.

5   In the United States, the mandatory reporting laws vary, with approximately half of the states requiring reporting to a social service department and half reporting to other agencies, usually the police (Brown, 1983). In Quebec, Canada, the law mandates reporting to the social service department responsible for child protection. Although it eventually changed, at the time of the research, social services did not have a policy to refer to the police (Cooper & Cormier, 1985).

6   Very few of these works give statistical evidence but simply state that the denial rate is high.

7   In both samples the most complete information on the sexual abuse came from files other than those of social services or the child protection service (NSPCC and DYP). In England most details of the abuse came from police records - in Canada from the files of a psychiatric service.

8   Quote from child abuse case conference report.

9   A psychiatrist commenting on the effect of this type of examination on a boy who allegedly had been sodomised stated 'If he had not been buggered by the man, he certainly was... by the doctor' (Ingram, 1979, p.24).

10   Conclusive evidence of intercourse consisted of a completely ruptured hymen. Sperm was found in only one case. Conclusive evidence of buggery was anal dilation to three-quarter inches.

6 Major Professional Interventions Following Disclosure of Sexual Abuse

Criminal proceedings - English sample

Criminal proceedings were brought in a much higher number of cases in the English sample than in the Canadian sample. That so few Canadian cases were investigated by the police, is probably largely due to the policy of the Canadian child protection services not to routinely refer to the police. In contrast, the policy of the NSPCC in Northamptonshire was to involve the police in all case conferences for children referred for abuse, a policy reflective of the general practice in most places in Britain.

Charges

All allegations of penetration and all but a small number of allegations of only non-penetrative sex were either disclosed directly to the police or referred to them by the professional agency which first dealt with the case, usually the NSPCC or the social services. As described earlier the police investigated the alleged offences against 89 of the 96 victims. While aware of the allegations in the remaining seven cases involving six perpetrators, usually by their attendance at the case conference, they did not investigate for a variety of reasons.

If the suspect confessed, or if the police obtained sufficient evidence to prosecute, charges were usually brought. Charges of incest had to be referred to the Director of Public Prosecutions (DPP) for approval before proceeding. The police referred 34 of the 89 cases they investigated to the DPP who made the following decisions: prosecution 28 (82.4%), no prosecution two, and formal warning one (three not known). The prosecution rate by the DPP is almost double the rate reported in Gorry's sample (49.1%, 1986, Table 4.15). It is difficult to explain the difference - perhaps the police officers in Northamptonshire exercised more discretion in their referrals to the DPP. Some initial charges were eventually dropped because of lack of evidence and sometimes the police exercised their option of issuing an official caution. Charges were brought against 16 of the 51 non-penetrating perpetrators (34%, 20 victims) and against 24 of the 33 penetrators (73%, 26 victims). [1]

Of the 46 cases where charges were laid 38 resulted in the perpetrator being held in custody. In 29 of these the accused was released on conditional bail (usually not to contact the family), in four he was released unconditionally and in five he remained in detention until his sentence. Of the eight who were not held in custody, three were granted unconditional bail and five, conditional bail. In 36 of the 46 cases which were prosecuted, the perpetrators appeared in crown court, ten in magistrates' court.

The length of time before a court decision is given has considerable impact on the family who are usually very anxious about what will happen to the perpetrator (Paulsen, 1968). Family members live in a state of emotional limbo where it is very difficult to begin the difficult process of healing. In 30 out of 46 cases (65.2%), four months or longer passed before a sentence was rendered - 17 waited four to six months, seven - seven or eight months, five - nine to 12 months, and in one exceptional case, 15 months elapsed. This is similar to the rate reported in Gorry's study of 66.4% (Gorry, 1986). (Of the remaining 11 cases, five took one to two months and seven took three to five months).

Probation reports   Social enquiry reports on the 40 perpetrators who were charged were prepared by probation officers who, in the majority of cases, made a clear recommendation for a prison sentence. While other aspects of the reports (for example, the offender's general background and family life) were usually well done - comprehensive and well written, they showed little understanding of the incestuous behaviour. Some were harsh (and a few even emotional), portraying the perpetrator as a dangerous sexual offender. Others were more positive but still unable to make a clear recommendation for probation. For example, in one of these, the officer stated honestly that he did not have enough knowledge about the subject, and if he knew of resources to treat the incest offender, he would recommend probation. Most of the reports were handed in only one or two days before the court date for sentencing.

This was of considerable concern to the director who felt the judge did not have sufficient time to read and 'digest' the information.

Charges, pleas and legal disposal of the non-penetration cases

Charges Police investigated the alleged offences of 45 perpetrators against 52 of the 59 English victims and of the 45, 16 were finally charged with offences for their behaviour with 20 victims. [2] The most common charge was indecent assault, followed by indecency with a child, brought against 14 and six perpetrators respectively. Other charges were attempted incest, attempted unlawful sexual intercourse and, in one instance, indecent exposure to a daughter. The 16 were charged with a total of 44 offences, 11 receiving one or two charges and only three receiving six or seven charges.

Of the 45 perpetrators investigated by the police, 29 were not ultimately charged for offences against 32 victims. Charges against three of them were brought and later dropped, in two cases because of insufficient evidence and in the third, perhaps because of his age. This was a 17-year-old youth, who admitted sexual contact with his 8-year-old sister and was cautioned [#11]. Three other perpetrators (four victims) were cautioned without being charged, two for a few sexual incidents [#24,#25] and [#47], but the third, a father, had admitted to sexual contact with his 15-year-old daughter which had allegedly occurred on more than 100 occasions [#3]. The police files stated they preferred to caution the father as he had no record and the sexual acts had commenced as a form of 'comforting and were not malicious'. (It is interesting that there was no evidence in the social service or probation files of this type of attitude towards the perpetrators. This suggests that in some instances the police may be less punitive than social workers and probation officers).

In a further three cases, other charges related to physical abuse of the victim were brought, either against the perpetrator [#9] or against the victim's mother [#19,#48].

Insufficient evidence was the reason noted in police records of six perpetrators (seven children) for the failure to lay charges. In one of these [#14], the police records stated that no charges were laid because of the ineptness of the officers who conducted the investigation. There was a lengthy time lapse between the referral to the police and their investigation, the interviews were poorly done and the information was inadequately reported to the police superiors and the case conference.

Prosecutions of siblings are reportedly rare (Gorry, 1986)[3] and in this sample none of the five cases where the accused was a sibling resulted in prosecution even though the victims were young - two were 7½ at referral [#11,#13], and one was 5½ [#20]. It was not clear whether grandfathers were given special consideration. Two of the four grandfathers were charged. One of those not charged had been involved in several incidents with his 8-year-old granddaughter and collapsed when disclosure occurred. After several brief interviews with him in hospital and consultation with his doctor and social worker the police issued a caution [#47]. This case illustrates the discretion sometimes taken in cases where the perpetrator is old and/or infirm (Barnes, cited in Manchester, 1978).

No obvious relationship could be discerned between the seriousness of offending and the likelihood of prosecution. Of eight men reportedly responsible for 20 or more incidents each, four were charged, but so were ten of 24 men involved in less than 20 incidents and three of the six men responsible for only one incident. While cases where the sexual contact was extensive and included digital penetration of the vagina were charged, so were cases where only fondling of the child's breasts occurred.

Plea and legal disposal Thirteen of the 16 charged pleaded guilty to at least one charge (four entered mixed pleas) and 15 were convicted. Five received sentences of imprisonment, five probation and five suspended custodial sentences.

With two exceptions [#18,#15] convictions in cases involving fewer than 60 non-penetrative incidents resulted in sentences of probation or suspended custody. One of the exceptions [#15] was a father who exhibited himself on fewer than five occasions to his 5½-year-old daughter and was sentenced to three months in custody. While the victim's tender age may have been a consideration in this case, two other cases involving victims of the same age [#16,#41] resulted in suspended custodial sentences. Apparent inconsistencies in sentencing were also evident in the cases of two other men, each involved in over 100 incidents with step-daughters who were aged 10 when the offences began. Although the relationship had persisted four years, one received a suspended custodial sentence of six months [#2], while the other was imprisoned for 18 months for a similar relationship lasting 2½ years [#1].

Charges, pleas and legal disposal of the penetration cases

Charges Of 33 perpetrators investigated for offences against 37 victims, 24 (73%) were finally charged for offences against 26 victims (70.3%). This was slightly higher than that reported in Gorry's study where 66.9% of the cases investigated for incest were prosecuted (1986). [4] Both rates are higher than the rates of prosecution for incest cases in England and Wales (for example, in 1977, the rate was 40%, in 1983 - 41%, Home Office, 1978, 1984). In contrast to the non-penetrative offences the relationship of the perpetrator and victim did not seem to affect either the decision to charge or the type of charge. For example, three of the four siblings suspected of penetration of five victims were charged and while one of the those prosecuted was only charged with indecent assault [#82], the others had charges of incest [#77] and buggery [#93].

The offences usually resulted in more than one charge (an average of slightly more than three charges per victim) and buggery led to a charge more often than intercourse.

Chi-square tests showed a significant relationship between the decision to charge and whether penetration had occurred - 16 out of 45 perpetrators investigated by the police for non-penetration offences versus 24 out of 33 for penetrative offences, chi-square = 10.43 (DF = 1, p = <.01).

Whereas the type of penetrative behaviour appeared to influence the number of charges, the frequency of penetration did not. For example, four perpetrators [#60,#62,#61,#65] who had had intercourse with their victims on more than 100 occasions had to answer to 13, 6, 3 and 2 charges respectively. Although in two of these cases [#60,#61] the duration of the relationship and age of the victim were similar, the first resulted in 13 charges and the second in only three.

Charges were as likely to be brought when the victim was in the later teens at the onset of the sexual relationship as when she or he was much younger. Eight of the 11 cases where the victim was 11 or younger when the sexual contact started eventually resulted in charges. Of the six cases where the age of onset was 14 or older, five resulted in charges.

Charges are more readily brought when the perpetrators' admissions about specific incidents correspond with the victims' statements. This is

one probable reason why the number of charges fail to reflect the true frequency of offending and why some seemingly serious cases were not prosecuted. Charges against nine perpetrators who had been involved with 10 victims were either dropped or never brought. In the cases of six of the victims this was due to the perpetrator's denial of the allegations and the lack of corroborative evidence.

In another three cases, the police failed to charge the perpetrators in spite of their admitting to the offences. In one involving a 15-year-old youth who admitted to several incidents of intercourse with his 13-year-old sister [#92], the police stated they believed that the girl had initiated the acts and issued a caution. In another involving a mildly retarded girl of 16 who complained of forced intercourse with her mother's co-habitee [#81], the police simply warned the offender and the mother. Although the third offender's sexual involvement with his daughter was extensive and serious, sexual contact commencing at the age of 7 and eventually proceeding to intercourse before disclosure at 16 [#63], failure to charge the father may have been because the offender was a psychiatric patient and the social services argued strongly for the police not to investigate until the clinical assessment was completed.

Plea and legal disposal   All but one of the 24 offenders were found guilty, and in fact 20 had pleaded guilty to all their charges. Of the 23 who were convicted, 15 received custodial sentences, four had suspended sentences, two had probation orders, and two had supervision orders. The length of sentence corresponds to the observations of Thomas (1970) who commented that the usual range of custodial sentences for the more typical case [5] of incest extends from two to four years.

Walker (1968) observed that, of all offenders, the person convicted of incest was the one most likely to be sent to prison. In this study it would appear that charges for penetrative sexual misconduct tend to attract more severe sentences. Sixty-five per cent of those convicted received custodial sentences, as compared to only 33% of those convicted for non-penetrative offences. This is similar to the 59.2% rate reported by Gorry (1986), but slightly lower than rates reported for incest cases in the whole country, for example, 74% and 75% in 1976 and 1977 respectively (Home Office, 1977, 1978).

Anal penetration was dealt with more severely than vaginal penetration even though the number of alleged incidents in each case were generally few. (In no case did it occur more than nine times.) The custodial sentences ranged from 3 months to 5 years and 3 months and the majority were 2½ years or less. Of the four sentences of four years of custody or more, three [#60,#85,#86] involved charges of buggery. One of these cases [#60] sentenced to five years, had also involved intercourse on over 100 occasions, but another case [#61], almost identical save for the absence of buggery, received only 15 months. Cases [#74] and [#80] further illustrate the marked differences in sentencing; in the first, an uncle who committed buggery six to ten times with his 9-year-old nephew over a four-month period received a 2½-year custodial sentence while in the second, a father who had had over 100 incidents of sexual manipulation and approximately five incidents of intercourse with his 14-year-old daughter since the age of 10, received a nine- month custodial sentence.

Although cases of intercourse without buggery usually attracted more lenient sentences, some were dealt with severely. For example, the father [#71] who received the longest custodial sentence in the sample, 5 years and three months, had initiated the sexual relationship with his daughter when she was 10½. At disclosure when she was 12½ six to ten occasions of intercourse had taken place and some oral-genital contacts as well. But these features were present in many cases receiving lesser sentences. For example, the father of a 13½-year-old girl who had initiated sexual contacts five years earlier and had committed more incidents of intercourse was sentenced to only 21 months imprisonment [#69].

The sentencing decisions were usually unaffected by the frequency of incidents. For example, in two cases where the victims had been subjected to intercourse on more than 100 occasions, [#62,#65], the perpetrator in the first case received a custodial sentence of 12 months while the second had a two-year custody sentence suspended for two years with a supervision order. In some cases, age of the victim, reported as a factor determining the severity of the sentence (Bailey & McCabe, 1979), did not appear to affect sentencing. For example, while the father in one case who vaginally penetrated his 6½-year old daughter on one occasion was charged with Indecent Assault and given a nine month custodial sentence [#87], another father who had intercourse with his 13-year-old daughter on two to five occasions was charged with incest and received the same sentence [#84].

The three young perpetrators who were charged for offences against their siblings were dealt with comparatively leniently. None of them was given custody and one youth, in spite of numerous incidents of buggery and deviant acts with a younger sibling over a three-year period, was given a three-year supervision order [#93].

Summary of police and sentencing decisions - penetration and non-penetration cases

In summary, within both the penetration and non-penetration cases there appeared to be wide variations in decisions to charge, number of charges and severity of sentences. Nevertheless, there was a clear trend for the penetration cases to be taken more seriously. In the cases investigated by the police, only 39.2% of the victims who had not been penetrated had charges brought against their perpetrators (20 out of 52), compared with 70.3% of the penetrated victims (26 out of 37). None of the seven cases in which the police elected not to initiate an investigation involved allegations of penetration. Discussions in the police records indicated that the decisions to prosecute were based almost entirely on the possibility of a successful prosecution. They considered such factors as the corroborative medical evidence (which rarely existed) and the clarity of the statements of the victim, suspect and witnesses. There was no indication that the wishes of the victim or the possible effect of the prosecution on the victim or family were considered.

Over half of those sentenced for penetrative offences received custodial sentences compared with only a third of the non-penetrating offenders. Half of the penetrative group received custodial sentences of two years or longer compared with only two of the 24 non-penetrative offenders.

It is likely that a number of features contribute to the differences in dealing with allegations of penetrative and non-penetrative behaviour, but it would seem that the police, the DPP and the courts view the latter as more serious, warranting more intensive investigation and more frequent prosecution, and that the courts reflect a similar view in their sentencing practice.

Criminal proceedings - Canadian sample

Charges

Of the 19 perpetrators about whom the police were notified of alleged offences against 21 victims (usually by a family member) 15 were investigated (four not recorded). Information on the police investigation is very scarce as it was only derived from the youth protection files, and in a few cases, from psychiatric files. In one case they did not interview the child, in another involving two female cousins, the police, against the wishes of social services, declined to lay a charge and, in an unusual move, the DYP called their lawyer for advice but finally no charges were laid [#4C,#35C]. Eleven men were eventually charged for offences against 11 victims and only four of these were cases of sexual intercourse. [6]

Four were tried in criminal court and three in juvenile court under article 33 of the Juvenile Delinquents Act (four not recorded). It is generally believed that the decision to try the accused in the lesser court was due to factors other than the severity of the offence such as familiarity with this type of disposal, availability of treatment resources and belief in a less punitive approach (Cooper, 1978). For example, case [#76C], tried in juvenile court, involved a father whose sexual abuse of his daughter included sexual intercourse for 6½ years as well as incidents of physical violence and buggery. This option is not available under the new Young Offenders Act implemented in Quebec in 1984.

The five probation reports that were able to be consulted were comprehensive and showed an understanding of incest behaviour, unlike in the English sample. Probation was recommended in all the cases, even one where the offending had been very serious (described below) [#76C]. This represented a striking difference from the English sample where most of the probation reports recommended a prison sentence. The Canadian approach was probably aided by their access to a psychiatric clinic which had expertise on the subject and they usually recommended treatment at this clinic as a condition of probation.

Pleas and legal disposal

Of the five perpetrators where information was available, four had one charge and one had three; with the exception of one who was eventually found guilty, all pleaded guilty to their charges. Two were remanded in custody after being charged and five were given bail on the condition of having no contact with their victim (four not recorded). Four waited between four to six months before their sentence, one waited one year (six not known). Both psychiatric and social enquiry reports were prepared in all the cases where information was recorded (six not known). [7] Of the five perpetrators when the information is known, two received a custodial sentence (one for one year [#26C], the other, charged with incest, for two years [#81C]) and three were put on probation. The sentences of probation included two conditions - not to have contact with the victim and to receive psychiatric treatment. Two completed their probation successfully but one violated his probation by resuming a sexual relationship with his daughter [#18C].

While the small number of cases do not allow for any meaningful analysis, it can be noted that in cases where the sexual relations were fairly extensive, severe sentences did not necessarily follow. For example, two men who had extensive sexual relations with their daughter, were charged under article 33 in juvenile court and received sentences of probation. The first had begun sexual fondling of his daughter at 5, and continued until disclosure at 12 [#5C], and the second [#76C], had committed over 100 incidents of intercourse as well as incidents of buggery and sadism. In contrast, another father [#81C] who had had intercourse with his 8½-year-old daughter approximately 15 times was charged with incest in criminal court and received a two year custodial sentence. These differences suggest that that the type of court probably had a bearing on the sentence. [8]

Relatively minor acts in terms of frequency resulted in the charges against one father who was charged under article 33 in the lower court. However, the nature of the acts, (on two occasions he showed his 13-year-old daughter pornographic pictures and gave her mild drugs in an attempt to encourage her to engage in sex play with a boy the same age) and the fact that he had previously been convicted for incest with an older daughter, probably contributed to the fact he was charged and his one year custody sentence.

Both men known to have received custodial sentences were paroled, one after serving nine months of a one year sentence, the other after serving 13 months of a two year sentence. Both had parole conditions, one that he not return home, the other that he follow treatment and both completed their parole without further offences.

Comparison of the Canadian and English legal decisions

Because of the small number of Canadian perpetrators who were charged (11 versus 40) and sentenced to prison (two [9] versus 20), it is not possible to compare the prosecution and sentencing policies of the two samples. The low prosecution in the Canadian sample reflects the policy of the child protection social workers at that time not to refer to the police. [10] The fact that the Canadian prosecution body used the lesser court for serious offences suggests that they may have been more lenient in their approach to the problem. While this option was not available to the British authorities, they could have given more non-custodial sentences.

Child abuse team decisions - English sample

Because there were considerable differences in the child protection authorities' procedures for responding to disclosed cases of child abuse in England and Canada, they will be described separately. A summary comparing the two will follow, a path analysis comparing the two samples is in chapter 8 and a discussion is continued in chapter 9.

Case conferences

The policy in Northamptonshire for professionals apprised of suspected child sexual abuse was to refer to the NSPCC who were responsible for holding and conducting a case conference or series of conferences to decide whether or not abuse had occurred. If it was felt that sexual abuse had taken place the child was placed on the 'at risk' register. Conferences were subsequently called either by the NSPCC or any other professional involved in the case to review the situation and make any other decisions deemed necessary to secure the protection of the child from further abuse. A range of professionals including the police, health visitor, medical doctor, agency social worker, legal advisor, and school personnel were routinely invited by the NSPCC to participate in the conference. Other professionals such as probation officers and psychiatrists were invited if it was known that they knew the child and/or family involved. These conferences were crucial in the decision making process as most of the major decisions about interventions were made at this time. The minutes of the conference including the discussions and decisions were written up by the NSPCC staff members and circulated to all the professionals invited to the conference.

Ninety of the 96 victims were the subject of NSPCC conferences [11] and in the majority of these cases (53 out of 90) the conference was held more than two weeks after the initial referral to a professional agency. In an exceptional case [#14] the NSPCC held a conference nine months after the initial referral and only after the case was referred again for physical abuse (six not known). Police and social service workers were the professionals most often involved in the initial conference. Eighty-four of the 90 conferences had social workers in attendance, 70 had police. Other professionals present were school professionals 73, health visitors 51, medical doctors 28, psychiatrists six. Forty-nine initial conferences had other professionals in attendance such as probation officers and legal representatives.

It is important to note that while some family members may have been interviewed by the police prior to the first case conference, none of the families had been clinically assessed. Much of the information provided at the conference was offered by professionals who had known one or more members of the family in the past. As Table 6.1 shows, with slight variations in the different categories, social services and the police played an equal role in providing the reports (or information) which influenced the various decisions. With the exception of the psychiatric reports, most of the reports for the important decisions of placing the victim on the register and removing him/her from the home were given verbally. Information on sexual abuse was often scanty and reported indirectly from third parties not attending the conference. Other information (for example, on the family) was frequently anecdotal and given by professionals who had not had recent contact with the family members. With a few exceptions, social services and the NSPCC had never interviewed the alleged perpetrator. [12]

Table 6.1 Source of reports available when decisions made - England and Canada

Decision	Total no. of decisions		Police		Soc. Serv.		Medical		Probation		Psychiatry		School	
	UK	Can	UK	Can	UK	Can	UK	Can	UK	Can	UK	Can	UK	Can
Place on 'at risk' register	81	78	*(72)6	(8)	(67)7	(7)71	(57)7	(1)14	(1)22	0	(7)(1)	6	(1)59	(3)8
Remove victim from home	42	34	(17)5	(5)	(17)5	(2)20	(12)2	(1)6	(1)2	2	(2)1	(1)1	(12)3	(1)
Apply for care order	27	19	(7)9	1	(6)12	(2)14	1	2	1	0	1	(2)1	2	0
Return victim home	13	18	(4)2	0	(4)7	15	(1)2	1	(2)1	0	1	3	(6)1	1
Court decision re granting care order	25	18	(1)12	0	(2)16	15	2	1	(1)	0	0	3	(2)	1
Close case at NSPCC or DYP	46	87	(16)8	0	(19)18	(7)43	(6)5	0	5(5)	2	(1)1	(3)6	(17)3	(4)6
Terminate care order	3	4	(1)	0	3	4	0	0	0	0	1	0	1	0

• Parentheses '( )' indicate those reports which were only given verbally - some of the written reports were accompanied by verbal reports.

Note: Information was not available for all categories.

The *decisions* taken prior to and at the first case conference and at the second and subsequent conferences regarding the victim, his/her siblings, the perpetrator and the family are shown in Table 6.2. By the time the first conference occurred, police had already started their investigation in 81 cases, had made application for eight place of safety orders (two had already been applied for by social services) and had laid charges against the alleged offender of 21 victims. It can be surmised that to some extent the whereabouts of the perpetrator might have some bearing on the decisions taken at the time of the first report. In over half the cases (55 victims), the alleged perpetrator was no longer living in the victim's home - in 41 of these he had been removed by the police, in seven he left because of pressure from social workers and in another seven his departure was voluntary.

In the cases of 22 victims proceedings were taken against the adult family perpetrator as well as civil proceedings (application for a place of safety order, care order [13] or supervision order).

Place on 'at risk' register

Seventy-five of the 96 victims were registered as 'at risk' (two were already on the register for other problems). In 11 of the 19 cases who were not, the decision appears to be justified because as a result of disclosure, the victim had little or no contact with the perpetrator. (In six of these the victim moved out of her home, in three the mother separated from the parent/perpetrator and in two the perpetrator and victim had never lived together). However, eight victims were left at risk of more abuse from the alleged perpetrator in that sexual abuse was still suspected by the professionals who took no action. It is known that at least five of them were re-abused.

A principal reason for the failure to intervene further in many of the eight cases seemed to be the reliance by the NSPCC on the police to undertake the investigation and they (the police) decided that either there was insufficient evidence for an enquiry or, if they investigated, they could not confirm the allegations. The severe pressure this placed on the victim is illustrated in one case [#1], where a 14-year-old boy informed a probation officer [14] that he had witnessed several sexual incidents, which he described in detail, between his 12-year-old sister and his 25-year-old step-father. Although the probation officer informed the conference that, in his view, the boy was not embellishing, the police decided there was not enough concrete evidence to investigate and the probation officer's suggestion that the girl be questioned was ruled out on the grounds that 'more damage might be done by acting too hastily'. The decision was for 'the school to keep a close watch to see if more evidence materialized'. The disinclination by some professionals to believe children's allegations of sexual abuse and hence their collusiveness in the abusive behaviour (de Young, 1982; Sgroi, 1975) is well illustrated by the remarks of a GP who suggested that the boy 'be advised not to pass allegations onto his grandmother as he runs the risk of being exposed as more people find out about this'. The inaction of the professionals placed a great strain on the boy who, within the next 1½ months, actually managed by himself to disclose the abuse in the family. He informed his mother who received confirmation from the girl that sexual manipulation including inter-femoral intercourse had taken place on a twice weekly basis for the past two years. The boy reported that after this disclosure and before the interventions of the police and NSPCC, he and his sister were subjected to a lot of verbal aggression by the step-father.

In another example, the step-mother of a 15-year-old girl living alone with her father, informed the NSPCC and police that he was making sexual advances to her (undoing her blouse while she was sitting on his lap and asking her to sleep with him with the warning not to tell [#14]).

The police only interviewed the step-mother and concluded that, obviously with the tendencies he appears to have, the fact that he is living on his own with these children isn't a healthy situation. However, at this stage we have no information to suggest that any offences have occurred.

Five months later the case was re-referred on similar grounds to the NSPCC who took care orders on all the children and removed them from the home.

The girl in the third case approached social services with the concern that her younger sister, aged 15, was being sexually abused by their step-father (she herself had recently had a therapeutic abortion and been taken out of the home on a care order and social workers were suspicious that she had been sexually abused by the step-father). No work had been attempted previously with the family, but the social worker stated at the conference that 'there was no way for a social worker into the home' [#53]. The decision was to ask the education officer to 'try to talk to mother at work. If mother is willing to discuss the home situation, the case will be passed to the long term social worker. If there is any evidence of sexual interference, the case will be referred to the police'.

In spite of the fact that two other professionals had had recent contact with the girl and had been concerned (a month previously she had been seen by a GP because of an overdose of pills and she had also told a teacher of being beaten by the step-father, intimating as well that he was abusing her sexually), there was no decision to interview the girl and ask her about possible sexual abuse. Four months later the step-father was arrested and charged for blackening the girl's two eyes. Questioning revealed that not only she but her younger sister, aged 13, had been sexually abused as well.

Table 6.2 **Decisions made after referral prior to first case conference, at first case conference and at second or subsequent case conferences for victim, perpetrator and family - England**

Decisions	Before 1st conf.	At 1st conf.	At 2nd or subsequent conf.		Total
Placement on 'at risk' register	2 [a]	75	4		81
Close case after referral	-	6 [c]	-		-
Apply for place of safety order & remove from home	10	2	1	13	
Remove from home on voluntary basis	12 [d]	8	9		29
Apply for interim care order	7	8	1		3
Apply for voluntary care order	0	2	1		3
Apply for supervision order	0	0	3		3
Apply for full care order	0	16 [b]	11		27
Prosecution of perpetrator	21	13	0		34
Referral of victim or perpetrator to a psychiatrist	7	23	0		30

[a] These were registered for other reasons
[b] An additional 4 victims were in care for other reasons
[c] All of the cases were ultimately closed; this refers to those closed as a result of the first conference
[d] Two other victims (#58,#57) had been out of home for other reasons for one and three years respectively

In the other two cases where re-abuse is known to have occurred [#94,#63], while the professionals accepted the allegations of intercourse, they took no action. In the first involving a 12-year-old girl who eventually gave birth to her step-father's child, the reasons for non-intervention are unclear. In the second case, even though both the mother and the step-father/perpetrator (who admitted a nine year sexual relationship with his step-daughter) requested individual counselling, only marital therapy was offered. Files indicate incest was not discussed and the father recidivated.

Four of the 19 cases not registered were registered at a second conference, two because of re-referral for sexual abuse with the same perpetrator, one for physical abuse and one because of the chance that the abusive father, charged for the offences that resulted in his first referral, might return home.

There were a number of cases which were registered and followed on a voluntary basis with no statutory interventions. In these the child welfare professionals tended to believe that abuse had occurred but, because the police could not prove an offence had taken place, felt they could only 'monitor' the family. For example, in a case where the father admitted to watching his 13-year-old daughter masturbate herself [#27], they decided they had no choice but to leave the girl in the home where she lived alone with the perpetrator. [15]

Close case after referral

Six of the 19 cases that were not registered were closed after the first conference, primarily because of a lack of medical and legal evidence. However, professionals were not certain that basing the decision on these factors ensured the child's safety. For example, in the case of an 11-year-old girl whose allegations of sexual interference by her twin brothers, aged 14 [#37], were not substantiated by medical tests (and the boys denied the abuse), the police, who conducted all the inquiries, requested the agencies 'to be alert to any worrying behaviour from any of the children, as an absence of medical findings does not necessarily totally rule out the possibility of sexual abuse within a family'. Considering that within the three years prior to the current attempted disclosure, allegations of abuse had been made by both the girl and her mother to three professionals including a social worker, (who had been unable to substantiate the claims), it is highly probable that sexual abuse had occurred.

While there are no known incidents of re-occurrence of sexual abuse in these six cases, in one instance a year after the case was closed, the perpetrator assaulted the victim physically, resulting in a re-referral to the NSPCC [#51]. The 10½-year-old boy had complained he did not like sharing his room with his 35-year-old mentally handicapped uncle, who was revealed by the later investigation to have regularly masturbated in front of the boy. Although the boy's recent deterioration in behaviour including soiling himself and aggressive behaviour towards other children which is suggestive of more serious abuse was noted by the conference, the only action taken was to suggest to the mother to give them separate rooms.

Remove victim from home

After disclosure, 32 victims were removed from their home either prior to the conference (22) or as a result of the conference (10) and placed in different settings, mostly an assessment center or a foster home. Slightly more were removed from their home on a voluntary basis without recourse to a place of safety order. It is not clear from the data what factors led the professionals to obtain a place of safety order. Reasons for the child being taken out of the home were similar in these as in other cases - for example, presence of the perpetrator in the home, the perpetrator being the only adult in the home, the victim wanting to be away from home, and hostility of the mother. At least nine of the victims were rejected by their mother after disclosure and in some instances the hostility was extreme. For example, when the 38-year-old mother of a 15-year-old girl learned that she had had sexual intercourse with her 21-year-old husband, she ordered the girl to get out of the house, saying that 'without her, she would have more chance of making a successful relationship with the perpetrator' [#78]. Another mother, upon learning of her daughter's sexual relationship with the girl's step-father, told her to 'get out of my sight'. In these cases there was no effort by social services to work with the mother to help alter her view of the daughter.

An additional ten victims were removed later after subsequent conferences, all but one on a voluntary basis. In two of these cases, no action had been taken previously because of lack of evidence; one discussed earlier [#14] had not been registered; in the other [#36], although all the professionals believed the 11-year-old girl's allegations against her step-father, they only placed her on the register. Six months later when the girl's mother had moved out of the home, the girl refused to return to the house, thereby forcing social services to become involved. (The perpetrator had never been seen by social services.) In six other cases the removal from home was due to either the mother's direct request (four) or her inability to take care of the victim (two).

The perpetrator's presence in the home was a factor in the decision to remove the victim in 18 of the 42 cases where the victim was removed. In 24, he had already left the home, often because of being charged and given a bail condition of not being in contact with the victim. However, the professionals, particularly social service workers, were often unsure of whether he would in fact stay away. However, as they almost never interviewed the perpetrator, they were unable to assess this for themselves and seemed to remove the victim as a precaution. This concern remained even when the perpetrator was sentenced to prison. For example, when the father of a 16-year-old girl was released from his prison sentence for sexual offences against her, the social workers became very concerned that he would return home (where his family wanted him) and took a place of safety order. They observed that 'all the children and Mrs._ were terrified (of father returning and of being split up) because they were aware that it was their father who had put them in this difficult position'. It was in fact the professionals who, because of their fear of recidivism, had placed the family in that position. They had never interviewed the father who probably had a good prognosis as he had stopped the sexual relationship on his own, was very remorseful and took full responsibility for his actions.

It is known from the available data [16] that it is likely that the majority of the victims removed from their home (29 out of 42) never returned. Of the remaining 11, six were allowed back after a period of one to four months and five after 10 to 20 months.

In a substantial number of cases, particularly in those where there were no plans to rehabilitate the family, contact between the victim and family members was non-existent. Even in cases where the removal was considered temporary, contact was minimal. For example, in a case where a man was convicted and sent to prison for molesting his two daughters ([#33,#34]) and a granddaughter [#23], three months after disclosure, all his children (two daughters and a son) were placed in separate foster homes because of their mother's inability to take care of them. Although social services planned to return them home, they only permitted a two-hour visit once a month with their mother, and a one-and-half-hour visit with each other. [17] Considering that they had 'lost' their father whom they apparently cared for, one would expect that efforts would have been made to ensure their extensive contact with each other and their mother. It is possible that they were as affected by the social service intervention as the sexual abuse, if not more so.

Chi-square tests showed a significant relationship between the age at referral ($p=<-05$), the nature of the abuse (whether penetration had occurred) ($p=<-05$) and the duration of the sexual relationship ($p=<-05$) and the decision taken at disclosure to remove the child from home. The relationship of the perpetrator (a father or father substitute) was significantly related to the decision to remove the victim from home both at disclosure and later, at subsequent conferences. At this point, the other factors showed no significance. This coincides with the data which showed that the whereabouts and legal status of the perpetrator, usually a father or father figure, was a major concern in all the discussions for some time after disclosure.

Care order

As shown in Table 6.2, application for a care order was made in 27 cases. [18] In seven of these they had been preceded by a place of safety order. The decision seemed to be based primarily to ensure that the victim and perpetrator had no contact when legal interventions were considered insufficient for this purpose. (This may explain why a chi-square test was significant [$p=<-05$], showing that the relationship of the perpetrator to the victim [a father or father-substitute] affected the initial decision to apply for an order.) In all but three of the cases (discussed below pp.164, 165), the care order was used to keep the victim out of the home but there was rarely any clinical assessment of the perpetrator and family to determine if there was any possibility for them to live together without risk. In fact there seemed to be an underlying assumption that once an individual had committed an incestuous act he would always be a threat. Thus, in the majority of cases social workers told the mother directly that if she chose to stay with her husband/perpetrator (or accept him back if he was out of the home), they would be forced to apply for a care order and remove the child(ren) from the home. This sometimes even involved direct messages to the mother to apply for a divorce. For example, in the case of two girls, aged 7 and 8 [#39,#12], whose father had admitted to sexually molesting them, the notes from the first case conference state that 'she is now reluctantly filing for divorce and it has been pointed out to her that unless she separates from her husband, steps would have to be taken to protect the children (a care order). She is very much under pressure, both from neighbours and the social service department to divorce her husband'. The family's GP described the social worker's message to the mother as 'holding a pistol to her head' and as taking the 'easy way out'. This pressure on the mother to choose between her perpetrator/husband and children was also brought in all the cases where the perpetrator was a sibling (i.e. one of her children), thus forcing her to choose between her children.

The sometimes strange rationalisations that the social workers used to justify their threats to the mothers can be seen in another case where a conference was called when a step-father was sentenced to prison for his sexual abuse of his 12½-year-old step-daughter [#1]. A child psychiatrist reported that the mother, whom she had assessed, wanted both her daughter and husband. Because of this, the psychiatrist recommended a care order as 'this would allow mother to have father back, and for her to feel less guilty about the decision as it would not he hers... mother's anger would be directed towards society for removing her child and she could maintain her self-image as a caring mother. [19]

In one case, however, where offering this choice to the mother might be judged as appropriate considering that she had only been with the alleged perpetrator for five months, this was not done [#55]. The case was referred because the 7-year-old girl was assessed to be at risk when her mother started to live with a man who had recently served a prison sentence for sexual offences against other children. The girl was removed immediately from the home and it was stated that it was 'up to the mother to prove she can care adequately (for the child)'. A judgmental attitude towards the mother may have influenced this decision. It was reported at the conference that 'she [mother] is known to be fairly easy with her favours, free or otherwise. She has two children whose fathers are unknown. Her younger brother has been charged with robbing, with violence and possibly murder. Basically, the family are not criminal but the house is very untidy...'. Although one social worker reported that 'although (the girl) has had a disrupted life, the emotional bonds have been warm... and there has been no reason to remove her from the care of her mother', even when the alleged perpetrator left several months later to live with another woman, the child was not returned.

In two cases the mother's hostility towards the victim influenced the decision to apply for a care order, but there was no attempt to ameliorate her negative attitude. Otherwise it was apparent from the comments by professionals recorded in the case conference minutes that the whereabouts and legal situation of the perpetrator were the main factors where care orders were applied for.

While it is apparent in the seven cases where the perpetrator was the only parent in the home that some statutory arrangements needed to be made for the victims, it is not clear why a voluntary care order was not requested, as was done in two similar cases [#38,#96]. In five of the seven cases the perpetrators' situations (four were in prison, one had a supervision order) could have been considered as protective of the victim. Even in cases when there was another parent in the home and the perpetrator was sentenced to prison (three) or was being treated at a probation hostel (one), the professionals still decided to apply for a care order.

In six cases the main reason for application was that the perpetrator was not going to be prosecuted due to lack of evidence. However, even when the decision not to prosecute was changed, as occurred in one case [#4], the professionals still decided to proceed with the application.

Probation orders were not used to monitor the living arrangements of the perpetrator. In one case where the perpetrator returned home after receiving his sentence of probation, the conference decided to remove the victim on a care order, only allowing her to return home when her parents separated.

In only three cases was there an attempt to allow the victim and perpetrator to be together and to use the care order as a means of supervising their contact. It is interesting to note that this seemed to be more the result of strong objections made to the care order (in one case by the victim and in two by a professional) rather than of factors in the case. In the first case, the girl had been removed from home on a voluntary care order because of hostility of her mother and placed in a foster home [#2]. After two months, during which she continuously expressed the desire to return home, she ran away and returned to her home, where her step-father had also returned after receiving a suspended custodial sentence. Rather than upset her further, social services decided to monitor her safety at home through a care order. In the other case involving two victims [#39,#12], (discussed earlier on p.162) the threat to the mother of removing her children from the home and applying for a care order if her husband returned was only avoided by the strong objections of the family's GP. The GP had not attended the conference where the decisions were made but learned of them in the minutes. He responded by writing:

> ... I do not consider, having examined the girls, that there is any psychological damage to them at present from the offences... but, there is no doubt that they are both undergoing extreme mental stress as a result of the break-up of the family unit.

As a result of his reactions, a comprehensive treatment plan based on a psychiatric assessment of the family was obtained and the following decisions were made: 'that the children are not to be removed from home if and when the family reunite' and that an application for a care order be made which 'would act as a constraint and ensure on-going supervision'. This was the only case in the whole sample where this was stated as a decision.

Application for care orders in two of the 27 cases were dropped, in both cases because the mother had separated or was divorced from her husband and the perpetrator had no more contact with the victim. Ultimately court proceedings for care orders were taken for 25 victims and in 21 of these care orders were issued, in one it was not (no information for three). The reasons for the failure of the court to issue a care order are not entirely clear, since the features in the case were not substantially different from the others. The victim had moved to live permanently with her mother and step-father and her father (the perpetrator) had received a two year suspended custodial sentence. It may have been due to the victim's unusually strong antagonism to social services and to the idea of a care order. She refused finally to talk to the social workers and strongly objected to a care order which she perceived as a punishment.

In all but three of the 25 cases, the victim was out of the home as a result of the care order, either because they had already been removed (21 cases) or were removed when the care order was issued (one case). Care orders were terminated for three victims, after 21 months, 24 months and 33 months (no information for 18). In one of these cases [#62], professionals terminated the order and allowed the victim to return home to her step-father, even though they knew the sexual relationship would resume. However, because she was over 16, they reasoned (correctly) that the sexual relationship would no longer be illegal.

Return victim home

Victims returned home Forty-two victims were out of their home as a result of disclosure of sexual abuse and as shown in Table 6.3, only 13 are known to have returned home and only seven of these within six months. In eight of the 13 who were allowed to return to their homes the decision was based on the fact that the perpetrator was no longer there (in four mother had separated or divorced, in three he was already out of the home at disclosure and would not return and in one he was incarcerated). It is clear in three of these eight cases that the fact that there were therapeutic and legal interventions was deemed insufficient to protect the victim. The three perpetrators had been removed from home and charged with offences. The first [#70] returned home when he received his sentence of probation which had no requirement to live out of the home. His victim was removed on a care order, only returning 15 months later, several months after her parents separated. In the second case [#17], even though the perpetrator was living in a probation hostel on a deferred sentence and was receiving extensive treatment, the victim was only allowed home after 10 months on the understanding that care proceedings would be initiated if her father returned. [20]

In the third case [#4], the step-father, who had left home when he was charged and returned after receiving a suspended custodial sentence, received psychiatric counselling and the couple were in marital therapy, but the girl was only permitted to return when her parents divorced. This was unusual on the part of social services who generally insisted on removing the victim in these circumstances. Their decision was probably due to the extensive therapy given the perpetrator and family which was largely conducted by an NSPCC worker who took particular interest in the case.

In five of the 13 cases where the victim was allowed to return home the perpetrator was still there. In three of these five cases, although the perpetrators had been charged and, in two cases, treated along with family members, the decision seemed to be based on factors other than a belief that sufficient intervention had occurred. The victims insisted on returning home - one ran home [#2], another [#18], who had been kept out of home even when her father was in custody, insisted on returning a year later after her father had returned upon his release [21] and the third situation [#62], is discussed earlier (p.166).

Table 6.3   Length of time victims out of their home after disclosure - England and Canada

Number of months before return	England N=42		Canada N=31	
	No.	%	No.	%
1 - 2	6		6	
4 - 6	1	19	1	
7 - 9	0		4	38.7
10 - 11	1		1	
12	1		0	
14	1		0	
15 - 16	2	11.9	3	19.4
19 - 20	1		2	
29	0		1	

Number of months elapsed, still away *				
2 -<12	8		5	
12 -<24	11	69.1	2	41.9
24 -<36	8		2	
36- 48	0		3	
48+	2		1	

*   When the data was collected the victim was still out of home at the number of months indicated.

In the other two cases, in spite of a feeling by some professionals that abuse had occurred, there was no legal intervention because of insufficient evidence and the victim was returned home with no further action being taken. In the first [#50], involving a 10½-year-old retarded girl who was blind and physically handicapped because of physical abuse as an infant (probably by her parents though this had not been proved), although the medical doctor was convinced sexual abuse had occurred, the police claimed, with no query as to who the perpetrator might have been, that they were certain the father had not abused her. The conference concluded that 'although there had been concern, as both parents had been interviewed by police, it was felt that this awareness had afforded extra protection for "...". In the second case [#36], discussed earlier (p.159), after taking no action at referral except for placing the girl on the register, six months later social services were forced to arrange for voluntary care when she refused to go home because her mother had recently left the home, leaving her and her siblings alone with the father. The girl returned several months later when the mother moved back to the house. However, because the family said they did not want regular contact with social services and the social worker was 'certain that mother will report any concern about the girl', the conference decided that 'over-involvement by a social worker may be detrimental to family progress'. [22]

Victims not returned home   The data indicate that in only six of the 29 cases where the victim was still away from home when the information was collected was there a slight possibility that they might eventually return. The majority lived in a residential setting (foster home or children's home) and only seven went to live with a family member. [23]

Reasons for the failure to return the victims home varied. In nine of the 29 cases, the perpetrator was the only parent in the home [24] and in eight of these, he was charged and either sentenced to prison, or given probation or a suspended custodial sentence. As discussed earlier, professionals did not appear to judge these legal measures as sufficient to protect the children. For example, in four of these (two perpetrators) the children were not permitted to live with their father when he was released from prison. While in the case of one of these perpetrators ([#84,#87]) the decision appears justified, given his denial of the offences and long history of physical abuse of the children, the decision in the second case can be questioned ([#38,#96]). After two years the prognosis in this case could have been assessed as good in that the father had readily admitted his offences and had co-operated well in treatment both during and after his incarceration and his two daughters, 14 and 16, continually expressed a desire to return home. As described in footnote #24, the mother of these victims had died after a long illness, thereby increasing the father's importance as a parental figure a year following disclosure.

In another nine cases the perpetrator was at home and no charges had been brought, usually because of insufficient evidence. [25] In other cases (four) the mother's high level of hostility towards the victim as well as the fact that the perpetrator was still living at home contributed to the decision to keep the victim out. There was no clinical intervention to attempt to work with the mother's hostility and in fact in one case [#19], where the mother had been physically abusive towards her daughter when she learned of the minor sexual contacts between her husband and daughter, the major intervention was to prosecute the mother, which, not surprisingly, only served greatly to exacerbate her anger towards the girl.[26] It is interesting to note that in two of these cases, although the perpetrators had been charged (one was given a suspended custodial sentence and the other was sentenced to probation), there was no effort to utilise the legal interventions to monitor the living arrangements of the perpetrator, with a view to avoiding placement of the victim out of the home.

Clinical interventions with both victim and perpetrator did not cause the victim to be allowed to return home. For example in a case involving two victims [#33,#34] there was a protective mother in the home and both parents had co-operated in a period of treatment, but the victims were still not permitted back when the perpetrator returned home on release from prison.

In the remaining five cases the victims were not returned home in spite of the fact that the perpetrator was no longer there. The reasons varied and included hostility of mother, inadequacy of mother who was unable to care for the children, behaviour problems of the victim, and judgmental assessment of mother by social services.

Other decisions

Victim's siblings (not in the study) In some cases decisions were made regarding the victim's siblings. Removal from home and the application for care orders were ones that involved them most directly and 28 children from 21 families were affected by these decisions as follows: removal from home voluntarily or on a POSO 7, application for care order 10, both 11. In a few cases these decisions were taken because the perpetrator, who was charged and sentenced to prison, was the only parent in the home. Records indicate that this was difficult for the victim's sibling(s) - for example in one case the victim's 10-year-old brother, who became withdrawn and detached at school, was described as being 'more emotionally distressed than the victim'.

In the majority of cases, however, the decision was based on concern that the child was at risk of sexual abuse from the perpetrator. In most of these the decision was taken without any clinical assessment or treatment of the perpetrator. For example, in a case where the male perpetrator, the only parent figure in the home. was alleged to have had a 10 year sexual relationship with the 20-year-old daughter of his former co-habitee, [#64], because he denied the accusations, no charges were brought. In spite of the fact that allegations involving a second girl were mild (he had been seen putting his hand up her skirt, an action both denied [#22], and that there were no allegations about sexual acts with the youngest girl (aged 14), both were removed from the home. The 14-year-old reacted badly to the separation (truanting from school, loss of appetite, withdrawal from friends) and there appeared to be no recognition of his importance to her. He was the only father she had ever known and her mother had died four years previously. While one professional asserted that she could only return to him when he was perceived as 'adequate', there was no description of what that entailed and there was no attempt to offer him counselling. One social worker questioned whether, in fact, they (the professionals) had done any better for the girl than her father.

Decisions to ensure separation of the perpetrator and other children in the household were taken even when, because of their age or sex, they reasonably could not be assessed as being at risk. In these cases professionals did not appear to recognize that most recidivistic perpetrators choose victims the same sex and approximately the same age as the victim they are currently alleged to have abused. For example, in a case where a step-father was alleged to have sexually molested his 12½-year-old step-daughter for eight months, the three other children in the family, including a 9-year-old boy and an 8-month-old baby, were removed from home on a POSO [#7]. In another case where a father received a 2½-year prison sentence for two incidents of sexual molestation of his 12-year-old daughter, except arranging for the father to receive some photographs of his children, social services made every effort to ensure that the father had no contact with his 10-year-old son who reportedly missed his father. [#88]. They were concerned for the boy, however, whom they perceived as being 'torn between his natural affection for his father and his loss of respect for and resentment of the man who behaved so badly with his sister'. It is interesting that, while their actions were aimed at separating the boy and his father, there was no direct statement about the nature of the risk that they perceived that the father posed for his son. [27]

While the purpose of applying for a care order in most of the cases was to separate the perpetrator from the child, in a few cases the care order was used to monitor the safety of the child who was living with the perpetrator. It is not clear why this measure was adopted instead of a supervision order which was used in another case, apparently successfully.

In other cases where there was a strong possibility of other children in the family being at risk, no action was taken. For example, in the case of a father who admitted his extensive molestation of his 15½-year-old daughter (over 100 incidents) to police [#3], the father, who remained home, was cautioned and the girl went to live with relatives. Although concerned about possible risk to another daughter at home, aged 12, they took no action, seemingly accepting the mother's assertion that 'it wouldn't happen to "…" because she's not like her [victim]'. Their only intervention was to have a social worker 'express concern for "…" to the parents' and to have the school 'watch her'.

Referral to a psychiatrist While decisions were made to refer 30 cases to a psychiatrist for an assessment and/or treatment of one or more members of the family, only 21, mostly perpetrators, were ever actually referred. Of the 21 assessments, only ten resulted in treatment.

Close case at NSPCC

In many cases the decision to close the case was not made at a conference. Instead, the request was made by the key worker, usually a social worker, whereupon letters were sent to the conference members and if there were no objections, the case was closed.

As Table 6.4 shows, a considerably smaller number than in the Canadian sample were closed because the perpetrator, who was living at home with the victim, was assessed to be not at risk of further abusing the victim. 'Other reasons' usually referred to the lack of contact between the perpetrator and the victim such as 'mother divorcing', and 'perpetrator not at home and there are no plans to rehabilitate the family'.

Similar to the Canadian sample, as Table 6.5 indicates, almost half of the cases investigated by the NSPCC, 37 (41.1%), were closed within one year, which included 19 who were not registered. However, a larger number, 53 (58.9%), were opened for over one year. [28] This may be a reflection of the tendency of the British professionals to rely upon the legal interventions made with the perpetrator. For example, in cases where the perpetrator (usually a father figure) was charged, they would wait until the perpetrator received his sentence before making a decision about the victim. If he was sentenced to prison, they would wait until he was released to see if he would go home before making decisions.

Treatment

As Table 6.6 shows, 57 of the 96 victims were 'monitored' in that one or two professionals, usually a social worker, but sometimes a health visitor or probation officer, saw the child and/or other family members to determine the child's situation and if the sexual abuse was re-occurring. 'Monitoring' was essentially a superficial contact or visit and rarely involved any in depth discussions of issues. In most cases these visits occurred only once a month, but in some, twice a month. Besides monitoring, 60 cases received some type of clinical follow-up, the most common of which was family intervention and this was the only follow-up in 25 cases. This tended to take the form of monthly or bi-monthly home visits by a social worker who dealt with practical, current problems (as opposed to in-depth, insight oriented counselling). Only 24 victims were given therapy (17 were seen individually, one was in a group, one received both types and five were followed in family therapy). While this was usually carried out by a social service's worker, in some cases the worker was from the NSPCC or a Child Guidance Clinic.

Table 6.4   Recorded reasons for closing the case (NSPCC - England; DYP - Canada)

Reason	England	Canada
perpetrator not at home with victim	21	15
victim not at home with perpetrator	14	3
perpetrator at home with victim but assessed as no longer abusive	3	13
victim over 18 (Canada)/16 (England)	8	5
other reason	18	33

Table 6.5 **Number of months case opened at NSPCC and DYP - England and Canada**

No. of months	England (N=90)[a]	%	Canada (N=95)	%
1 - 2	17 [b]		7	
3	0		6	
4 - 6	3 [bc]		3	
7	0	41.1	2	41.05
8	4 [a]		3	
9	2		6	
10 -11	5		4	
12	6		8	
14 - 15	3		2	
16	2		1	
17	0		20	3
19	1		1	21.05
20 - 22	6		5	
24	6		8	
27	0		3	
28	1		3	
30	2	6.7	3	12.63
36	1		1	
42 - 43	2		1	
48	0		1	
Time elapsed [d] case still open				
5 - 9 mths. +	7 [c]		0	
1 year +	17	32.2	2	
2 years +	3		4	8.42
3 years +	1		2	
4 years +	1			
Not known	0	0	16	16.84 [e]

[a] Six were not conferenced at the NSPCC

[b] 19 of these were not registered

[c] One of these cases was transferred to another area of jurisdiction

[d] Still open when data collected

[e] These 'not knowns' reflect a lack of information in the DYP files. It appeared that they had closed (most around one year) but information about the exact date (or reasons for closing) was missing

What is significant is that social service files revealed that in both their monitoring and treatment of the victim, the sexual abuse tended not to be discussed. This was further corroborated by a number of social workers interviewed by the researcher. While this may have been due to a disinclination of the workers to discuss sexual abuse, it was sometimes due as well to the victim's situation. For example, one worker stated that in one of her cases where the girl was out of home for a year as a result of disclosure, she spent most of her time attempting to help her client overcome the trauma of losing her family.

Table 6.6   Types of intervention - monitoring and treatment * - England and Canada

Intervention	England N = 96	Canada N = 95
Monitoring only	16	7
Monitoring (treatment not known)	8	0
Treatment and monitoring	33	0
Treatment only	27	61
No monitoring or treatment	8	12
Not known	4	15

* includes family intervention

Sixteen perpetrators were followed on an individual basis, in most cases by a probation worker who saw him once or twice a month. The quality of this intervention varied - while the data indicate that some probation officers discussed the perpetrator's sexual and emotional problems related to the offence, most did not. For example, in a case involving a father who received a suspended custodial sentence for his sexual contact with his daughter [#73], the probation officer saw him and his wife together every two weeks for two years. The father had been highly incestuous (for example, he had written love letters to his daughter who had replied and once stated that she was very fond of the father and 'just thought it [the incest] was the natural thing to happen'. The discussions, which appeared to be directed by the father, a musician, were superficial and in fact, in several sessions he played his instruments for the probation officer! When he started to meet his daughter outside the home (which was reported to the officer by the daughter's boyfriend), the officer did not question him about it. Three of these perpetrators were seen by psychiatrists who seemed to be able to discuss the pertinent issues more easily.

In only eight of the 73 cases involving an incestuous father or father substitute was there an effort to engage all members of the incest situation (victim, perpetrator and mother) in an integrated treatment programme. [29] The approach taken in these eight cases appeared to be primarily the result of a developing awareness by the professionals, particularly the NSPCC, of new programmes to deal with intra-family sexual abuse, particularly the American Giaretto model (Giaretto, 1976, 1981). (The majority of these cases were disclosed between 1982 and 1984). While there was an effort by the different agencies and professionals to integrate their interventions in these eight cases by communicating regularly, in only four did this involve a plan (if the therapy progressed well) to reunite the family, which in fact occurred. In the other four cases, in spite of a good prognosis (perpetrator admitted the offences and co-operated well in treatment), the professionals appeared to be fearful to allow the family to reunite. For example, in one case where a step-father had initiated disclosure of his sexual relationship with his 11-year-old step-daughter, in spite of individual therapy with the step-father and couple counselling, the girl was still not allowed to go home after two years. [30]

While there was an obvious effort by the professionals to model the treatment of the integrated Giaretto programme (Giaretto 1976), in some cases there was a misapplication of the model, with unfortunate consequences for the family. For example, in a case discussed earlier ([#7], pp.173, 174) where the 12½-year-old victim as well as three siblings were immediately removed from home, therapy was initiated with the couple by an NSPCC worker who, referring to the Giaretto model, stated that 'it is important to have some form of power which would keep the family engaged even when sessions become intensely uncomfortable'. This resulted in a decision to keep the three siblings out of the home until the worker felt that the couple was sufficiently involved in the therapy. [31] One of the children ran home from his placement and finally, due to a lack of placements and over the protests of the NSPCC worker, after three months social services returned all three children home.

Attempts to apply the Giaretto model (1976, 1981) where all parties are involved, also meant that social service and NSPCC workers tried to work with the perpetrator, which was generally unusual for them and sometimes resulted in considerable awkwardness in the interviews. For example in the case just described [#7], two workers confronted the perpetrator, who was obviously depressed and anxious, in front of his wife, by reading out the police statement of his alleged offences. This caused him to leave the room abruptly, very upset, whereupon his wife became worried that he would be leaving her as well. While the workers were concerned about his reaction, they justified their action by stating that 'he needed to tell the truth because there would be no progress until he did'. A few days after the interview the step-father, inebriated, became involved in an argument with his wife and struck her, whereupon he was arrested and put in jail. As a result of this event, on the grounds of witnessing domestic violence, all the children were eventually taken into care and removed.

Professionals generally revealed a lack of awareness of the stress and possible trauma for the victim when interviewed with the perpetrator. For example, in the case just discussed, the worker interviewed the girl, no longer living at home, with her mother and step-father. While noting the extreme tenseness the girl exhibited throughout the whole interview, the worker interpreted it as proof of her dislike of her step-father. In another case where, on his own initiative, a father, living alone with his 14-year-old daughter, disclosed his incestuous relationship with her to the NSPCC, the worker arranged supervised access visits between the girl and her father who was awaiting sentencing. The records describe the girl as feeling 'lost and unhappy' at the end of the sessions which were very tense. It was only when the father outrightly refused the visits and his daughter declared she wanted to wait 'until his case was dealt with' before seeing her father that the visits were terminated. Their attempt to interview the perpetrator and victim together was probably an effort to follow the Giaretto programme which involves conducting an interview with the two in which the perpetrator apologizes to the victim. This only takes place, however, when considerable individual work has been done with both parties, and, unlike in these cases, after the legal disposition.

No monitoring or treatment follow-up occurred in eight cases; in some this was due to a lack of proof and the victim was left at risk; in five this appeared to be because the victim was not assessed to be at risk as there was no longer any contact with the perpetrator. However, in at least one of these cases it can be surmised that the situation was not psychologically resolved for the victim, an 11-year-old girl allegedly molested by her twin brothers for three years. Because the situation resolved itself in that she went to live with her natural father, no follow-up was done with her. Considering that there had been partial disclosure to professionals several times during the three years, with no action taken, and she was the one forced to leave the family, some counselling would seem to have been indicated. The nature of the events surrounding the successful disclosure make the lack of follow-up even more surprising. Apparently the girl was sexually assaulted three times by a male friend of the family who admitted the offences.

Child abuse team decisions - Canadian sample

When a case of alleged sexual abuse is reported to the DYP, a process referred to as a '*signalement*', the case is usually assigned immediately to a social worker who has to prepare for the DYP a report containing a psycho-social assessment and recommendations for any treatment or statutory interventions. Recommendations approved by the DYP are then put into effect by the social worker. If at referral the situation requires immediate removal of the child from home ('*urgent measures*'), these are carried out either by the intake worker at the DYP or the social worker who has long term responsibility for the case. Until the case is closed at DYP, reports on the progress of the family are supposed to be submitted to DYP at three monthly intervals.

Reports

The major source of the reports (most of which were written) was the social agency followed by a medical service (Table 6.1). The largest number of reports was provided for the initial decision to register the child 'at risk', followed by those for the decision to 'deregister' the case. The initial assessment reports which clearly described the goals of the interventions and the later case review reports, which stated whether the goals were obtained, were comprehensive in terms of family background and the victim's functioning. However, considering that alleged sexual abuse was the reason for referral, it is surprising that in these cases details about the sexual incidents were often vague and in some cases non-existent. (The only cases where this information was provided in detail were those seen by a psychiatry clinic - 29 cases). [32]

In almost half the cases (47 of 95) the social worker's initial report was sent to the DYP within two months, 27 were submitted between two and six months but quite often (21 of 95) there was a delay of six months or more. (In ten of these the report was not submitted for 15 months or longer). In these cases it is apparent that the DYP were not aware of the safety of the child. While in some of these cases they sent reminders to the social worker, in others they did not. In a quarter of the cases (25 of 95) more than two reports (not including the deregistration report) were written before the DYP closed the case.

Assessment interviews

It is said to be good practice in the initial assessment for the victim and perpetrator to be interviewed separately and without other family members being present (Cormier and Cooper, 1982, Sgroi, 1982). This allows them to disclose more fully and with less emotional discomfort and trauma. Social services were the only professionals to interview the victim and perpetrator together (with other family members). In some cases, the only interview the social worker conducted with the perpetrator was together with the victim, sometimes with another family member (usually a spouse) present as well. This may explain in part why so often the social worker did not appear to have obtained details of the sexual abuse. Assessments will be discussed further in relation to the different decisions.

Table 6.7 displays the decisions taken by the DYP in respect of the victim, siblings and perpetrator at various stages, some of which were taken and acted upon before the initial report (containing the major assessment and recommendations) had been received. [33] It can be surmised that to some extent the whereabouts of the perpetrator might have some bearing on the decisions taken at the time of the first report (three not known). In the cases of 53 victims, the perpetrator was still living in the same house as the victim and in 39 he/she was not (three not known). In 14 of the 39 cases he had left voluntarily and in 25 either the mother had left home or he had not been living with the victim at the time of disclosure.

Table 6.7 **Decisions made after referral prior to first report or at first report for victim and perpetrator - Canada**

Decisions	Before 1st report	At 1st report	At 2nd or subsequent reports	Total
placement on 'at risk' register		75	3	78
take urgent measures and remove from home		8[a]	3	11
remove from home on voluntary basis	9	10	1	20
take voluntary measures		50	2	52
'seize the court'		7	12	19
referral of victim to psychiatrist	6	11[c]	3	20[c]
referral of perpetrator to a psychiatrist		15	0	15
recommend police investigation		4	1	5
recommend prosecution of perpetrator		6	0	6
close case		12[b]	-	-

[a]   In addition three victims were already out of home
[b]   Most of the cases were closed by the time the data was collected
[c]   In an additional 14 cases the whole family (including the perpetrator) was referred to a psychiatrist

After the initial assessment of the 95 cases '*signalled*' (referred to the DYP), 12 were closed (not 'retained'), 78 were 'retained' as warranting protection and two (already followed by the DYP under suspicion of sexual abuse) were registered again (no information for three).

In six cases where there was an application for a statutory order ('urgent measures' or 'seizing the court') proceedings were also taken against the adult perpetrator.

Close case after referral

The main reasons for closing four of the 12 cases not 'retained' seemed to be that the abuse had occurred when the victim, who did not live with the perpetrator, was visiting him and the victim's non-abusing parent was judged to be able to provide protection from further abuse.

The decision not to retain the '*signalement*' in some of the remaining eight cases seemed questionable. The assessments were sometimes poorly done, clearly leaving the child at risk. In one, although the step-father admitted sexually abusing his 14-year-old step-son (and had admitted sexual abuse of this boy to the DYP several years earlier), the boy was allowed to remain at home and no treatment was offered to the family [#21C]. In another two cases social workers judged the victims not to be at risk because a mother or mother figure had rejected them after disclosure, forcing them to leave home. One 11½-year-old girl, however, continued to want to return home on weekend visits, and another actually did return home after one month. [34] In the first of these two cases the alleged perpetrator, a male co-habitee, had not been interviewed and very few details of the sexual abuse had been obtained. In the second, although the accused step-father had previously admitted sexual abuse of his two step-sons (also in the study), this was not mentioned in the assessment.

In another non 'retained' case a 14-year-old boy and his mother admitted having shared a bed for most of his life, but the social worker, who took one and a half years to complete the assessment, seemed reluctant to pursue the matter [#9C]. In yet another such case, the worker's assessment of the girl's allegations of intercourse as the 'products of a very vivid and pubescent imagination' was severely rebuked by the DYP, but the conclusion (by the DYP) was that there was 'no choice but to close this incorrectly evaluated case' but it would be used as a teaching tool [#93C]. Several factors may have influenced the worker' assessment - the family were wealthy and the accused father, a professor, adamantly denied the allegations. Furthermore, the interview with the father was conducted in front of his wife and daughter, making it difficult for him to admit the abuse. The worker disliked the girl' attitude towards her when she saw her alone and noted in her report that she gave the worker 'frequent dirty looks'.

Finally, shortly before disclosure of father-daughter incest in another case [#76C], the mother left her husband, also leaving her daughter to live alone with him even though she knew of the sexual abuse. In spite of this, the worker assessed the girl to be no longer at risk as she was now living alone with her mother. Furthermore, in spite of the seriousness of the abuse which had consisted of intercourse, buggery and sadistic acts lasting 6½ years, they did not take any measures to ensure the girl's well-being. Shortly after her case was closed, she referred herself to an out-patient psychiatry clinic for severe anxiety.

Remove victim from home

It is interesting that in approximately one half of the cases where the victim was removed from the home in the period shortly following disclosure, it was done without recourse to 'urgent measures'(10). Instead, it was usually worked out with the family as one of the 'voluntary measures', thereby giving the family some control over the situation. The nine who had left home prior to the first assessment had done so shortly before disclosure and for reasons apparently related to the disclosure. [35] The decision to take 'urgent measures' and remove the victim immediately from the home (eight cases) was due to various reasons including the victim not wanting to be at home and hostility of mother (three cases), to protect the victim from the alleged abuser (one case) [36] and because the alleged perpetrator was the only parent in the home (four cases). Ultimately 31 left (or were removed from) home as a result of the disclosure.

In most of these cases, social services made efforts to maintain links between the victim and other family members. The exceptions were those cases where the mother was hostile towards the victim.

Chi-square tests showed a significant relationship between the initial decision to remove the victim from home and the nature of the abuse (whether penetration had occurred), the victim's age at the onset of the abuse, and the length of the sexual relationship ($p=<.05$). The nature of the abuse was also significantly related to later decisions to remove the victim from home.

Voluntary measures

In the majority of cases (52 out of the 80 'retained' by the DYP), some type of agreement on disposal and treatment was able to be negotiated with the family in terms of 'voluntary measures'. Even when 'urgent measures' were employed at disclosure, with one exception voluntary agreements were eventually worked out with the family. These were usually signed by both parents, including the perpetrator, and by the victim if he/she was 14 years of age or older. After three or six months they were reviewed and in most cases (32 out of 52) were renewed for another three or six months, with any alterations or additions considered necessary. The measures generally included agreements about where the victim and perpetrator were to live, the treatment of the different family members (where to attend treatment, frequency) and about issues relevant to the particular family that had contributed to the sexual abuse. For example, in a case where a 14-year-old girl disclosed that when her mother had been away on vacation her father had got into bed with her and fondled her breasts, stomach and thighs [#28C], further investigation revealed that both parents and their 10-year-old son frequently walked around the house naked. (On one occasion the mother had sung 'happy birthday' to the boy in the nude). The measures in this case were very specific and included the following stipulations: no more nudity in front of others, the bathroom door was to be locked by the person using it, the girl was not to stay alone with her father if mother went away and the girl and her parents were to see the social worker (separately) once a week and once a month respectively.

In a more serious case, where an 11-year-old girl revealed that her father had been molesting her on a daily basis for three months [#17C], the voluntary measures included the following conditions: the girl was to stay in the home, the father, who was to attend a psychiatric clinic, was to live outside the home until his evaluation and treatment had started, his visits to his children were to be arranged by telephone and supervised by his wife, and the girl and her mother were to see a social worker regularly.

In only 12 cases where 'voluntary measures' were employed initially, was it eventually deemed necessary to take stronger measures and 'seize the court'. In half of these the decision to employ 'voluntary measures' as the initial intervention seems to have been appropriate in that the families were appropriately assessed and the events which ultimately caused the workers to 'seize the court' were largely unforeseen. For example, in one, the parents started to break some of the conditions of the voluntary agreement, the mother by allowing her husband, the perpetrator, to visit the home and the father, by trying to meet his daughter outside of the home. In others, even though the perpetrator was no longer living at home, either the victim's behaviour (running away, drug abuse) warranted placement or the relationship between the victim and her mother deteriorated to the point where the victim needed to be placed outside the home.

In the other six cases, however, the available data indicate that the worker's initial assessment which led to the decision to offer 'voluntary measures' was inadequate, leaving the victim vulnerable to further abuse. As seen in the following examples, the workers' failure to adequately explore the nature of the sexual abuse diminished the chances for the 'voluntary measures' to succeed. In the case of a 15-year-old girl who disclosed a four-year sexual relationship with her father [#86C], the 'voluntary measures' which contained the condition of a provisional placement for the girl, were signed by the parents without any discussion of the sexually abusive incidents having taken place with them! Furthermore, as little work was done with these parents, who were in a state of mourning because of the accidental shooting death of one of their sons, it is not surprising that six months later they refused to sign the second set of 'voluntary measures'. Similarly, in another case [#27C], the social worker devised a treatment plan for the family which involved conditions related to the alleged abuse (for example, father not to go into his daughter's room), without any discussion of the sexual abuse with either parent. Three months later the social workers were forced to remove the girl from home when her father telephoned the police asking that she be put in jail (for minor rebellious behaviour). In another where the alleged sexual relationship of the father and his 11-year-old girl was never discussed after the initial interview [#59C], the girl and her siblings were allowed to continue to live alone with their father (mother had left the family) and family therapy (which did not involve discussions of the sexual abuse) took place for one year. Shortly after it ended, charges of paedophilia were laid against the father for incidents with other children in the community and the agency 'seized the court' for all the children.

While in the cases just discussed appropriate assessments might have allowed the 'voluntary measures' to work and avoided the necessity of 'seizing the court', in another case a more adequate assessment might have led to a decision to 'seize the court' immediately [#80C]. In this case, a 16½-year-old girl who disclosed her sexual relationship with her brother when she became pregnant and had a therapeutic abortion, managed to convince the social worker not to interview her parents. Facts later revealed that her father was also sexually abusive and had continued to molest her after the abortion. Ten months after the initial disclosure she went to the police when her father struck her.

Seize the court

In seven cases workers 'seized the court' shortly after disclosure. A common reason seemed to be their perception that this was the only way to ensure the safety of the victim either because of the seriousness of the abuse or the inability of the non-abusing parent[s] to protect the victim or both. For example, in one case [#26C] the father, whose abuse of his eldest daughter had been disclosed three years earlier, had also started secretly to abuse his 13-year-old daughter. Although the mother knew about the incest with the eldest daughter and, in fact, had separated from her husband, she eventually allowed him to return home for several weeks during which time the abuse of the second daughter occurred. Although the worker was very concerned about the safety of this child and her two younger sisters, because of her perception that the children would be 'very traumatized' if separated from her (mother), she decided to try and keep the children with their mother and monitor the case more closely with court measures. One of the conditions recommended to the Youth Court was that the father was to have no contact with the children. In addition, extensive treatment was carried out with the mother and children by social services and the father was referred for psychiatric treatment. This case illustrates how, with appropriate conditions, the proceedings for parental rights can be used to ensure the safety of a child and his/her siblings, and, at the same time, avoid inflicting trauma on them by separating them from their mother. In another case [#87C], discussed earlier, the father had always been obsessively involved with his 7-year-old daughter and, in addition, had been investigated for exhibiting himself to children.

While in most of the cases the decision to 'seize the court' appears to have been justified, in one where two sisters, aged 12 and 17 [#75C,#74C], disclosed sexual abuse by an uncle, the decision to 'seize the court' for the younger girl seemed to be related more to the discomfort the agency felt about their inadequate assessment of a case of sexual abuse of another sister four years earlier [#82C]. At that time the uncle admitted to incidents of intercourse which had occurred when the girl visited him to collect money which was helping to support the family. The worker, accepting the girl's belief that her two sisters had not been molested, did not interview them and, feeling that the mother could protect them from any possible abuse from the uncle, who did not live with them, closed the case. [37]

Ultimately the DYP went to court to obtain parental rights in 18 of the 19 cases where a decision had been made to 'seize the court'. The exception illustrates the social services' ability to make a creative use of their power to 'seize the court'. Although the parents in this case had signed 'voluntary measures' which included the condition of attending a psychiatric clinic, they failed to do so for two months [#49C]. When the worker 'seized the court' they began to comply with the condition and the court action was dropped. In fact the parents' failure to comply with the agreed upon measures may have been partly due to the worker's failure to continue to work with the father's admission. After the first interview where he admitted the abuse, the worker did not see the parents again to discuss his actions.

Parental rights were granted to the DYP in 17 cases (no information for one) and it is interesting that being 'in care' did not necessarily mean that the victim could not live at home. At the time of the court decision, five were living at home and 11 were already out of their home (usually since disclosure). (No information for two). Of the five at home, one was removed and of the 11 not living at home, nine stayed out and two returned. In four of the six cases where the victims lived at home, the perpetrator was also living in the household but was assessed to be not at risk of recidivating, usually because of the close supervision which the youth court allowed and the mandated treatment he and other members of the family were receiving.

While the perpetrator was at home and judged to be still a source of risk for the victim in the case of five of the ten victims who were removed from home and not returned, it is of interest to note in one of these ([#84C], the social worker did not conduct a full assessment and in the case of another two victims molested by their father [#3C,#73C], there was no effort to treat the father who, although he admitted to the abuse, was described by the worker as 'crazy and untreatable'. [38] It may be that treatment and a more comprehensive assessment, as occurred in the cases where the victims lived with the perpetrator, might have allowed at least these three victims to live at home under the protection of the court.

While the perpetrator was no longer in the home in the case of the other five victims not allowed to live at home, other factors contributed to the decision to keep them out of home including their high ambivalence about returning and serious behaviour problems.

The court decision for seven of the victims was that they would be in the care of the court until their eighteenth birthday.

Return victim home

Excluding the three victims already out of home at referral, ultimately 31 lived away from home for a period of time after disclosure, at least 14 for a year or more (see Table 6.3). The decision to allow the 18 victims to return home was not affected by the perpetrator still being in the household; in fact in ten of the 18 cases, he/she was at home and assessed to be no longer a risk. (All of them were followed in treatment and only one of these victims is known to have been reabused, the second time by a different family perpetrator [#79C.) In the other eight cases, either the victim had not lived with the perpetrator at disclosure (one case), or the mother had separated from the abusive mate (seven cases).

The minimum length of time out of home for the 13 victims still out of home when the data was collected ranged from two months to four years. For at least five of these, the removal from home was permanent (usually because they went to live with another parent). Similar to the cases where the victim was returned home, the perpetrator's presence did not seem to be a major factor in the victim's failure to return home in many of the cases. For example, for at least five the principal reason was the victim's very poor relationship with their mother who did not want them home and in some of these the perpetrator joined with the mother in rejecting the victim. Unfortunately, rather than working with the mother and/or the perpetrator to change their attitude, the workers tended to help the victim adjust to the separation.

Other decisions

Victim's siblings (not in study)   Social work intervention with the victim's siblings was rare. The court was 'seized' for ten siblings, three of whom were removed from home on 'urgent measures'. A further three children, not processed through the courts, were removed from home on a voluntary basis. (Total: 13 children from seven families.) The decision to 'seize the court' was taken primarily because of a perceived danger of recidivism (either the perpetrator had abused other children in the family besides the victim or he was highly resistant to treatment). In one case he was the only parent in the home and had physically abused the victim's siblings. Parental rights were granted to the DYP in all cases.

Referral to a psychiatrist   The importance of treatment in the initial plans of the social workers can be seen in the number of cases where there was a decision to refer the victim and/or the perpetrator or family to a psychiatric service (total 49, Table 6.8). All but five of the referrals were carried out. Psychiatric help was generally requested for assessing the feasibility of treatment as a means of dealing with the sexual abuse. Treatment was preferred to punishment in most cases, as can be seen by the small number of recommendations for a police investigation or prosecution.

Close case at DYP

As shown in Table 6.5, almost half of the 95 cases investigated by the DYP were closed within one year (41%); only about a fifth were followed for over two years. In almost a third of the cases, the closing summary either did not appear in the DYP files or was brief with few details. The recorded reasons for closing those cases retained by the DYP varied (Table 6.4). Most are listed under 'other reasons' which includes such factors as 'mother judged capable of protecting the victim', 'victim receiving psychological help and can alert the therapist of re-abuse' 'family engaged in therapy and the victim has a boyfriend', 'no more incidents of sexual abuse'. In a number of cases no reference was made to the safety of the victim from further abuse.

Treatment

Of the 95 cases referred for alleged sexual abuse, 61 received some kind of therapeutic intervention, 12 were closed and not treated and seven were followed by a monitoring type of intervention (14 not recorded). (See Table 6.6). Monitoring was usually chosen because the victim had minimal contact with the perpetrator and the chances of recidivism were assessed to be slight. In at least eight of the 12 cases not treated the assessment by social workers appeared superficial, in that important issues were not investigated and disclosure was incomplete, leaving the victim at risk. For example in a case of a father whose two daughters, aged 4½ and 3, [#51C,#72C], made clear statements about his sexual approaches, social services agreed not to pursue the matter. They did not appear to recognise the potential collusiveness of the mother who initially did not want her husband approached as she believed 'he'd rather break up the marriage than admit to sexual involvement with his daughters'. The social worker did not interview the father alone but with his wife, when he denied the abuse. Mother later told the worker that father had accepted treatment from a private therapist to whom he had admitted the allegations. However to 'protect the therapeutic relationship', she refused to divulge the therapist's name. The worker, who believed abuse had occurred but did not seem to recognise some denial and collusiveness on the part of the mother, wrote in her closing summary - 'I found her to be sincere and responsible in her concern for the children, her desire to help her husband and maintain her marriage and home'. One may speculate that this mother's educational level (a masters degree) and father's wealth (reportedly a millionaire), both unusual features in persons seen by social services, also influenced the worker's decision to close the case.

Parental status could also have been a factor in the case of a 12-year-old girl (discussed earlier on p.188 [#93C]) who accused her father, a university professor, of having had intercourse with her. Faced with a non-empathic and judgmental social worker, (a fact confirmed by the DYP), the girl retracted her claim. Even though the DYP believed her original allegation, closure was agreed, probably because much time had elapsed. As described later, it is known that recidivism occurred in at least two of the 12 cases which were not treated [#82C,#79C].

Therapeutic interventions other than monitoring were used in 61 cases, 48 of which involved a clinical intervention with the victim. The victim was the person in the family most likely to receive individual or group therapy, followed by the perpetrator and mother. Forty-eight victims received some type of therapeutic intervention (excluding family intervention and monitoring) - 25 were seen individually, a further 11 attended a group as well as individual therapy and 12 were in family therapy only). Treatment was extensive for approximately a third of the victims - in 33 cases some type of therapy was used for one year or more (three years for seven cases).

Although it has been viewed as detrimental to the victim to be the only family member to receive treatment as he/she may see him/herself as responsible for the sexual abuse (Cormier & Cooper, 1982) in seven cases this occurred. In 15 cases the interventions were made only with family members other than the victim - usually because of the victim's young age or the fact that he/she refused treatment.

In only 16 cases was there an integrated treatment programme according to the Giaretto model (1981) in that the victim, father/perpetrator and mother received counselling (the first two in individual treatment and the mother either alone, with her husband or in family therapy).

It is generally acknowledged that in order to prevent recidivism, it is important to treat the perpetrator who has the main responsibility for the sexual abuse, particularly if he/she continues to live with the victim (Cormier & Cooper, 1982; Sgroi, 1982a; Giaretto, 1981). The treatment may be on an individual basis or in a group. However, in 16 of the 21 cases where the perpetrator and victim still lived together after disclosure, this did not occur. (Most were seen with other family members.) In one of these cases the perpetrator reabused the victim [#70C] and in another, the perpetrator abused other children outside the family [#59C].

Social services provided most of the therapy for the victims, psychiatry treated 13 victims and the majority of perpetrators and marital couples. A psychiatric service also treated half the families who received family therapy and a third of the mothers who received counselling. The remainder were treated by social services.

Summary of child protection decisions - England and Canada

The following is a summary of findings which includes a comparison of the English and Canadian samples.

Structure

The structure of the decision making process in the two samples was different. In the English group the main mechanism through which decisions were made was the case conference conducted by the NSPCC, which was attended by a wide range of professionals, including the police. Social workers and police had an almost equal input into the decision making. Most of the contributions to decisions to place the victim on the register and remove him/her from home were given verbally. (See Table 6.1) By the time of the first conference, no clinical assessment had been done of most of the families. In general the only formal interviews were conducted by the police who saw the perpetrator and often the victim and other family members as well. Social workers rarely interviewed the perpetrator either at this point or later.

In contrast recommendations for interventions in the Canadian sample were prepared in a written report for the DYP by a social worker who had assessed the family including, in most cases, the perpetrator. Other resources such as psychiatry were used in some of the assessments. Police were involved in only a few of the Canadian cases and they had no part in the decision making of the social workers.

Assessments

The assessments prepared for the Canadian cases contained extensive material on the family's background and the present functioning of its individual members, as well as a clear description of the planned interventions and their goals. Follow-up reports stated whether the goals had been met, what the new goals were and what further interventions would be made. In contrast, in the English cases, no reports were prepared by the time of the first conference when most of the major decisions were made. Information provided at the conference was frequently anecdotal and offered by professionals who had not necessarily had recent contact with the family.

While there was slightly more material on the nature of the sexual abuse in the assessments of the Canadian cases than in the minutes of the conferences on the English cases, details were generally scanty in both samples. The detailed accounts that were available came from police records in the English sample and from psychiatric assessments in the Canadian sample. (See Tables 6.2 and 6.7 to compare the decisions in the two samples).

Decisions

Placement on 'at risk' register The two samples were similar in that the authorities in both groups registered the majority of cases referred to them, leaving a minority not registered, sometimes because of the minimal contact with the perpetrator. However, other reasons for the decision not to register these cases differed between the two authorities.

Because of an inadequate assessment (mostly a failure to interview the perpetrator and to collect enough information on the alleged abuse), the Canadian professionals judged the victims not to be at risk. In contrast, the English authorities believed abuse had occurred but due to insufficient evidence to prosecute the perpetrator, took no other action. The English social workers relied entirely on the police to investigate the allegations and tended not interview any of the family members. In both samples a few of those not registered can be considered to have been at continued risk; the degree of risk varied - while all of the English victims were left to live with the perpetrator, only a few of the Canadian victims were. Two of these Canadian victims are known to have been re - abused, [39] five of the English victims, who were not registered, were sexually abused again by the same perpetrator.

Removal of victim from home   Slightly more English victims left their homes as a result of disclosure (42 versus 31). In both samples most victims who left home did so on a voluntary basis either before the first case conference [40] (shortly before disclosure or after disclosure) or as a result of the conference. Most of the reasons for this decision were similar in the two samples and included the following: the perpetrator was the only parent in the home, the victim did not want to be home and the hostility of the mother towards the victim. However, unlike the English sample where victims were removed from home on a statutory order because of the presence of the perpetrator, only one of the Canadian victims was removed because of this, [41] usually because the professionals felt they could ensure the victim could live safely with the perpetrator through a treatment programme which was part of 'voluntary measures' signed by the family, including the perpetrator. All but one of the Canadian victims removed from home on 'urgent measures' were later dealt with by 'voluntary measures'.

Unlike in the Canadian sample where social services generally worked at maintaining links between the victim and other family members, the English social workers did not. In a substantial number of cases (particularly those where there were no plans to reunite the family) the links were non-existent.

Returning victim home

58.1% of the Canadian victims removed from home as compared to 30.9% of the English victims returned home. A much higher percentage of the Canadian victims who were still not at home when the data was collected, were expected to eventually return home (61.5% versus 20.7%). Half of the Canadian victims who were allowed to return to their home did so, even though the perpetrator was there; however he was assessed to be no longer abusive. In none of the English cases was a perpetrator, still living at home, judged to be non-abusive. In fact, the reason for returning many of the English victims was that he was no longer at home. In a few other cases, while the victim was seen as at risk of more sexual abuse, other factors prevailed, notably the insistence of the victims to return and lack of evidence to prosecute.

The basis for the Canadian professionals' confidence in these cases appears to have been the therapeutic measures taken with the families, including the perpetrator. Alternatively, even when therapeutic as well as legal interventions had been made in the English cases, professionals still did not perceive these as adequate to protect the victim. In fact, most of the discussions in the English case conferences centred on the where-abouts and legal status of the perpetrator. One of these Canadian victims who was allowed to return home was reabused, but by another family perpetrator.

The principal reason in the Canadian cases for not returning the victim home, similar to a small number of the English cases, was the hostility of the mother towards the victim. Neither Canadian nor English professionals attempted to work with these mothers to modify their attitude and in one English case, the mother was actually charged for physically assaulting the victim when she learned of the sexual contact between her and her husband.

Voluntary measures

The main intervention in most of the cases in the Canadian sample was the application of 'voluntary measures', a contract signed by the victim's parents, including the perpetrator, and the victim if he/she was 14 or older, which contained conditions designed for the particular needs of the family. In approximately half of these the measures were renewed at least once and in some cases, three or four times before the case was closed. The measures were specific and based on the assessed needs of the family and included items related to issues such as treatment, rules of behaviour in the home and in cases where the perpetrator did not live with the victim, agreements about access visits such as supervision and frequency of the visits. In the majority of these cases the voluntary measures appear to have been appropriate and successful. However, in a small number (six out of 12 where eventually the court had to be 'seized') the assessments on which the decisions were based were poorly done, usually because of an inadequate exploration of the nature of the sexual abuse. A more comprehensive assessment might have resulted in the measures being effective.

Parental rights

The decision to take the parental rights of the victims from the parents (in Canada described as 'seizing the court' and in England as applying for a care order) was made in 19 Canadian and 27 English cases. While the Canadian authorities took this decision in more cases in the second case conference than in the first (after trying other interventions) (seven followed by 12), the English professionals made the decision in more cases in the initial conference (16 followed by 11). The principal reason for applying for a care order in all but two of the English cases was the legal situation of the perpetrator and his possible contact with the victim. The English professionals did not appear to see the care order as a means of monitoring the living situation of the victim or the treatment of the family so as to allow the perpetrator and victim to live together. Rather, they viewed the order as a means of removing and keeping the victim out of the home if the perpetrator did not leave, or, having left, if he returned. Even when legal interventions were taken with the perpetrators in the group (18 out of 27), the professionals still felt that a care order was necessary. Their attitude appeared to be that once an individual had committed an incestuous act, even with treatment he would always be at risk of repeating the abuse. This led them frequently to threaten the victim's mother that if she chose to live with the perpetrator (usually a husband or co-habitee but sometimes a child), the victim and sometimes her siblings, would be removed from home and a care order applied for.

While it is apparent in the cases where the perpetrator was the only parent in the home (and some of these were charged), that some statutory arrangements needed to be made for the victim, it is unclear why the less intrusive supervision order was not used, as was done in two similar cases. (In this type of situation the Canadian professionals used less severe interventions, such as removal of the victim from home under voluntary measures.)

In contrast, the principal reasons for most of the decisions by the Canadian authorities to apply for parental rights was the seriousness of the abuse and/or the perceived inability of the mother or other caretakers to protect the victim from the perpetrator. The decision appears to have been justified in all but one case where the workers seemed to be reacting more to the inadequate interventions they had made previously with an older sister. In most of the cases, other options, particularly voluntary measures, had been attempted but had failed adequately to protect the victim. In one case the application was used to motivate the parents to follow the agreed upon measures and was eventually dropped when they complied.

In those cases where it was felt that the perpetrator was likely to reabuse the victim if they lived together, the court order was used to ensure that the perpetrator lived out of the home. However, even in most of these cases, unlike in the English sample where the treatment of the perpetrator did not appear to be of concern to the professionals, there were provisions in the order for the treatment of the perpetrator as well and, in some, the treatment of the father/perpetrator and his wife, with a view to possible reunion in the future, if appropriate. However, the clinical interventions were not adequate in all cases. In four of the five cases where the victim was not returned home because the perpetrator, living at home, was judged to be still abusive, either the clinical assessments were incomplete or treatment was not offered the perpetrator. Some were not returned home even though the perpetrator was no longer there, usually because of behaviour problems and ambivalence about returning.

More of the Canadian victims where care orders were granted (six out of 17) were allowed to live at home, some with the perpetrator who, due to the treatment he and the family had undergone, was assessed to be not a risk to the victim. Ultimately only three of the 25 English victims where care orders were granted were allowed to live at home with the perpetrator. This was more the result of the strong objection of some of the parties involved than of a carefully thought out decision - in one the victim ran home and in the other (two victims) a professional objected strongly to removing the victims from home.

Besides the civil proceedings (place of safety order, care order and/or supervision order), legal proceedings were also brought against the family perpetrator approximately three times as often in the English cases.

Decisions regarding victim's siblings

There were more interventions with the victim's siblings in the English sample than in the Canadian - 28 English children were removed from home and/or had applications for care orders. Only 13 Canadian children had similar decisions. Most of these decisions were based on the perceived risk of the perpetrator to these children. In some cases the English professionals, without a clinical assessment of the perpetrator, removed children who were a different sex than the victim or much younger.

Closing of case by child protection authorities

Almost half of the cases in both samples were closed within one year. A larger number of English cases remained open for over one year, probably because of the reliance by the English professionals on what legal interventions were made with the perpetrator.

Treatment (See Table 6.6)

i) A much larger number of English victims were followed by 'monitoring' (57 versus seven) and it was the only follow-up in 16 of the English cases and in all of the seven Canadian cases. This intervention involved a limited, superficial contact (once or twice a month). While the reasons for this choice in the English sample are not clear, its choice in the Canadian group was due to the low risk for the victim who had little or no contact with the perpetrator.

ii) The cases of 12 Canadian victims and eight English victims were not followed either by monitoring or a treatment intervention. In eight of the Canadian and all of the English cases the victim can be judged as being left at risk; in these Canadian cases the professionals did an inadequate assessment and the English professionals often did not proceed because of a lack of legal proof. In two of the Canadian and five of the English cases the victims were reabused by the same perpetrator.

iii) While approximately two-thirds of the cases in both samples received some type of therapeutic intervention following disclosure, the recipients targeted and the therapies used differerd considerably. Twice the number of Canadian victims were followed in treatment (exclusive of family treatment) (48 versus 24) and the majority of these victims in both samples were given individual therapy, followed by group counselling and family therapy. While the samples were similar in terms of the number of cases where the perpetrators received individual treatment (23 cases), the source of the treatment varied. Whereas most of the English perpetrators were followed by the probation service, the majority of the perpetrators treated in the Canadian sample were seen by a psychiatric clinic. Records indicated that the probation follow-up consisted of monthly or bi-monthly sessions and in most cases the emotional and sexual problems of the perpetrators related to the incest were not discussed. This was not the situation in those cases followed by a psychiatric service in either sample. Ultimately more Canadian perpetrators received treatment because they were usually included in the family therapy sessions, unlike in the British sample. Failure to treat some Canadian perpetrators (either individually or in a group) who were living with the victim led to reabuse in four cases (three perpetrators).

Individual counselling of the mother and marital therapy occurred in only a minority of cases in both samples.

Professionals used family intervention (monthly or bi-monthly home visits by a social worker who dealt primarily with current, practical problems rather than deeper issues) in many more of the English cases (47 versus 29). While this was the only follow-up in 25 of the English cases, in all but five of the Canadian cases it was accompanied by another type of therapeutic intervention.

In three of the English and seven of the Canadian cases the victim was the only family member to receive treatment.

In only eight of the English cases and 16 of the Canadian cases was there an integrated program of treatment where the father/perpetrator, the victim and the mother received therapy (the perpetrator and victim followed individually and the mother either alone, with her husband, or in family therapy). While the goals in these Canadian cases where the perpetrator was out of home always included his return to the family, this was not a goal in half of the English cases, in spite of a good prognosis.

While the English professionals were attempting to follow the Giaretto model from California in these cases, there was some misapplication of the concepts of the American programme with consequences for the family.

Notes

[1] These 84 perpetrators actually represented 81 perpetrators as there were three who had victims in both groups. The 40 perpetrators eventually charged represented 40 individuals.

[2] Three of the 16 received additional charges for offences other than those related to the sexual molestation of the victims; two being charged for physical abuse of the victim, [#2,#18], and the third charged for indecent assault on a young boy and breach of a probation order [#16].

[3] Manchester (1978) suggested that in situations where the sibling perpetrator is young, with no great age disparity with his victim and where both have participated in the act equally, the public interest would favour not to press a charge even when the was a reasonable chance of conviction.

[4] The difference in rates may reflect the fact that Gorry's sample included only those whose alleged offences constituted the crime of incest, as legally defined. The current study used a broader definition to include non-blood relatives.

[5] A typical case is described as 'involving a series of acts over a short period of time, often with a family living in cramped conditions, and a father whose normal sexual relations with his wife had been interrupted' (Thomas, 1970, p. 119).

[6] Prosecutions are undertaken by crown attorneys who are acting for the Solicitor General of Canada who is appointed by the executive branch of government (Clarke, Barnhorst & Barnhorst, 1977).

[7] The impact that psychiatric reports and careful monitoring and treatment of an incest perpetrator can have on the sentence he receives may be seen in the follow-up of one serious case [#18C]. The father, on probation for incidents of sexual fondling of his daughter which led to the current referral, subsequently resumed the sexual relationship. He impregnated her and was charged with incest. In spite of the severity of the recidivism, after one year of being followed by a psychiatric clinic which submitted several extensive reports to the court, he was eventually given a sentence of probation for the new offence.

8   The maximum penalty for those found guilty under Article 33 was two years imprisonment.

9   Of the five where information about sentencing was available.

10 A new 'incest protocol' adopted by the youth protection authorities in 1985 required social workers to inform police when they received referrals for child sexual abuse. The implications of this radical change in policy is discussed in the last chapter.

11 The social service department conducted the case conference concerning four victims on their own without involving the NSPCC. Another two cases, a girl and her male cousin [#86,#91], allegedly abused by the girl's father, were handled primarily by the police. Although the NSPCC were aware of the cases, neither child was placed on the register and conferenced. The girl was followed at a Child Guidance Clinic, and the boy was not seen by any agency. Note: although these cases were not formally conferenced, decisions were made by different professionals about interventions and they are included with the others in the discussion on decisions and in Table 6.2.

12 Unless stated otherwise, the quotations in the following material are from the minutes of the case conferences.

13 One of these was a voluntary care order.

14 The boy was not on probation but spoke to him because he was known by the boy's grandmother.

15 The original allegation reported to the police by the girl's mother (and told to the mother by the girl) was that the father had masturbated both himself and his daughter. He denied this and the girl retracted her original statement.

16 The follow-up on these cases varied from six months to three years and over (Table 7.1), but it is apparent that for most of these victims, the decision was to never allow their return home.

17 Furthermore, the victims were described as doing well and the social worker remarked how 'the children seem remarkably unmarked by their experience'.

18 When disclosure occurred, another four victims were already in care for other reasons - in two cases for physical abuse by mother, in one for severe neglect and in one because of stealing. These care orders were continued.

19 Ultimately the girl remained at home under a supervision order and the stepfather returned home.

20 This was the only case in the English sample where deferred sentencing with treatment was used. Because of his successful completion of the treatment programme, the father was ultimately given a sentence of probation.

21 It is interesting to note the amount of interventions relative to the amount of sexual abuse (two incidents of fondling) that were made in this family. The

father received a one-year custodial sentence and the girl was removed on a Place of Safety Order.

22 It is interesting to note that in the conference where they discussed what action to take when the mother left the home, only one professional raised the issue about the possibility of another girl in the home, age 9, being at risk of abuse by the father. No one responded and the issue was dropped.

23 One of these, a 5-year-old girl who was returned to her mother [#20] had been taken away from her shortly after birth by social services because of being physically abused by her. Mother was now living with a man with a long criminal record for non-sexual offences who, according to probation, had 'changed dramatically'.

24 Earlier, it is stated that in seven cases the perpetrator was the only parent living at home (p. #124). This was at the time of disclosure. The mother of another two victims died during the father's incarceration [#38,#96] making a total of nine victims with the perpetrator as the only parent.

25 In one of these there was no inquiry [#59] and in another discussed earlier (p. #125) [#14], the police admitted that their inefficient investigation was the main reason no charges were laid.

26 Furthermore, after the police could not provide evidence of the abuse which father denied, the social workers tried to find other reasons for the girl's allegations which had been clearly stated, by saying 'father had probably just spoken to _ in a suggestive way which is just his manner and would not be deliberate'. They also suggested that perhaps the allegations had been initiated by a visit the maternal grandfather had made to the home. He was known to have sexually abused the girl's mother in the past. This illustrates well the collusive way professionals may act in an effort to avoid their own painful feelings about sexual abuse (Summit, 1986).

27 When the wife divorced her husband, the judge decreed that he was to have no access to the children without applying to the court. When he was released from prison, the father sought legal assistance to gain some access to his son.

28 See Note 'e' in Table 6.5 explaining the 'not knowns' in the Canadian sample.

29 This refers to a programme of treatment whereby the father/perpetrator and victim are treated separately (either in individual or group therapy) and the mother is seen either alone, with her husband or in family sessions (Giaretto, 1981).

30 In this case there also appears to have been some over-simplified application of the concept of the connection between the occurrence of sexual abuse and a poor marital relationship as at one point the therapist said to the couple, 'If your relationship doesn't improve, then this must put _ at greater risk'.

31 Giaretto has never suggested using the removal of children from the home to force parental co-operation but rather supports the use of prosecution of the perpetrator to ensure his involvement in treatment.

32 These 29 cases were seen at a forensic psychiatry clinic where the researcher had access to the files. More than 29 cases were followed by a psychiatrist.

33 To facilitate the discussion these are counted under the first report.

34 This was known from sources other than the DYP - i.e. a psychiatry clinic which treated the family for other problems.

35 For example, two were in hospital - one boy because of injuries sustained when he was masturbating anally [#1C], and a girl who was hospitalised for her acting-out behaviour [#95C]. Both disclosed while in hospital.

36 Although the 7-year-old girl was not even living with her father, the alleged abuser, at the time of disclosure but with her paternal grandparents, due to the father's over-preoccupation with his daughter and the grandparents' past failure to protect her, social services moved her to a foster home whose identity they hid from the father. They were concerned he would 'kidnap' her [87C].

37 The court was not 'seized' for the 17-year-old [#74C] because she was no longer living at home.

38 Strangely, after the two girls were followed in treatment for 14 months, the DYP allowed them to return home without any reference to the danger of reabuse.

39 The five Canadian victims who were reabused by the same perpetrator were registered. Details of the reabuse are contained in the subsequent section of follow-up.

40 In the Canadian sample this refers to the first report but for ease of discussion 'conference' will be used.

41 This was an exceptional case where the father/perpetrator did not even live with his daughter, but was obsessively preoccupied with her. (Details on p. 189 [#87C]).

7 Follow-up of Victim, Perpetrator and Family - England and Canada

Major changes

The periods of follow-up for which data was available about the victim was in most cases six to 12 months or one to three years, but some were followed for less than six months or over three years (Table 7.1). During these follow-up periods many victims experienced a change in the person(s) with whom they were living. [1] This occurred for twice the number of English victims as Canadian victims (68 versus 31). Some were living with only one parent-figure (with whom they had been living at disclosure) while others lived away from home with new people (in placement or with another relative or parent). The highly negative effects of placement and the separation of children from their parents has been extensively documented [2] and in cases of incest the child feels she/he is being punished (Cormier & Cooper, 1982; Maisch, 1972). Fifteen of the 19 Canadian and 20 of the 29 English victims living away from their home were in placement. In a third of the Canadian and over half of the English cases, the principal reason for placement was the social worker's perception that the victim was still at risk of further abuse from a perpetrator who had not been charged and was living in the home. Hostility of the mother towards the victim was another. Negative parental responses to disclosure have been cited as aggravating trauma in sexually abused children (Anderson, Bach & Griffiths, 1981; Tufts, 1984).

Another frequent change was separation of the victim's functional parents, which occurred twice as often for the English victims as for the Canadian victims. Forty-eight per cent as comparerd to 24% were either separated or divorced after disclosure. [3]   All the reasons for this difference cannot be discovered, but it may be relevant that charges had been brought against the father/perpetrator in almost all of the English cases, but in only one of the Canadian cases. [4] The English rate is similar to the 44% rate of separation reported in Maisch's study which was based on a court sample (1972).

Several researchers have observed that a number of victims experience intense feelings of guilt which are due primarily to the fact that the family had broken up as a result of disclosure (DeFrancis, 1969; Rosenfeld et al., 1979). [5]   Considering this, a substantial number of victims in this study, particularly in the British sample, likely experienced guilt after disclosure. [6]

At follow-up more Canadian than English victims were living with the perpetrator (26 compared to 17) and a few of them (two English, one Canadian) alone with him. While the youth protection authorities in both samples were aware of these living arrangements, the basis for the decision by the British authorities appears to have been different for many of the cases. While some type of intervention had been made in the majority of the 26 Canadian cases (mostly under voluntary measures), there was little or no intervention in the cases of at least nine of the 17 English victims, still living with their perpetrator and possibly at risk of further sexual abuse. In these nine cases professionals believed the allegations but for various reasons took no action. The prevailing attitude appeared to be that if the police took no action, there were few, if any, interventions that social services could make.

It is known that the perpetrator repeated the abuse in three of the 26 Canadian cases (discussed below) and six of the 17 English cases. These latter cases were ones where some professionals clearly believed sexual abuse had taken place.

Table 7.1 Follow-up of victim, perpetrator, and victim's family after disclosure - England and Canada

Length of follow-up: Victim N=	<6 mths.		6-12 mths.		>1-<3 yrs.		3 yrs.+		Total	
	Eng.	Can.	Eng.	Can.	Eng.	Can.	Eng.	Can.	Eng.	Can.
	19	17	37	32	27	24	13	22	96	95
living[w] both parents	4	1	9	17	5	8	2	3	20	29
living[w] mother only	6	3	15	5	12	10	5	9	38	27
living[w] father only	4	2	1	1	3	0	1	0	9	3
living[w] perp. alone or[w] others	3	2	8[a]	16[a]	2	7	4[a]	3	17	26
living away from home or[w] others[b]	5	0	12	3	7	6	5	10	29	19
still in school	4	2	14	22	8	20	4	16	30	60
quit school	0	1	1	2	1	0	0	1	2	4
completed school	0	0	0	0	2	4	3	2	5	6
working	0	0	0	0	2	0	0	0	2	0
poor school performance	0	0	2	2	1	1	0	2	3	5
truancy	0	0	1	1	2	0	0	0	3	1
poor performance & truancy	0	1	1	2	1	2	0	5	2	10
running away	0	1	1	2	1	2	0	5	2	10
suicidal attempts	2	0	1	1	0	3	1	2	4	6
drug &/or alcohol abuse	0	1	2	0	0	1	0	0	2	2
delinquency	0	0	0	0	0	1	2	1	2	2
further sexual abuse by perpetrator	3	0	2	2	0	0	1	3	6	5
sex. abuse by others	0	0	0	1	0	1	0	3	0	5
pregnancy	1	0	0	0	1	0	2	3	4	3
poor relationship[w] mother	4	0	4	8	0	10	0	13	8[c]	31

Table 7.1 continued

		<6 mths.		6-12 mths.		>1-<3 yrs.		3 yrs.+		Total	
		Eng.	Can.	Eng.	Can.	Eng.	Can.	Eng.	Can.	Eng.	Can.
Victim	N=	19	17	37	32	27	24	13	22	96	95
poor relationship[w]											
perpetrator		1	0	0	3	0	5	0	7	1	15
Perpetrator[d]											
lost employment		2	0	2	0	4	3	2	0	10	3
sex. abused others		0	0	1	0	1	1	0	2	2	3
suicidal attempt		2	0	1	0	2	0	1	0	6	1
Family											
moved to other residence		1	0	5	0	2	2	1	3	8	5
separation/divorce of parents		5	0	14	2	10	4	6	9	35	15

Note: Information was not available for all variables
[a]   Only one of these was living alone with the perpetrator
[b]   This was usually placement
[c]   This information was largely unavailable for the English sample
[d]   This is counted for perpetrators rather than victims

Symptoms of victim/s

The serious difficulty in linking the victim's symptoms post-disclosure directly to the sexual abuse per se and separating them from other family problems has been described (see, in particular, Steele & Alexander, 1981 and Maisch, 1972). Social workers, particularly in the English sample, frequently voiced concern about a lack of symptoms in the victims. For example, in a case of a 14-year-old girl who had been molested numerous times by her father, a single parent, for whom she expressed considerable affection, the worker stated that she would be 'far happier if "..." had some form of reaction because of her traumatic experience' [#65]. When investigation in another case of a 5-year-old girl who had what was thought to be a 'love bite' on her face revealed that the father, whom they suspected, had several convictions for exhibitionism, although the child was loving and well-adjusted, the social worker stated that 'it is easy to predict that there would be a vast degree of disturbance in "..." as she gets older...' [#48]. These assumptions about the significance of an absence of symptoms would, to some extent, influence the professionals' decisions.

The majority of victims in both samples showed no signs of emotional disturbance and interestingly, none of the victims who had been reabused by the perpetrator showed signs of disturbance. (This may indicate that the absence of upset in the victim may be a factor encouraging reabuse by the same perpetrator). The general absence of symptoms corresponds to other studies which reported no ill effects (Burton, 1968; Gibbens & Prince, 1963; Lempp, 1979; Luckianowicz, 1972; Yorukoglu & Kemph, 1966). More Canadian than English victims exhibited symptoms at follow-up (27 out of 77 where information was available, 35.1% versus 16 out of 60, 26.7%). [7] No particular symptom predominated in the English sample, but the most common features in the Canadian group were 'poor performance at school', followed by 'running away', usually running from a difficult relationship with their mother, the only parent in the home. This concurs with the findings of other studies (see, for example, Kaufman et al., 1954 and Rosenfeld et al., 1977).

Other studies have found a higher rate of drug and alcohol abuse occurring in victims than in non-victims (Briere, 1984; Herman, 1981; Peters, 1984) and links between delinquency and sexual abuse have also been reported (Reich & Gutierres, 1979; Wisconsin, 1982). For most of those in this study who exhibited the more severe signs of disturbance (drug and alcohol abuse, delinquency and suicidal attempts) the behaviour was transitory rather than chronic.

The proportion of victims who attempted suicide within three and half years following disclosure (4.2% British, 6.3% Canadian) is much lower than that reported by de Young (1982) who found that 68% of her sample of 60 incest victims had attempted suicide at least once, either during the incestuous relationship or within two years following its termination. The incidence in the present research corresponds to the 3.9% reported by Goodwin (1982b) in her study of 201 treated incest victims followed for two and a half years. Her slightly lower rate may be due to the shorter follow-up period of her study. [8]

In some cases in this study, it is clear that the victim was reacting to the results of intervention. For example, shortly after she and her two sisters had been removed from home (where they had lived with their father, the alleged perpetrator, a single parent), one 16-year-old English victim who was described as 'pale, tired and run down', exhibited 'tremendous withdrawal symptoms, was impossible to talk to and dropped her old friends', tried to kill herself [#22]. She denied any sexual incidents and wanted to see the perpetrator. Her three siblings, meant to have shared the same placement, were actually sent elsewhere. In two other English cases the attempted suicides could be attributed in part to social service's interventions. One 14-year-old girl who, after disclosure, was removed from home to an assessment centre, took an overdose of pills when she had to leave there to go and live with her natural father who was ambivalent about her coming. One month after a successful disclosure, another girl, who had previously been followed by social services because of her single parenthood, was hospitalised following an overdose of pills after an argument with her social worker [#60].

Of the 16 Canadian and seven English victims who had symptoms both before and after disclosure, at least two and three respectively had had problems even before becoming acquainted with the perpetrator. Factors besides the sexual abuse that may have contributed to the signs of emotional disturbance in the other victims were as follows: in the Canadian group - neglect or emotional abuse by the non-perpetrator parent (five), a mentally ill parent (four) and serious family disruptions (frequent marital separations, numerous live-in partners of mother sometimes resulting in placement (six); in the English sample - sexual abuse of other children in the family by the same perpetrator (two), chronically depressed mother (one), lengthy illness and recent death of mother (two), and severe marital problems (one). This supports the view of Lukianowicz (1972) and Westermeir (1978) who suggested that negative consequences for the victim are sometimes linked to disturbed, problematic families.

Nine of the English and 11 of the Canadian victims had shown no signs of emotional disturbance prior to the disclosure. While it is not possible to determine precisely why symptoms appeared after abuse had supposedly been ended, the data provide hints as to possible contributing factors (e.g. in the Canadian group - very poor relationship with mother (five), missing their father (the perpetrator) who was in prison (two), and change in living situation including one placement (four); in the English sample - sexual abuse of other children in the family by the same perpetrator (two), living in placement and missing father (the perpetrator and only parent) (two), living in placement and missing family (three), anxiety about whereabouts of father (the perpetrator) (one), no action by professionals and left to live with the perpetrator (two).

Recidivism of sexual abuse by same perpetrator

In the Canadian sample, 10 victims were reabused after disclosure, five by the same perpetrator, two by other family members and three by persons outside the family. In the English sample the six victims known to have been reabused were abused by the same perpetrator. De Young (1982) reported that 38% of her sample were also victimised by someone other than their perpetrator (father or step-father). A somewhat similar rate occurred in this sample (27.1% English, 31.6% Canadian) if victimisation that occurred during the incest relationship is included, as in de Young's study. Explanations for the reabuse of the victim include the following: that the identified victim becomes fascinating for others (Summit & Kryso, 1978), that the victim becomes prematurely 'sexualised' by her premature sexual experiences (Nash & West, 1985), the mother is unable to supervise her daughter or provide her with accurate sexual information (Finkelhor, 1979) and that the incest victim may accept the identity of 'harlot' or whore (de Young, 1982).

In all six of the English cases, and in three of the five Canadian cases of victims reabused by the same perpetrator, victim and perpetrator were living together. [9] The recidivism was serious in some of the cases in both samples (duration and frequency of sexual contact and some girls became pregnant). Inadequate professional interventions contributed to the recidivism in most of the Canadian and all the English cases.

Canadian sample

In most of the cases the reabuse consisted of one or two incidents but in two [#18C] and [#79C], the consequences were serious in that the victims, both 13, became pregnant. The first girl had a therapeutic abortion, the second gave birth.

An example of the inadequate social service intervention in these cases is a case involving a highly resistant father whose wife stated she had witnessed him sexually abusing his two daughters, aged 2½ [#71C] and 7 years [#70C], in spite of several reports of charges of sexual abuse against the perpetrator in another province, the only intervention social services made was to offer family therapy which the father consistently failed to attend. Four months after the first disclosure, mother phoned the police claiming that her husband had sexually molested the 2½-year-old again.

In another case the social worker did not believe a girl who alleged that her 23-year-old step-father (married to her 40-year-old mother) had had sexual intercourse with her [#79C]). In her report to the DYP she described the grandmother who supported the girl's story as 'a vicious unreliable source' and wrote that 'though "..." had been faced with the evidence from the gynaecologist that her story could not be true, she maintained it for a long time but finally admitted she had made it up to harm him [the perpetrator]'. The worker concluded that the girl had probably 'learned her lesson'. The DYP did not accept the worker's assessment and asked that it be rewritten in a less judgmental and more accurate way, but, contrary to the girl's wishes, supported the worker's decision to return her to her family and close the case. A year and a half later the girl gave birth to a child by her step-father.

Social service decisions failed to prevent recidivism in another case [#18C]. The parents separated following disclosure and the perpetrator (a father) was followed at a psychiatric clinic and his wife and daughter at a social service agency. In spite of knowing that the mother greatly wanted her husband to return home, social services stopped seeing the mother and daughter eight months after disclosure. They did not inform the psychiatric clinic who would have strongly disapproved of their decision on the grounds of the mother's high degree of collusiveness and the father's strong emotional attachment to his daughter. [10] Unbeknownst to either service father returned home and one month later the daughter became pregnant. [11]

English sample

The reabuse was serious in at least four of the six cases and lack of intervention (including non-registration) or inadequate intervention appear to have contributed to the reabuse in all six cases. In the first, three years after the initial disclosure which had occurred when she was 12, the girl gave birth to her step-father's child [#94]. Conferenced initially at the NSPCC, who believed abuse had occurred, the case received no interventions except for voluntary treatment at a Child Guidance Clinic. While the reasons for this minimal intervention are not clear in the files, a social worker who knew the case suggested to the researcher that they were reluctant to break up the family.

In the second case which involved allegations of sexual molestation by a mother of her 1½-year-old son [#49], the professionals focused on her treatment of an older son who had been scalded and who was eventually permanently removed from her care. Besides the allegations of sexual abuse made at the first case conference, the only other reference to her behaviour was made nine months later in a psychiatric assessment presented at the conference which stated: "..." sleeps in his mother's bed and mutual fondling is frequent'. The matter was not discussed at the conference and the case was eventually closed. [12] Thirdly, in a case where a 16-year-old girl disclosed a nine year sexual relationship with her step-father [#63], while social services conducted a thorough assessment of the family and the incestuous abuse, they did not carry through with an adequate treatment plan. Although the step-father, who readily admitted the abuse, requested individual treatment, the worker insisted that he would only be seen with his wife in couple counselling. After two sessions he stopped coming and several months later made another sexual approach to his daughter. When she informed social services, their only action was to help her leave home. They did not confront the father. The other three cases [#1,#14,#53] are described earlier (pp.154-156). [13, 14]

Sexual abuse of victim by others

There were no known examples of this in the English sample, but there were five reported cases in the Canadian group, two of whom were sexually abused by family members - one by her father [#80C] and one by her brother [#59C]. The first girl ([#80C]) revealed sexual abuse by her brother when she became pregnant and had a therapeutic abortion (she had also run away from home after an argument with her father), but instead of pursuing a full assessment, the social worker agreed to her request not to speak to her parents. Three months later she disclosed that her father had also sexually abused her for some time and had continued the abuse after the first disclosure. The inadequate interventions in the second case ([#59C]) are described in the following section. The other three victims were sexually abused by persons outside the family - one by foster parents six months after disclosure, one by a staff member in a juvenile residential treatment center and one was raped by three youths. The reabuse of victims by caretakers chosen by the professionals responsible for them, reported by others (Pagelow, 1984; Smith, 1987;

Green, 1988b) is particularly distressing as it represents one of the severest forms of iatrogenic abuse. These children may be more traumatised by the later abuse than that experienced in their family.

Recidivism of perpetrator with other victims

Social services appear to have inadequately assessed two of the three Canadian cases where the perpetrator abused children other than the victim following disclosure [#82C,#59C]. In the first case the perpetrator admitted an allegation by his niece [#82], but the fact that he was not living with her and her two younger sisters seemed to influence the workers to close the case. At the time they failed to interview the two younger girls, accepting the victim's view that her sisters were not being molested. Four years later it was disclosed that in fact they were being abused [#74C,#75C]. In the second case [#59C], the disclosure of sexual abuse of the 11-year-old girl by her father had occurred when she and her four siblings (including three sisters) were given emergency placements because of his physical abuse of them. Depressed and unemployed, he was their sole caretaker. The children were returned to him and all were followed in family therapy. No details of the alleged sexual abuse were provided in the initial assessment and although family therapy continued for one year, the subject does not appear to have been discussed. Shortly after the therapy ceased the father was arrested for pedophilic activities with other children in the neighbourhood and in addition, it was disclosed that the girl had also been sexually molested by her brother.

The two known cases of recidivism in the English sample involve a 16-year-old sibling perpetrator accused of an incident of voyeurism and a 23-year-old perpetrator (brother-in-law of three victims in the study) who was accused of sexual incidents with two boys after his release from custody. There were no reports of treatment in either case.

Other circumstances noted at follow-up

Ten perpetrators from the English sample as compared to only three Canadian perpetrators are known to have lost their job as a result of disclosure followed by imprisonment. These were all fathers or father-figures and, as observed by others (Cooper, 1978; Tyler & Brassard, 1984), the families suffered financial hardship as a result. Five of the

English perpetrators, none of whom had a previous psychiatric history, became seriously depressed after disclosure and investigation by police, four to the point of attempting suicide; two were hospitalised. All recovered with counselling. Depression among perpetrators has been described by others (Cormier et al., 1962; Maisch, 1972). In three studies of suicide attempts and successful suicides of incestuous perpetrators (Maisch; Morrison, 1988; Wild, 1988), all of the incidents followed prosecution or conviction. Goodwin (1982b) has suggested that the lack of suicide attempts among the incest fathers in her sample (N=201) was because very few were prosecuted. This may explain the absence of attempts by perpetrators in the Canadian sample, most of whom were not involved in criminal proceedings. [15]

The families of at least eight English and five Canadian victims are known to have changed residence following disclosure. In the English group this was often due to the family's humiliation from the publicity of the abuse in the newspapers, a negative sequelae observed by others (Howard League, 1985; Tyler & Brassard, 1984; West, 1987). One mother, whose husband went to prison (reported in the press) described the move as a way 'to escape the memories'. The mother in another case reported in the newspapers received anonymous phone calls and was rejected by her friends and neighbours when she accepted her husband back home [#70]. Because of the harassment, the victim changed schools. This family, like others, felt everyone knew about the incestuous abuse because of the newspaper's account. Even though the victim's name was not mentioned, her father's was, as well as his age, the street he lived on and his charges. The heading was 'Shame of Sex Assault' and reported the magistrate's statement that 'he would have to live with being ostracised by society'. Unfortunately, the ostracism affected his wife and daughter as well. Some were verbally harassed by neighbours and one father/ perpetrator had been threatened by neighbours with iron bars. [16]

There were no recorded instances of cases from the Canadian sample being reported in the newspapers. This may be due to two factors (1) the low number of criminal prosecutions and (2) the Canadian press is less interested in sex 'scandals' than the British. The Canadian government survey found 'that the practice of Canadian newspapers which were reviewed with respect to restricting the publication of information which might serve to identify young victims of sexual offences was one of commendable restraint and circumspection' (Canada, 1984, Vol.1, p.441).

Notes

1. Situations where the perpetrator (usually a parent) was no longer living with the victim as a result of disclosure are counted as an alteration in the living arrangements of the victim. Only two of the victims (in the British sample) are known to have stated she did not want to live with the perpetrator any longer.

2. For a review see Chapter 7 in *Lost In Care* (Millham, Bullock, Hosie & Haak, 1986).

3. Separation or divorce of parental figures occurred in the cases of 35 out of 73 English victims with intact families at disclosure and in 15 out of 61 Canadian victims.

4. Prosecution often entailed a temporary separation of the marital couple when the perpetrator was charged and on bail and in some cases, a more lengthy separation when the perpetrator was sentenced to prison. Also, social workers in the English sample often pressured the mother to separate in order to keep the victim home.

5. In DeFrancis's study (1969), 64% of the sample of 250 victims expressed guilt, and in most of these cases the guilt was related to the problems created by disclosure rather than to the sexual abuse.

6. As noted previously, there were only two cases in the English sample and none in the Canadian where it is reported that the victim stated she did not wish to live with the perpetrator who was at home.

7. These symptoms exclude pregnancy.

8. The marked difference between these findings and those of de Young is difficult to explain. Even when the number of victims known to have attempted suicide before disclosure are included (one English, two Canadian), the rate in this sample is still much lower. While the de Young sample may be a clinical one (she does not clarify this), and therefore more likely to have a higher incidence of suicide attempts than the current sample, so is Goodwin's sample.

9. In one of the three Canadian cases where recidivism occurred in spite of the fact that the victim and perpetrator were no longer living together [#91C], the girl ran away from her mother in order to be with her father, the perpetrator; in another [#18C], the mother pressured her husband to return home in spite of the conditions of his probation and against the advice of her social worker.

10. Personal communication, clinic director, September 1984.

11. Because of the serious consequences of the reabuse authorities in the DYP investigated to determine how the interventions had failed. They exonerated the psychiatric clinic, claiming that social services should have informed them.

12. The mother was actually charged with GBH of her older son, but was found not guilty. When the conference members met to discuss removing the 1½-

year-old from the register, the allegations of sexual abuse were not discussed and the main reason for their recommendation to remove him from the register seemed to be 'to confirm to mother that she'd made progress in his management'.

[13] In another case described earlier, (p.166) [#62], it is highly likely that the intentions of both the girl and her step-father to resume a sexual relationship when they began to live together again, declared to various professionals (there was no mother in the home) were carried out. However, there was nothing social services could do as she was 17 years old and the perpetrator was not a blood relative.

[14] Subsequent to disclosure, other victims in the English sample were physically abused, two by the perpetrator and one by her mother's new co-habitee. All were removed from their home.

[15] While the percentage of suicide attemptors who are physically abusive to their children has been estimated as between 3% and 5% (Roberts & Hawton, 1980), there are no known figures of the proportion who are incest perpetrators.

[16] One perpetrator was not given bail because of threats in the community against him [#85] and another who was sentenced to prison received threatening letters while incarcerated [#23,#33,#34]. The cases of both men had been publicised in the newspapers.

8 Path Analysis of the Combined Samples

Introduction

In order to compare the Canadian and British systems, and because of the amount and complexity of the data, a path diagram was used. Use of a causal model has been suggested by Asker (1976) as a means of facilitating 'the clearer statement of hypotheses and the generation of additional insights into the topic at hand'. A causal diagram 'not only specifies the relationships between the independent variables and the ultimate dependent variable of interests... but also makes explicit the relationships among prior variables' (p.9). Although the data do not meet all the assumptions for using multiple regression (for example, some of the distributions are not normal), it was decided that a path diagram would be useful in providing a global picture of a complex system. Kerlinger (1986) has pointed out the validity of employing such a model even with the limitations noted above.

The following composite variables were calculated:

1) Frequency-duration of sexual abuse. The scores ranged from 1 to 8 with the highest meaning that the victim experienced one or more of the sexual behaviours including sexual manipulation, penetration (anal or vaginal), and oral-genital contact for four years or more or on 100 or more occasions or both. A score of 1 indicated that the behaviour(s) was experienced only once or less than one month.

2) Severity of abuse. This was coded by adding points for penetration, oral/genital contact by the victim on the perpetrator, participation of other children or adults in the sexual acts, and violence or threats of violence by the perpetrator to the victim. Scores ranged from 0 to 4 with 0 assigned to those who experienced only sexual play and 4 assigned to those who had all the features listed above.

3) Previous disclosure of sexual abuse to professionals. This referred to previous attempts to disclose sexual abuse with the same perpetrator to professionals. The scores ranged from 0 (no previous disclosure) to 1 (previous disclosure).

4) Social work response. This variable, reflecting the amount of intervention, was created by adding points for removing the victim and/or the victim's siblings from home, applying for parental rights for the victim and/or the victim's siblings, and not returning the victim home. Scores ranged from 0 (none of the social work interventions listed) to 5 (all of the interventions).

5) Court action. This score ranged from 0 (no court action) (1) to 3 (prison sentence) with 2 assigned to those cases where the sentence was probation or a suspended custodial sentence.

6) Therapy for victim and/or family. The scores ranged from 0 to 4 and were coded by adding points for therapy with the victim, with the victim's parents and family therapy.

7) Original victim symptoms. This was coded by adding points for delinquency, truanting, absconding, school performance, drug and alcohol abuse and suicide attempts. Scores ranged from 0 to 7 with the latter assigned to those who had all the behaviours.

8) Improvement in victim symptoms. This was calculated by first creating a composite variable for 'follow up of victim symptoms' which included the same items as in 'original victim symptoms'. This score was then subtracted from the score obtained in 'original victim symptoms'.

9) Parents separate. This code was limited to cases where the perpetrator was a parent-figure. Those victims where parental figures did not separate after disclosure were scored 0 and those who separated received 1.

10) Victim moves. Scores consisted of 0 (victim did not move) and 1. The latter was applied to those whose perpetrator was a parent figure or a sibling and the victim had moved out of home after disclosure. (This excluded those victims whose perpetrator was a grandfather or uncle, as it was assumed they would not be living together at referral).

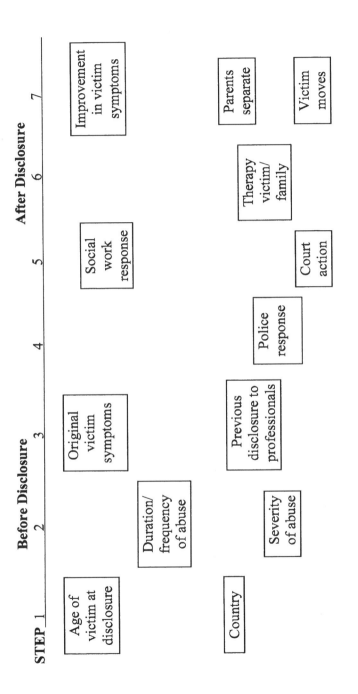

Figure 8.1 Causal model

Figure 1 shows the causal model that was used.   There were 13 variables, including the ten composite variables.   The single variables included source (country), age of child at disclosure, and police response. The causal diagram consisted of seven steps, or levels and the causal process was divided into two main parts, before disclosure and after disclosure with three steps occurring in the first part, and four in the second.   Each variable in levels 2 - 7, in turn, was regressed on all the variables to the left of it.

There was some difficulty in deciding where to place some of the variables in the diagram.   For example, 'social work response' actually occurred in essentially two stages, decisions were made shortly after disclosure at the first case conference and then, in some cases, several months later at a second or subsequent conference.   The first decisions were made at approximately the same time as the police were deciding whether or not to lay charges and before the court decisions and the second group of decisions were made after the police decisions and usually after the court decisions.   Dividing the social work response into two composite variables, and placing these in their respective positions to the police and court variables, would have complicated the diagram and ignored an important aspect, the total amount of the social work intervention in each case.   Thus it was decided to combine the two sets of social work response into one composite variable and place it after the police response and at the same time of the court action.   The causal relationships between these variables will have to be understood in function of this possible distortion of reality.

Similarly, the variables at step 7 placed at the end of the diagram, particularly 'parents separate' and 'child moves' could have been positioned at an earlier stage.   The former could have been put right after police response as some couples separated when the perpetrator was arrested.   Others, however, separated shortly after the social workers made their first decisions and others did so at the end of the process. Some of the victims moved before the police responded and others after the social work response.   Thus the outcome variables and their causal relationships to preceding factors will have to be considered in this light.

The significant relationships found in the regression analysis were further explored by cross-tabulation and calculation of chi-square, as a more conservative estimation of significance.

There was a considerable amount of missing information for some of the variables; for example, follow-up information was available for only approximately half of the English cases.   In order to carry out the multivariate analysis described below, the missing variables were counted as 'nos' (negatives) as otherwise, the sample would have been too small.

Table 8.1 shows a correlation matrix for the 13 variables used in the path analysis. The significant relationships found in the regression analysis are shown in Figure 2. [1] Beta coefficients for all relationships that were found to be significant at p < .05 or better are shown, (22 in all). [2] Some of these relationships were obvious (e.g. age of child at disclosure and frequency and duration of abuse, 'police response' and 'court action' and 'original victim symptoms' and 'improvement in victim symptoms') and not of theoretical interest in this study. The fact that they were found, however, tends to suggest the validity of the path analysis approach.

Differences between Britain and Canada

One of the most interesting findings is the number of significant differences between the Canadian and British systems. The diagram in Figure 2 indicates five significant differences in the two samples as follows:

i)   The negative beta coefficient on the path to 'severity of abuse' shows that the sexual abuse was more severe in the British sample. There was a larger number of British victims who had been penetrated, either vaginally or anally (37 versus 20) and there were slightly more English victims who had been physically assaulted by the perpetrator during the sexual act (10 out of 76 versus 3 out of 73). It can be noted, however, that while the variable 'frequency/duration' of abuse was not significantly related to country, as observed earlier, Canadian victims were abused more often and for longer (Tables 4.5, 4.6 and 4.8, pp.78, 79 and 86 respectively). Table 8.2 comparing the composite variable 'frequency/duration of abuse' for Canada and Britain indicates this trend (DF=8, p=.01). Furthermore, if the age of onset of the sexual abuse is considered in an estimation of the severity of abuse, there was a larger number of Canadian victims whose abuse began under the age of 8 (28.5% versus 18.8% - Table 4.4).

Table 8.1   Correlation matrix for composite variables in path analysis of English and Canadian data

	Age of victim	Source of country Eng/Can[a]	Severity of abuse	Freq./dur. of abuse	Previous discl. to prof.	Orig. victim sympt.	Police resp.	Social work resp.	Court resp.	Therapy victim/family	Improv. in vict. sympt.	Parents separate rate
age of victim	1.00											
source	.07											
severity of abuse	.08	-.15*										
freq./dur. of abuse	.34***	.05	.27									
previous disclos. to professionals	.03	-.12	.21**	.03								
orig. victim symptoms	.25***	.01	-.00	.10	.08							
police response	.06	-.66***	.25***	.19**	-.002	.03						
soc'l work resp.	.15*	-.13	.20**	.12	.11	.01	.03					
court response	.05	-.43***	.21**	.24***	-.001	-.06	.76***	.16*				
therapy-victim/family	.01	.14	.18*	.25***	.06	.06	.08	.09	.13			
improvement in victim sympt's	.08	-.25***	.03	-.1	-.08	.60***	.10	-.05	.02	-.11		
parents separate	-.06	-.13	.05	-.02	-.02	-.04	.19**	.13	.07	.15*	.05	
victim moves	.001	-.03	.31***	-.15*	.18	.06	.02	.16*	.01	.21**	-.15*	.47***

Note: N=191 except for correlation involving police response, where N=186; [a] Canada = 1; * p<.05; ** p<.01; *** p<.001

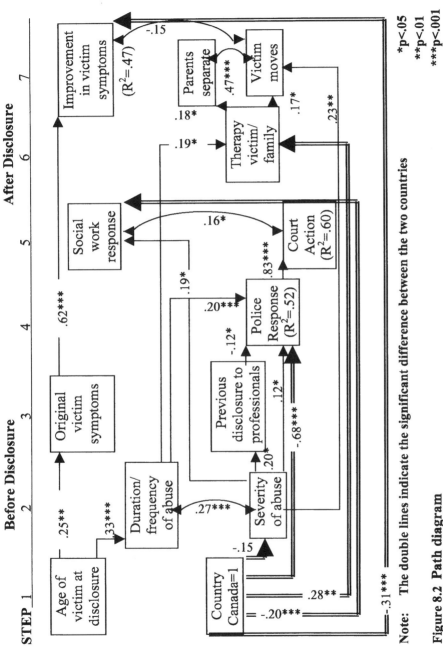

Note: The double lines indicate the significant difference between the two countries

Figure 8.2 Path diagram

Table 8.2   Frequency and duration of sexual abuse by country

| | England | | Canada | | |
Frequency/Duration	No.	%	No.	%	Total
0	13	13.5	23	24.2	36
1	9	9.4	5	5.3	14
2	11	11.5	5	5.3	16
3	4	4.2	7	7.4	11
4	15	15.6	5	5.3	20
5	17	17.7	8	1.6	25
6	7	7.3	9	9.5	16
7	4	4.1	4	4.2	8
8	16	16.7	29	30.5	45
Total	96		95		191

It is possible that duration and frequency of sexual abuse is more indicative of trauma than the type of sexual abuse. Browne and Finkelhor (1986), in a review of the various studies of these factors, concluded that 'there is a strong, if not conclusive, evidence to establish the connection' between trauma and duration and frequency (p.167), and that 'it is premature to conclude that molestation including more intimate contact is necessarily more traumatic than less intimate contact' (p.169). It may be that, in spite of the fact that fewer of them were penetrated, the Canadian sample can be considered as more seriously abused than the British.

ii) There was a highly significant difference in the police response by country, which is further illustrated in Table 8.3.

Table 8.3   Police action by country

| | No. of victims | |
Police action	England	Canada
no charges	34	84
charged	62	11
Total	96	95

A much larger number of English cases were investigated by police (89 versus 16) and many more resulted in a prosecution. This is clearly the result of the different policies of the child protection authorities in the two samples - while the police were routinely involved in the case conferences in the British sample, in the Canadian sample they were involved in only those cases which had been referred to them by persons other than social workers. As a result of the much higher number of English cases which were investigated by the police, many more of the cases from the British sample were prosecuted and sentenced in court (Table 8.4).

Table 8.4   Number of cases resulting in a sentence and type of sentence - England and Canada

Sentence	England		Canada	
	No.	%	No.	%
not sentenced	49	51	84	88.4
suspended custodial or probation	18	18.8	3	3.2
prison	26	27.1	2	2.1
not known	3	3	6	6.3
Total	96		95	

The table also demonstrates that only 9.1% of the Canadian cases which went to court received prison sentences (2 out of 11), compared to 40% of the British cases (26 out of 47).

iii) The significant path from 'country' to 'social work response' indicates that the social work response in Britain was more intrusive for both the victims and their siblings. As observed earlier, in the British sample more children were removed from home and for a longer period of time, more applications for care orders were made and fewer victims, once removed, were returned home. (For example, the number of cases where applications for parental rights were made was 27 in England; 19 in Canada and 5.4% of the Canadian victims removed from home, as compared to 30.9% of the English victims, returned home. The higher amount of intervention is shown in Table 8.5 which describes the degree of intervention in each country (0 indicates no intervention and 4 indicates the highest amount).

Table 8.5   Social work response by country

Degree of intervention	England	Canada
0	42	51
1	15	14
2	21	22
3	11	6
4	7	2
Total	96	95

The significant relationship between 'severity of abuse' (which was higher in Britain) and 'social work response' (which was more intrusive in the English sample) suggests that the British social workers were influenced by whether penetration had occurred. A chi square test showed a significant relationship between the fact of penetration and the decision to remove the victim from home ($p=<.05$).

Another factor that may have influenced the British social workers which was included in the composite variables was the identity of the perpetrator. If the perpetrator was a father or father-figure, the social workers were more likely to remove the victim ($p=<.05$) and apply for a care order ($p=.05$). Given that this type of perpetrator was more likely to be living at home (as compared, for example, with an uncle or grandfather) and that the British professionals tended to view all perpetrators as 'intractable', their decision is understandable. However, the Canadian data showed no comparable significance.

iv) The figure which shows a significant path between 'country' and 'therapy for victim or family', demonstrates that Canadian social workers offered more therapeutic interventions to the victim and the family. As Table 6.7 indicates, more of the Canadian victims received individual and group counselling, and more families were seen in family therapy. This was usually incorporated into 'voluntary measures', which, unlike in the British cases where more coercive measures were taken, were the main intervention in most cases.

v) The negative beta coefficient on the path from 'country' to 'improvement in victim symptoms' shows a significantly higher rate of improvement in victim symptoms in the British sample. This finding must be treated with considerable caution, however. As observed earlier, more Canadian victims had three or more problems prior to disclosure, thus less improvement in this group could be expected. More importantly, as can be seen in Table 8.6, information on the presence or absence of various symptoms in the follow-up was missing in almost twice as many British cases as Canadian cases in most categories. As the 'not knowns' were counted as having no symptoms [3] this could have caused a considerable over-estimate in the numbers 'improved' in the British sample. Also, the finding may reflect the position of the variable in the path diagram. As noted in the discussion on Figure 1, the placement of this category at the end does not reflect the reality for a number of cases where follow-up occurred earlier.

Table 8.6   Victim symptoms at follow-up and number of cases 'not known' - England and Canada

Symptom	Number of cases 'not known'	
	England	**Canada**
running away	57	27
suicide attempt	56	24
drug and.or alcohol abuse	62	30
delinquency	56	24
poor school performance and/or truancy	61	43

Police/court system

As described above, police response was very different in the two countries. It was significantly related to both the 'severity of abuse' and the 'frequency/duration of abuse'. Since the police were involved in so many more of the British cases than the Canadian ones, this finding is probably related more to the British police system than to the Canadian. In fact a chi-square test showed a significant relationship between the type of sexual act (penetration or no penetration) in the British sample ($p<.05$) but did not in the Canadian sample.

It is interesting to observe from the path diagram the apparent lack of relationship between the social work responses and the legal reactions (both police and court). This is particularly curious in the British sample, where there was a high degree of communication and apparent cooperation between the police and social workers through the mechanism of the case conference. As observed earlier, most of the discussions in the case conferences revolved around what legal actions were being taken with the perpetrator - whether he was being charged, or if charged, sentenced to prison. They appeared to act on the principle that a failure to take either of these actions indicated that the social workers had to act to prevent the victim from having contact with the perpetrator. Thus, it was hypothesized that the professionals would decide to use the more intrusive types of interventions (removing the victim from home, applying for care orders) only when there were no legal interventions taken with the perpetrator. This hypothesis was based on the clinical principle that, except in unusual circumstances, it is better to remove the perpetrator rather than the victim from the home (Sgroi, 1982a). The data reveals, however, that British social workers intervened even when the police laid charges. For example, in 12 of the 19 cases where care orders were applied for at the first conference, in five of the nine where a place of safety order was applied for and in 21 of the 43 cases where the victims were placed out of home, charges were laid by the police.

A similar, although less marked, trend in the British social work interventions took place in relation to the sentencing of the perpetrator. For example, in 19 of the 43 cases where the victim was placed, and in 14 of the 19 cases where applications for care orders had been made, the perpetrator had been sentenced (ten and five to prison respectively).

In Canada, there were few social work interventions when action was taken by police or the courts. For example, in only one of the 11 cases where charges were laid was a place of safety order also applied for, and none of the five cases where the perpetrator sentence is known, was the victim placed away.

Thus, it would appear that in a good proportion of the British cases where legal action was taken, the professionals did not believe that this was sufficient to protect the victim. As previously discussed, while it is obvious that in a few of these cases where the perpetrator was the only parent in the home that some protective intervention needed to be taken, [4] this was not the situation in most of the cases where it was felt that even with legal and therapeutic interventions, the perpetrator and victim could not live together. It should also be noted that the probation order was not used to monitor the living arrangements of the perpetrator (that is, whether he was allowed to live with the victim).

Figure 2 illustrates the separate functioning of the police and court system from the social services system and also shows that unlike the social services system which is mildly related to the outcome variables, the police.court system does not show any direct path. ('Social work response' has a relationship with 'parents separate' that approaches significance (-.14) and 'therapy/victim or family' which is also a social work activity, is significantly related to 'parents separate' and 'victim moves'.) This could be seen as a reflection of how the perpetrator is dealt with quite separately from the victim and the family, by different systems. As observed earlier, in only a very few British cases was there an effort to integrate the treatment interventions with the perpetrator and the rest of the family.

Outcome

The significance of the paths from the different variables to the three outcome variables ('improvement in victim symptoms', 'parents separate' and 'child moves') needs to be interpreted with caution. As discussed earlier, the positioning of these variables at the end of the diagram is not a reflection of the reality for all the cases. For example, some of the parents separated and a number of victims moved immediately after disclosure and prior to the court action, the therapeutic interventions and to some of the social work responses.

i)   The significant path from country to 'improvement in victim symptoms' and the severe limitations of the validity of the significance has been discussed earlier. There is an interesting concomitant relationship between 'improvement in victim symptoms and child moves' that suggests that if a victim is moved from home, there are less chances that his/her symptoms improve.

ii) There is a significant path between 'severity of abuse' and 'victim moves' which suggests that those cases involving penetration and violence are more likely to result in the victim moving out of home. This is probably due to the social service interventions for, as the diagram shows, there is a significant path between 'severity of abuse' and 'social work response'.

The significant concomitant relationship between 'parents separate' and 'victim moves' may reflect the situation where the chances of a victim moving are increased when the parents separate and the mother may not keep the child.

iii) Because of the difficulty in positioning the 'therapy-victim or family' variable, the significant path between it and 'victim moves' does not necessarily mean that the therapy resulted in the victim moving. It is more likely that there may have been more treatment in those cases where the victim no longer lived with her family.

Notes

[1] There are discrepancies between the numbers in the correlation matrix (Table 8.1) and those in the path diagram (Figure 1). This is due to the fact that the numbers in the former are first order correlation coefficients while those in the latter are path coefficients which represent the strength of relationships when other variables in the model are controlled. It was decided to discuss the findings in the path diagram as they were considered more useful in studying the differences between the two countries.

[2] Three additional paths that were near significance were between 'country' and 'court action', 'age of victim at disclosure' and 'social work response' and 'social work response' and 'parents separate'. As it was not felt these would contribute to the discussion, they were omitted.

[3] Excluding these cases would not have allowed a multivariate analysis as the sample would have been too small.

[4] It is not clear, however, why in these cases a supervision order could not have been taken, as was done in one of these cases.

9 Conclusions and Implications of the Study

Description of samples

Introduction

This research set out to examine, in two different settings, the kinds of decisions about interventions that professionals make in cases where intrafamilial child sexual abuse has been alleged and the impact these decisions have on the family and its members. To do this, records of all cases disclosed between January 1979 and July 1984 in two areas, Northamptonshire, England and Montreal, Canada were examined. The study allowed for a comparison between a child welfare system where police were routinely informed of the allegations of sexual abuse and were involved in the decision making (England) and one where they were not (Canada). The principal finding was that while the two samples were basically similar in terms of their characteristics, the interventions were quite different with more coercive interventions made in the British sample. Follow-up ranged from under six months to over three years and the observable impact on the victims and their families was greater in the British sample. More victims experienced a change in their living situation (who they lived with), more of the parents separated or divorced and more of the perpetrators (fathers or father-figures) lost their job. The recidivism rate was approximately the same. In reviewing the contrasts observed, an attempt is made to provide some explanation for them. Based on these findings, proposals for appropriate interventions are made.

Samples

With a few exceptions, the two samples were remarkably similar and generally corresponded to those described in other surveys. Most of the perpetrators were male and biological fathers, followed by father-substitutes. The majority of the victims, most of whom were in their early teens at the time of disclosure, had experienced only non-penetrative types of sexual acts.   A minority had been subjected to buggery, oral/genital contact or other deviant types of sexual behaviour and violence during the acts was rare. There were more victims in the English sample who had been penetrated, vaginally or anally. However, more Canadian victims were younger when sexual abuse started and their sexual relationships lasted for a longer period of time. Unlike some surveys, alcohol was a factor in only a minority of cases.

Approximately one-third of the victims in both samples had made previous attempts to disclose the sexual abuse to professionals, none of whom took effective action. Consequences were serious for a number of them, including pregnancy and an escalation of sexual molestation to vaginal or anal penetration.

Victim symptoms

With the exception of three characteristics (low intelligence, truancy and poor school performance) which occurred in almost twice the number of British victims, the victims in both samples had similar characteristics. The literature emphasises the frequent occurrence of serious symptomatology in the victims. In contrast, while approximately half the victims in this survey exhibited symptoms at the time of disclosure, in most cases they were limited to poor school performance or behaviour problems at school. Symptoms of truancy and absconding were not chronic, only occurring on a few (or less) occasions. Only a few in each sample had multiple (three to five) symptoms; but the survey focused on the effects on social functioning, features that could be observed in behaviour. Other possible initial sequalae such as emotional reactions (guilt, fear, depression and anger) and self-perception were more difficult to measure. Thus more victims may have experienced initial negative sequalae than this study revealed. However, since it can be assumed that in some cases at least, painful emotional reactions and negative self-perceptions would manifest themselves in behavioral symptoms, it is likely that the results indicating a lack of severe symptomatology in the majority of victims are generally valid.

There has been some suggestion that the lack of symptomatology may be due to the victim's masking of disturbance as a means of coping with the abuse (de Young, 1982), an interpretation that has implications for professional practice. Even though a child or adolescent is functioning well, this does not rule out the possibility that he/she is being sexually abused. Social workers were upset by the absence of symptoms in some of the British cases and it is likely they allowed this to influence them in making unnecessary interventions. This may have the unfortunate result of creating trauma where none exists. Schultz (1980a), for example, suggests that by assuming trauma where none exists, 'a self-fulfilling prophesy emerges that manages to produce the problem it claims to abhor, but which, in fact, must have in order to sustain the ideology it is based upon' (p.40). An absence of symptoms may indicate that in fact, some children are not adversely affected by sexual abuse and can recover quickly, as long as the professional interventions are not damaging.

Family characteristics

The family characteristics of the samples were largely similar to those reported in other studies. Families tended to be large and few included both biological parents of the victim. There was a multiplicity of behavioral and psychological problems in the parental figures in both samples including spousal violence, history of marital separations and physical abuse of the victim and other children in the family. British families, where the unemployment rate was 46.9%, appeared to be slightly more problematic than the Canadian families (22.1% unemployment rate). They had higher rates of parental instability reflected in fighting and separations (46.9% versus 24.2%), more spousal abuse by the perpetrator (27.1% versus 10.5%), more prior referrals to a social service agency (71.9% versus 56.8%) and more British perpetrators had health problems.

Some victims did not have a mother-figure in the home at referral and a significant number (34.5% English, 29.6% Canadian) had mothers with serious emotional or physical health problems. Also, the parents of a number of victims had a history of sexual abuse. One-fifth of the victims in both samples had been sexually abused by someone other than the current perpetrator and a significant number had siblings who had also been sexually abused.

As a result of the familial problems, approximately one-quarter of the victims in both samples had been referred to a statutory social service agency prior to the disclosure, mostly for physical abuse.

The meaning of the high rate of problems in the parents and family is not clear, that is, whether the sample is representative of the majority of incest cases, or whether, by virtue of being problematic (and often poor), these families were more likely to come to the attention of social services.[1] The greater visibility of the deviance of the poor has been generally accepted. (See, in particular, Skolnick and Woodworth, 1967.) While Finkelhor and Baron (1986) observed that 'it is generally acknowledged that the child welfare system is heavily biased towards identifying abuse in lower social strata' (pp.68-69), referring to representative community surveys conducted by Russell (1986), Miller (1976) and Peters (1984), they concluded that, unlike child physical abuse which empirical studies have shown is strongly related to low socio-economic status (Pelton, 1981; Straus, Gelles & Steinmetz, 1980), [2] there is little connection between social class and sexual abuse. Thus, the fact that a substantial proportion of these families were so problematic may reflect their greater visibility to child welfare authorities rather than that they represent the typical incestuous family.

Different professional responses in two samples and their impact on the families

It has been noted that professionals cannot decide whether sexual abuse is an illness, a crime or a family problem and interventions are based on how one perceives it (MacFarlane & Bulkley, 1982, cited in Finkelhor et al., 1984). Furthermore, these perceptions are affected by professional roles and ideology. An American study examining the different views of different professionals (N=790) reported that the most discrepancy is around the issues of prosecuting the offender and preserving the family unit (Finkelhor et al., 1984). Interventions by the two professional groups in this study clearly showed that they had divergent views on these issues. Canadian professionals viewed incest as both a family problem and an 'illness', more responsive to therapeutic interventions than legal ones, and they worked towards rehabilitation of the victim within the family. In contrast, their British counterparts seemed to view it primarily as a crime; social work interventions were mainly supportive-management type interventions rather than therapeutic ones aimed at change and focused on the victim and the remnants of the family after removal of the perpetrator. Although, except for the nature of the severity of the abuse, [3] the two samples were remarkably similar and the interventions were quite different with the British professionals intervening much more, both in terms of child protection interventions and police action and subsequent criminal prosecution. British professionals removed more victims from home, kept them out for a longer period of time, allowed fewer to return (see Table 6.3) and took out more care orders. They also intervened more with the victim's siblings. A much higher number of English cases were investigated by the police and ultimately prosecuted (40 versus 11) and 20 English perpetrators, compared to only two Canadians, were sentenced to prison. This higher degree of intervention by the British authorities is particularly interesting if one concludes that by virtue of a younger age of onset and lengthier abusive relationships, the Canadian victims were more seriously abused. [4]

Impact on the family

While it is not possible to measure the impact on the family with any precision, given the literature on iatrogenic effects and with the elementary measures that were used in the study (such as child placement, police investigation, incarceration of the family perpetrator, and marital break-up), some speculations about the impact of the decisions on the victims and families can be made. Many more English victims were exposed to the stress of police interrogation, medical examination and incarceration of the perpetrator. Twenty British victims, as compared to only six Canadians, underwent both statutory proceedings by the protection authorities and police investigation. More were removed from home and not returned, more stayed out for a longer period of time and more experienced a change in their living situation. In a few of these cases there was probably no alternative but permanent separation of the victim from the home because of the amount of familial problems that were resistant to change. However, in the British sample, rehabilitation of the family was not a goal, regardless of the potential for a safe return of the victim to the family in some cases.

The interventions made in both samples were supposedly geared to protecting the victim from further abuse, but in view of the excess of interventions in the English cases, it is interesting that the number known to have been reabused by the same perpetrator was very similar (five out of 95 Canadians, six out of 96 English). Notwithstanding, the differences in policy, in most of the cases of reabuse in the Canadian sample and in all of the English cases, inadequate social work intervention was a major factor. There was no police intervention in four of the reabused English cases and in none of the Canadian. British professionals could argue that their 'failures' were due to the lack of police involvement, but, considering that the police were involved in only a minority of the Canadian cases and yet the recidivism rate was approximately the same, this argument is very questionable. It would appear that use of the police does not affect recidivism and only serves to punish the offender. When the iatrogenic effects of the police and court procedures are taken into account, use of the criminal justice system in these types of cases would appear to be highly contraindicated. The similar rate of recidivism in the Canadian sample indicates that a clinical approach involves no greater risk to victims than the invocation of the criminal justice system. This approach, however, needs to be based on a good assessment, which was not the case in most of the cases in both samples which recidivated.

Professional interventions in these samples compared to other studies

It appears that there has been a trend for professionals to intervene more in cases of sexual abuse than physical abuse. Finkelhor (1983), in an analysis of interventions made in all cases of child abuse reported to child protection authorities in America in 1978, reported that foster placements occurred in more cases of sexual abuse than in cases of physical abuse. Julian and Mohr (1979) reported similar findings that more foster home placements (32.4% versus 9.6%), more civil court proceedings (33.3% versus 11.1%) and more criminal action (31.4% versus 11.1%) occurred in cases of child sexual abuse. Krugman (1988), discussing the impact of the 'discovery' of child sexual abuse on child welfare services in America, observed that these cases 'added the additional task of a criminal investigation to an already difficult civil process' (p.293) and that as a result, there has been a backlash movement by those critics who feel the child protection system has gone too far. Similar criticism has been raised in England following the events in Cleveland (Bell, 1988; Home Office, 1988) and more recently in Orkney (1992) which were marked by excessive professional intervention .

Although the Canadian professionals intervened less coercively than their British counterparts, it appears that this had not always been the case, at least in terms of child welfare interventions. [5] The 1977 Youth Protection Act coincided with the onset of the data collection for this research. A study done in Quebec prior to this showed that social work interventions were more severe in cases of sexual abuse than in physical abuse (Comité de la Protection de la Jeunesse (CPJ), 1984).

This study, based on 6,299 maltreated children known to the child protection authorities in Quebec between 1975 and 1978, reported that 75% of the sexually abused children, as compared to only 48% of the physically abused children were placed outside their homes; moreover their placements were longer (three years as compared to two) and there were more civil court procedures (62% versus 42%). When these figures are compared with those of the current study, it is evident that after the implementation of the new act with its focus on rehabilitating the family whenever possible, and during the period of the study (1979-1985), the Quebec authorities intervened less intrusively in cases of child sexual abuse. The current Canadian sample showed that only 33% were placed away (55% of these being returned home within two years) and that parental rights were applied for in only 20% of the cases. [6]

Reports in the UK, however, show that sexual abuse still warrants more attention from authorities than do other forms of maltreatment. Creighton and Noyes (1989), in a survey of British cases on NSPCC 'at risk registers' from 1983 to 1987, reported that the sexual abuse cases were assessed as needing more investigation and alternative care than cases registered for other reasons. Recommendations for adult court proceedings were also more frequent in sexual abuse cases. The average number of planned actions per case was 1.9 for sexual and 1.5 for physical abuse. The seriousness that British professionals view these cases can be further seen in the rates of police prosecutions of cases registered at the NSPCC between 1977 and 1982 (Creighton, 1985). The only rate that was higher than the 52.5% reported for sexual abuse was in cases of child deaths where the parents were still alive (78%).

Thus, in summary, it would appear that while in both countries, as elsewhere, decisive intervention is particularly frequent in cases of child sexual abuse, the current study indicates that after the new Youth Protection Act was passed in 1978 and until 1985 when the new incest protocol which advocated the automatic involvement of police was accepted (Cooper & Cormier, 1985), there was a movement towards less intervention in Quebec. [7]

Disclosure initiates a major crisis for the victim, perpetrator and other family members and, it may be said, also for the professionals mandated to deal with it (Summit, 1986). The main preoccupation of the family members, often including the victim as well, is disintegration of the family (Swanson & Biaggio, 1986). The initial actions taken by professionals following disclosure (assessment and interventions) are crucial in determining the future management of the case, both as regards the contact the family will have with the agency and the ultimate outcome (Cormier & Cooper, 1990; Sgroi et al., 1982; Simmons, 1986).

Four main factors seemed to govern the decisions taken by professionals - (1) the structure of the decision-making process (2) the goals of the child protection authorities (3) the role of the police and (4) the professionals' attitude towards sexual abuse. To facilitate discussion, decision-making is discussed in relation to these different factors, in particular, the last two. In addition, the decisions on statutory interventions and treatment are discussed further under separate headings.

Structure of the decision-making process - Canada and England

The different structures in which the two child welfare systems operated greatly affected the way assessments were done and decisions taken. The main element in the decision making of the English sample was the case conference which provided a forum for all the professionals who knew the child or family to meet, pool their information and decide about interventions. In contrast, in the Canadian sample decisions were made as a result of a psycho-social assessment done by a social worker under the supervision of a senior worker. The resulting decisions were relayed back in a report which included a detailed social history and proposed goals and methods of interventions to the Department of Youth Protection who reviewed them and either approved or questioned them. The worker could consult any other professional who had information on the child/family (such as a teacher, medical doctor, psychiatric service) or could request an assessment from a specialist (psychologist or psychiatrist). (For example, referral of a father/perpetrator to a psychiatrist was done in a number of cases.) [8] This range of potential sources of information can be seen as the equivalent of the different English professionals who attended the case conference and supplied information. As seen in Table 6.1, which explains the sources of reports used in the various decisions, written reports were available to aid many more of the decisions made in the Canadian sample. An exception was the court decision on care orders, where the English professionals supplied an equivalent number of written reports.

After reading all of the case conference minutes of 90 of the English cases, this researcher felt that the process was less than satisfactory. The quality of the information varied considerably, some of it first-hand, but perhaps acquired some time before, and some second- or third-hand. Usually, the only information on the nature and extent of the abuse was supplied by the police officer. The literature suggests that up-to-date information is crucial for appropriate decision making in these cases (see, for example, Sgroi et al., 1982) and should include the nature and extent of the abuse, history of the victim, perpetrator and family, relationships in the family (perpetrator/victim, victim/mother, marital), attitude of family members about the abuse, and family strengths. Information on some of these areas was offered by different members but was quite often out of date, and of variable quality depending on the nature of the contact the professional had had with the family, as well as his/her professional level of expertise. As a result, crucial decisions were made, particularly at the initial stages, on the basis of incomplete data and inadequate clinical appraisal.

A review of British studies on social work practice in child welfare cases was strongly critical of the quality of the assessments and concluded that 'the whole basis for planning is shaky. Decisions are made on inadequate evidence and it is not surprising if goals are unclear or if there is a lack of congruence between goals and what is actually done - or not done' (Department of Health and Social Security (DHSS), 1985b, p.21).

The case conference structure, initially established in response to the death of Maria Colwell and the resulting inquiry (Colwell, 1974), was part of an overall re-organisation of administrative structures including the creation of the area review committees and the 'at risk register'. It has, as part of its purpose, (a) the task of sharing knowledge about the family including its history and information about individual members (b) to diagnose the problems and assess the family, including the degree of risk to which all children are exposed and (c) to formulate an immediate treatment plan and long term goals (British Association of Social Workers Working Party, cited in Jones, McClean & Vobe, 1979; Malcolm Page Inquiry Report, 1981). In his testimony to the Cleveland Inquiry, David Jones from the British Association of Social Workers stressed that 'it is absolutely essential that those involved with the family, social workers, and others, conduct the fullest assessment of the family background. A full family history is being shown repeatedly to be of vital importance' (Home Office, 1988, p.214).

In spite of the establishment of this improved structure to ensure good child welfare practice (particularly communication), there appears to have been an increasing unease with its efficacy, particularly with the case conference procedure. Although the 'collective decision making' function of case conferences was advocated by government circulars (DHSS, 1976), Packman (1975), among others (see, in particular Hallett and Stevenson, 1980) have suggested that the conference may be primarily a means of sharing anxiety and avoiding responsibility and produces a sense of false reassurance. 'Elaborate procedures are ...defensive rituals - a means of dealing with anxiety, and fending off criticism should anything go wrong' (p.181). Such defensiveness is understandable given the hostile public criticism that social workers have routinely been exposed to in child abuse death enquiries in England (Packman, 1983; Greenland, 1990), but it does not contribute to good clinical practice.

Writers with more specific criticisms have observed that the conferences are expensive (Howells, 1974 ; Freeman, 1983; West, 1987), sometimes badly chaired (Geach, 1981; Hallett & Stevenson, 1980) and too large (Geach). Hallett and Stevenson have suggested that the difficulty in achieving the effective co-operation is caused by differences in role perspectives, status and professional attitudes. Another factor militating against co-ordination is the value-laden subject matter of abuse and the difficulty different professionals have on agreeing on what constitutes being 'at risk' (Freeman, 1983). There are also serious questions about the issue of confidentiality and the infringement on civil liberties (Geach, West).

Some of the most serious concerns which are highly relevant to this discussion have been about the inefficiency of the conference in eliciting facts and its inappropriateness for planning action. Howells (1974) pointedly observed that 'correct information is essential for assessment. Right assessment leads to right actions... *assessment of families should not be dependent on past information from others, but on careful and accurate assessment*' (p.106) (added emphasis). Bedford (1987), commenting about the importance of good assessments in child abuse wrote:

> Although human relationships will never be an area of precise prediction it is important to have a structure within which assessment and treatment plans can be made. If risks can be carefully analysed, then it is more likely that decisions about intervention and the intervention itself will be successful (p.2).

A report by the Society of Clinical Psychiatrists (Chapman, et al., 1985) was strongly critical of child abuse case conferences, stating that:

> The crucial decision whether, and when, it is safe to allow the child to return to its parents is a technical decision requiring the highest degree of professional competence... even if some of the individual participants should happen to be adequately equipped to make such a decision, it would be quite unrealistic to expect them to do so in such circumstances. The nature and degree of a parent's emotional problems and their probable response to treatment can be assessed only in the course of a personal diagnostic-therapeutic interview (cf. Woodmansey, 1982), and not by any kind of debate, and still less by a debate arising out of

differences of opinion that are inevitably based largely on emotional prejudices (pp.8-9).

Some critics have advocated retaining the procedure but with various alterations, for example better preparation for the conference with key people presenting a brief (one page) written summary of their evidence, compulsory chairmanship training for all potential chairmen, meeting within 72 hours of the initial referral (Jones et al., 1979), no written records of the proceedings other than the decisions so as to ensure absolute confidentiality (Teebay, 1983) and training in presentation skills and information evaluation techniques (Bell & Pennington, 1990).

Others, however, have advocated a different system of assessment and accountability, usually on the lines of a multi-disciplinary assessment. Howells (1974), in a critique of the Maria Colwell case and inquiry, observed that 'the biggest weakness of these conferences is the way in which they obscure the source of responsibility' (p.104).

He argued that 'nothing sharpens expertise more than responsibility... professional intervention will be efficient if one person only is responsible for deploying the welfare services for a particular family. Behind the worker responsible for a family can stand a number of specialists in various aspects of the welfare services, available for consultation and support, but not immediately responsible' (p.104). With this system the expert's main responsibility is to make decisions. In their later study of the assessment and management of child abuse in Britain, the Society of Clinical Psychiatrists (Chapman et al.,1985) came to a similar conclusion and stressed the importance of having the responsibility for the case assigned solely to one supervisor who 'gives continual comprehensive support to the case workers and will have the final decision on all questions of placement and access' (p.11). They further argued that one person must be in charge and free from any interference.

Based on their research of battered babies, Smith and Noble (1973) made a somewhat similar recommendation. Observing that workers tended to rely on the case conference which, in their view, was 'extremely inefficient' (p.395), they proposed that decisions and case management be conducted by a hospital-based multi-professional team. While the concept differs in the number of decision-makers, the idea is basically similar to those above in that the decisions are made by specifically identified people who are seen as experts.

The idea of a multi-disciplinary form of assessment of the incestuous family (see, for example, Simmons, 1986), or at least an assessment carried out by more than one person to avoid counter-transference problems (Cooper & Cormier, 1990; Schetky, 1988a) seems to be gaining general acceptance.

While there are obvious benefits from having a procedure, as in the British sample, that allows face to face sharing of information, particularly so that pertinent professionals in contact with the family are all made aware of the allegations of abuse, it is highly questionable whether the conferences should form the main basis for crucial decision making. It has been argued that they should be seen as advisory bodies only and that different professionals must feel free to act independently according to their professional judgment (Jones et al., 1979), an issue recognised as well in the government circulars (DHSS, 1976). However the data showed, as others have reported (Hall, 1978; Dingwall et al., 1983), that conference members rarely disagreed on the final decisions [9] - and also that major decisions, like removal from home, were always carried out. It is perhaps interesting that the decision which was not always carried out, referral to a psychiatrist, was a treatment option while the others involved control.

In the Canadian sample the system of assessments made by one worker in consultation with a supervisor generally conforms to the models outlined by Howells (1974), Smith and Noble (1973) and Chapman and his colleagues (1985). It is apparent that the value of such an assessment system is dependent on the level of competence of the interviewer. In a number of cases Quebec social workers did not do an adequate assessment. Nevertheless, considering the emphasis in the literature on the importance of a comprehensive psycho-social view of the family situation and the problems inherent in the case conference model for achieving this, and considering the uneven quality of the information in the conferences in the English sample, it would seem that the assessment process allowed by the child protection structure in the Quebec sample has, on the whole, a much better potential for providing the type of evaluation needed.

Goals of the child protection authorities

The professionals' goals of verification of the abuse and protection of the victims from further abuse were common to both countries. However Quebec professionals seemed to have a further goal of helping the victim recover from the incest and, if possible, of rehabilitating the family, as long as this did not place the victim at risk. In contrast, while the British professionals were also clearly concerned about the welfare of the victim, their focus was mainly on ensuring separation from the perpetrator rather than on treatment. Rehabilitation of the family unit was actively opposed.[10] A British study on the management of child abuse by the Social Services Inspectorate (1986) observed that while in the majority of cases the initial assessment for immediate protection was good, 'comprehensive assessments for long term planning were conspicuous by their absence... shoddy work can expose children to the dangers of risk at home or unnecessary alternative care' (cited in Bedford, 1987, p.11). This view was borne out in the British study sample where the actions of the child welfare workers most often appeared to be reactive rather than pro-active.

Role of the police

The British professionals relied heavily on the police to investigate allegations. Social work decisions largely followed the lead of the police, who routinely attended the case conference. In contrast, police had no role in the decision making of the Quebec child protection services and only became involved in a few cases when some outsider (for example, a family member) had informed them of the allegations. As a result, the Quebec social workers had full responsibility for decisions and management.

Verification of allegations The British professionals generally depended on the police to initiate and carry out a verifying investigation, which generally included a medical examination. Verification in the Canadian sample was conducted by the social workers and occurred in two phases: first, there was an initial brief assessment by the intake worker at the Department of Youth Protection who decided whether there was sufficient evidence to proceed further. If there was, the second stage consisted of an extensive assessment by a social worker. The evidence was 'softer' in the Canadian sample. For example, even if the alleged perpetrator denied the allegations but the professionals believed the child's statement that abuse had occurred, they would register the case, proceed to have contact with the family and continue to evaluate the situation. This tended not to occur in the British sample and resulted in five of the six cases of reabuse.

Professionals' attitudes towards sexual abuse

A theme which ran through many of the decisions was the professionals' view of sexual abuse. In both samples there was clear evidence that they saw sexual abuse as a horrible and frightening event, if not outrightly disastrous. While the fear and hostility focused on the perpetrator, it was also expressed in decisions about the victim and siblings. Like the British professionals, Canadian social workers demonstrated attitudes of fear and/or repugnance towards the problem but, because of the policy of the importance of rehabilitation of the family, whenever possible, these feelings had considerably less impact on their decisions. This was further reinforced by their 'clinical' approach to the problem demonstrated in their assessment and treatment procedures, which included preparation of a report containing details of the treatment goals and the means by which they would be obtained. In contrast, the strong role of the police in case management in the British cases allowed British social workers more opportunity to express and act upon their negative views and to both avoid and punish the perpetrator.

The emotional reaction to sexual abuse was particularly apparent in three areas (i) the decision to take little or no action (ii) decisions to apply for Place of Safety Orders and/or care orders and (iii) therapeutic interventions with the perpetrator. The latter two were particularly influenced by a view of the perpetrator as untreatable.

The decision to take no action or to only monitor   Summit (cited in Finkelhor et al., 1984) has observed that due to the emotional reactions provoked by the subject, sexual abuse is often either denied or treated as an emergency. This was evident immediately after the referral in the decision in some cases to take no action or to only monitor the case. While there were much fewer intrusive interventions by the Canadian professionals, there was a tendency for professionals in both groups either to ignore the case completely and take no action, which left the victim at risk, or to do a lot. (The fact that approximately one third of the victims in both samples had previously attempted to disclose the sexual abuse to professionals who failed to take adequate actions, further illustrates their tendency to sometimes ignore the problem.) Eight of the 19 British victims who were not registered or monitored (compared to three of the 12 Canadian victims) were viewed by the professionals to be at risk. While none of these three Canadian victims are known to have been abused later, five of the eight British ones were.

Avoidance and denial of the painful topic of sexual abuse was demonstrated by Canadian professionals, who based their interventions on a clinical assessment of the family, when they either did not interview the perpetrator or did it inappropriately, failing to collect enough information on the nature of the abuse (for example, interviewing the perpetrator in

example, decisions were taken to apply for a POSO and/or care order when charges were laid but they were concerned he would not be sentenced to prison, and also when a prison sentence was completed and the possibility arose that the perpetrator might return home where the victim was living. These decisions were also taken when there were no charges (seven cases). Even in those few cases where the perpetrator had been offered and had participated in some treatment, this was not deemed sufficient to ensure the safety of the victim in his presence.

Because of their reliance on the criminal justice system and their view of the perpetrator as untreatable, the time it took for a criminal case to proceed affected their ability to return the child home quickly (or at all). This apparent effect of delay in the adult court system on care decisions and decisions to return the victim home, is of concern when considered in the light of the findings of Millham and his colleagues (1986) who found that if a child is in care for longer than six weeks, he has a 78% chance of spending six months in care and a 63% chance of still being in care after two years.

The Canadian social workers were not immune to a similarly negative view of the perpetrator. Their failure to see some of the perpetrators for assessment, their frequent failure to obtain detailed histories of the sexual abuse from the perpetrator or even others, and their attempt, in some cases, to treat the perpetrator under voluntary measures without mentioning the abuse, all indicate a similarly nihilistic view. In at least four cases these problems resulted in a failure of the voluntary measures and a decision to 'seize the court'. (In one of these they referred to the father as 'crazy and untreatable'.)

The process of identifying child abusers and its effects on interventions have been discussed by several theorists including Newberger and Bourne (1978) who argue that child abuse in general has become medicalised and then legalised, in part because of the painful emotions it arouses. Focusing on a narrow medical issue rather than larger issues like family problems, helps professionals avoid upsetting feelings. Citing Parsons (1951), they further state that once abuse is defined as a sickness, though treatment, not punishment is warranted, the type of treatment depends on whether the abuser is curable; helping the abuser is generally seen as less important than the need to protect the child.

If the abusive behaviour cannot quickly be altered and the child remains 'at risk', the type of intervention will differ accordingly (for example, the child may be more likely to be placed in a foster home). The less 'curable' is the abuser, the less treatment will be offered and the more punitive will society's response appear (pp.310, 311).

Freeman (1983) has pointed out that medicalising the problem of child abuse allows us to distance ourselves from the abuser and concentrate on 'them' rather than us. He argues that Zigler's view that child abuse should be placed on a 'continuum on which everyone can be placed' (1979, p.176) rather than a classification system that identifies two groups, abusers and non-abusers, would allow a more empathetic approach to the abuser. 'Instead they are seen as "freaks"'... identifiable targets upon which to vent anger' (Freeman, p.108).

While these comments are about abusers in general, they are particularly relevant to sexual abusers of children and would seem to explain, at least in part, the professionals' view of the perpetrator as untreatable, particularly evident in the English sample. [12] Evidence of this largely unexamined, highly negative view of incest fathers can be found in a report on the study of father-daughter incest commissioned by the DYP in Quebec in 1981 (Messier, 1987). The report, with no criticism of the social workers, described their reaction to the incest father as follows: 'The caseworker's reaction to the abuser can only be one of disbelief, aggressiveness, horror and disapproval' (p.77). The study's surprising proposed solution to the problem further indicates the great difficulty professionals have in facing the abuser in a clinical, non-judgmental way. After acknowledging that treatment of the father would be difficult if he detects the worker's feelings, Messier concluded that, similar to alcoholics who are best treated by other alcoholics, so incest fathers are best treated by other incest fathers in a group format.

Conte (1984) has suggested that the 'greatest unmet need in cases involving adult sexual use of children is that of treatment for the perpetrator' (p.564). It is essential to prevent recidivism, particularly if there are plans to rehabililtate the family (Cormier & Cooper, 1982; Giaretto, 1981).

There is an interesting similarity between the samples in the rarity of individual treatment of the perpetrators and their wives (the victims' mothers), which suggests that they were difficult to engage. This has been noted about mothers (Cormier & Cooper, 1982) as well as father perpetrators (Giaretto, 1981; Sgroi, 1982a). It is likely that the fear and repugnance felt by professionals (Finkelhor, 1984; Giaretto, 1981; Messier, 1987) not only prohibited many workers from even seeing the perpetrator (particularly in the British sample) but also interfered with engaging him in a therapeutic process. [13]

This emotional avoidance of the incest abuser is well illustrated in the title chosen by Horton and his colleagues - *The Incest Perpetrator - The Family Member No One Wants to Treat (1991)*.

Actually, when family therapy is included, more perpetrators in the Canadian sample received treatment than would appear. In most cases family therapy in Canada included the perpetrator (usually a father figure) while in the British sample it did not as the perpetrator was usually no longer with the family. However, treating perpetrators in a family group is generally not recommended and when used at all, should be utilised towards the end of the therapeutic regime, after the victim, mother and father/perpetrator has had individual and/or group therapy (Finkelhor, 1984; Giaretto, 1981; Cormier & Cooper, 1982).

In some of the Canadian cases the perpetrator's problems did not get addressed by the social worker and perhaps the decision to see the perpetrator in the family group was a way of avoiding dealing with him directly. Walters (1975), noting the prevalence of social workers' avoidance of the incest perpetrator, has referred to this as 'treatment by osmosis' (p.134). It is possible, however, that simply by dint of so much exposure to the social worker and the reminder of his abusive behaviour, the perpetrator learned to deal with it. The Canadian professionals probably did not find it any easier to deal with the perpetrator than their British counterpart. However, because they were obliged to become involved with the perpetrator, at least in the initial stages, due to the goal of maintaining families together whenever possible, it may be that in some, if not many of the cases, this forced `exposure' served to reduce some of their fear and hostility.

A major argument for the necessity of using the criminal process for the abuser is that without it, he will continue to deny the offences and not co-operate in treatment (Giaretto, 1981; Graves & Sgroi, 1982). The fact that a significant proportion of the perpetrators in both samples admitted their incestuous behaviour, makes this questionable. While approximately three-quarters of the British perpetrators admitted to the police, at least one-half of the Canadian perpetrators admitted their offences to a non-legal professional in the course of the assessment (most were not interviewed by the police). [14] The higher rate in the police interviews may be due as much to the police's superior interviewing skills as to the likelihood that perpetrators might be more inclined to confess to them. Thus, it may be that (a) perpetrators make admissions to 'therapeutically' oriented professionals as readily as to police and (b) the denial reported by some professionals is as much a problem of the professionals as of the perpetrators. An example of this can be found in Messier's report of the treatment of father-daughter incest cases in Quebec, where she commented with surprise on the fact that while approximately half of the fathers admitted to the incest, only half of these co-operated in treatment (as assessed by the workers). (Messier, 1987) This suggests, as it did to her, that there is a problem in continuing to engage the perpetrator in a therapeutic process once an admission is made. However, considering the social worker's highly negative views of the father already noted, this is not surprising.

A further indication that incest perpetrators do not necessarily need the coercion of the criminal court to accept treatment is that most of the Canadian perpetrators who accepted treatment, did so as part of their contract with the youth protection authorities through 'voluntary measures' and had not been charged in criminal court.

It is surprising that more incest perpetrators in the British sample were not followed in treatment since the principle argument offered for using the criminal justice system is to utilise it as leverage to force the perpetrators to accept treatment (as noted above). However, there was only one case where sentence was deferred while the accused was treated in a probation hostel - in the other cases treatment was not used as a condition in either probation orders or parole. (Most of the perpetrators who received individual therapy were seen by a probation officer and it can be questioned how much the sexual abuse was dealt with.)

In summary, there seems to be no clinical basis for the punitive approach with incestuous fathers or the view of them as untreatable. It is important to make a clinical distinction between incest and pedophelia and realise that the majority of incestuous abusers are not primarily pedophilic; thus children outside the family are, in most cases, not at risk (Cooper & Cormier, 1990; Langevin et al., 1985; West, 1987). [15] This is a clinical distinction that can be made in a good assessment.

'Compassion versus control' [16] *- the degrees of coercive intervention with the victim and family*

Iatrogenic trauma for child abuse victims can derive from civil procedures as well as criminal ones. 'Children's entitlements to the company and stimulation of their parents and the continuity of their home lives may be violated by civil proceedings no less than by criminal, despite the best interests rhetoric the former may use as justification for intervention' (Dickens, 1984, p.90). Intervention in sexually abusive families requires a combination of therapeutic 'compassion' and 'control' (Rosenfeld & Newberger, 1979), the balance depending on the family's situation (for example, their acknowledgement of the problem and willingness to work towards change), which alters over time. The value of non-coercive work has been described by Howells (1974) who wrote that 'policy should be aimed at co-operative and non-coercive work with (abusive) families, with an emergency service able to rescue a child in dire straits... families approached in a helpful way, especially with patience, will respond to approaches that ultimately lead to co-operation in solving their own adverse situations' (p.110). This suggests that non-coercive measures be used as much as possible, without endangering the victim.

The first task for professionals who learn of allegations of sexual abuse is to decide whether removing the victim from home is necessary to ensure his/her emotional and physical safety. Given the negative consequences for victims to be separated from home that have been described (see, in particular, Ch.7 in Millham et al., 1986), this decision needs to be taken with great care. 'Removal has been described as the coarsest implement used by the state on the family. Involuntary separation of the family is probably the most drastic disruption to family stability. It has been portrayed as a terrifying and painful experience which damages the child's personality and normal growth' (Martz, 1979, p.91).

Many argue that removal of abused children may be as damaging, if not more so, than the abuse and should only be used as a last resort (Martz, 1979; Thomas, 1974; Turbett, 1979). For example, Gentry (1978) asserts that the child's removal from the incestuous family is justified 'only when the other family members are too passive or fearful to place limits on the offender, or when supportive homemakers, volunteers and other family supports cannot be provided' (p.359). While approximately one-third of the victims in each sample left home or were removed from home shortly before or after disclosure, in both samples more victims did so on a voluntary basis than by statutory measures. This was sometimes managed by the child herself or aided by the social worker. In the British sample there was no discernable difference between those who left home voluntarily and those where place of safety orders were used. Those removed under statutory measures arouse concern because of evidence that precipitant removals are more disturbing for children because of the lack of planning involved (Martz, 1979; Millham et al., 1986). Packman (1986) has pointed out that these children 'rarely have the comfort of familiar adults around them, or any foreknowledge of where they are to go... ' (p.198).

The question of the urgency of the placement in cases of child sexual abuse may be different than in cases of physical abuse where professionals fear that another incident of physical abuse might occur. Given the different nature of incestuous abuse (motivation, actions), the perpetrator is unlikely to initiate a sexual encounter with the victim immediately following disclosure. Instead, he is more likely to attempt to pressure the victim to change her story (Sgroi, 1982a). One study showed that the decision to remove a child from home was related to characteristics of the child protection services rather than to the incident that precipitated the referral or to family characteristics (Shireman, Miller & Brown, 1981). (For example, referrals made to the police resulted in more emergency placements.)

In this study it was not possible to determine exactly how many of the removals of victims from their home, either voluntarily or on a statutory basis, were actually required. However, it appears that the decision was appropriate in a number of cases in both samples where the child requested it, mother was hostile or the perpetrator was the only parent figure in the home. More siblings of the victims were removed from home in the British sample, often inappropriately, as the children were too young or the wrong sex to be considered at appreciable risk. [17]

The greatest power that child welfare professionals have over children is their authority to invoke care proceedings. While this occurred in a disturbingly high number of cases in both samples, there were more care orders applied for in the British sample (27 versus 19) and, unlike in the Canadian sample, usually with a view to permanent separation of the victim and perpetrator. This higher rate may reflect the recent trend by British social workers to take more statutory powers than before, a trend that has caused considerable alarm, resulting in several major studies. (In particular, see Millham et al., 1986, Packman, 1986 and Vernon & Fruin, 1985). 'In 1962, less than half of the children in care had been admitted compulsorily or else their parents' rights had been taken over by the local authority. By 1980, the proportion had risen to three-quarters' (DHSS, 1985b, p.7).

Perhaps a more crucial question than removal from home was the length of time victims stayed out of home and the number who did not return. Ultimately more English victims left home as a result of disclosure (42 versus 31), fewer returned (13 versus 18) and much fewer were expected to ever return home (six out of 29 versus eight out of 13). The problems facing these children have been described as 'distress, affective deprivation, placement breakdowns and diminished academic achievement... (and) the omnipresent risk that over time social isolation and even institutionalisation will develop' (Millham et al., 1986, pp.44, 45).

There was evidence in some English cases where the removal was not permanent that the victim's access to mother and siblings was severely restricted. However, it was not clear whether the majority of the English victims who were living in a residential centre or foster home and not expected to return, were able to maintain links with their family. If the social workers behaved like those described in the Dartington project (Millham et al., 1986), it is likely that contacts were not maintained. That study showed that social workers paid little attention to the importance of family ties, sometimes applying specific restrictions, but more often not helping children maintain contact with their family. Once a care order had been obtained, their visits with the children and families declined significantly over time. The study also showed that the chances of remaining in care and away from home were greatly affected by the links the child maintained with the family.

The 1989 Children Act has made considerable changes regarding children's contact with their parents, imposing a duty on the local authority 'to allow reasonable contact, by giving interested parties the opportunity to test the authority's plans and decisions in court, and by giving the court ample powers both at the time of the making of the care order and subsequently' (Allen, 1990, p.121). Hopefully this will alleviate the serious problem of lack of contact found in this study and others.

It seems clear that the Canadian professionals attempted to use the least amount of coercion possible, only resorting to more intrusive measure when necessary. For example, the British authorities applied for more care orders initially than later (16 versus 11), while their Canadian counterparts applied for more later (seven versus 12). In the Canadian sample minimum coercion was facilitated by the option of 'voluntary measures' which was the main intervention in the majority of cases and usually used before taking the more invasive step of applying for parental rights ('seizing the court'). It is interesting that a survey of Quebec social workers showed that they viewed the measures as a means of treatment rather than coercion (Sommerville, 1984). While there was certainly a coercive element in the measures in that failure to sign or to follow them could result in more drastic action, it allowed workers the opportunity to attempt to engage the family, including the perpetrator, in a therapeutic process. It was also used in a number of cases to keep the perpetrator out of the home for a period of time.

Much has been written about the powerlessness of abusive parents in the face of statutory child welfare agencies and their hostile feelings towards these authorities (see, for example, Packman, 1986, Millham et al., 1986) and how engaging people's will is ultimately more effective in bringing about long-term change than employing control. Pickett and Maton (1977) have described their way of doing this as follows: 'We explain the processes of decision making that have to occur once a diagnosis has been made - and keep parents informed of the decision making process, as far as is possible. Their sense of powerlessness should not be unnecessarily reinforced' (p.62). The voluntary measures represent a formalising of this process and appear to be a valuable tool to encourage participation. They were also valuable in that they not only included conditions of therapy but ones that related specifically to victim protection (for example, access of the perpetrator to the victim and where a child slept).

British studies have observed the failure of social workers to 'consult, inform and work with parents' (DHSS, 1985b, p.20) when compulsory measures are considered (or taken) and Packman (1986) concluded that:

> Social workers need to spell out, at an early stage in negotiations, their own ultimate legal powers and responsibilities for children's welfare... how it is done, as with all social work, is of crucial importance. Presented as a threat, or as sanctimonious moralising, it is unlikely to be either effective or appreciated. Frankly and honestly presented in the context of a genuine concern to help, and as an integral part of that concern - the ultimate safety net - the power to control and compel can be both understandable and even helpful to some parents (p.205).

This would seem an apt description of the process that goes on in the negotiations of 'voluntary measures' with the family.

The tendency of the British social workers to be controlling and intrusive has been observed in other research (Packman, 1986; Millham et al., 1986) which showed that compulsory measures were imposed 'at a time and in a manner that is unconstructive and often counter-productive' (DHSS, 1985b, p,19). The studies found that while the principle was to get control in order to plan, constructive planning was frequently absent. It is clear that the Quebec social workers were at an advantage in their ability to employ voluntary measures and Pickett and Maton (1977) have criticised the lack of 'provision in this country (Britain) (for the professionals or families) for a more contractual basis for social work intervention' (p.76).

However, it can be argued that they could have been less intrusive and still protected the victim. Employing a supervision order or a voluntary care order, particularly the latter, could have provided a means of engaging the family without the coercive elements of a court imposed care order. Packman (1986), on the basis of her research findings, strongly recommended that a voluntary care order be used whenever possible and 'not, as it appears at present, a course to be taken reluctantly or apologetically' (p.199). At the very least, the care orders could have been used to supervise the victim in the home, as was done in a few of the Canadian cases and as has been recommended by Pickett and Maton (1977). 'For a child to be on a care order but living at home on trial provides for by far the most effective form of supervision in the home' (p.74). This occurred in only three English cases (two perpetrators) and only because of the strong insistence, in one case, of the victim, and in the other two, of a medical doctor.

In addition, more therapeutic work could have been done, notwithstanding the limitations in the British system. In at least three other British programmes operating at the time of the study, therapeutic casework has been offered within the statutory framework (Baher et al., 1976; Dale & Davies, 1984; Pickett & Maton, 1977).

It has been noted that compulsion is against the ethos of most British social workers (DHSS, 1985b). If this is truly so, their intrusive interventions are curious. The causes are undoubtedly complex and some discussion follows later.

The spirit of the 1989 Children Act is to maintain a child with the family when it is consistent with his welfare. Two aspects of the act which may allow more negotiation with parents, as in the Quebec legislation, are as follows. Firstly, the reception of children into voluntary care is replaced by providing 'accommodation' for children, the change of terminology reflecting the wish to eliminate any elements of compulsion from the service (Allen. 1990). The local authority will be required to determine, where 'reasonably practicable the wishes and feelings of the child's parents...' (Allen, p.61). While the act does not refer specifically to agreements between the social services department and the parents, it is expected that regulations concerning such agreements will be forthcoming from the government. This proposal was contained in the Government's 1987 White Paper which said, 'Where the local authority provide for the care of a child away from home with the voluntary agreement of the parents, matters such as initial placement, schooling and access, and subsequent changes to these arrangements should be settled by mutual agreement' (cited in Allen, p.66).

Secondly, the powers of the local authority in supervision orders is expanded to include requirements imposed directly on the child's carers. This reflects a recommendation of the Child Care Law Review who felt that by doing so, supervision orders might be used more widely (DHSS, 1985a). They refer to the 1978 Child Welfare Act of Ontario, Canada, which has a provision called 'care by agreement' (Palmer, 1989), which is similar to the 'voluntary measures' of the Quebec act. However, the Law Review did not go as far as the Ontario legislation as regards the discretion about what requirements can be imposed, arguing that 'if the courts have an unfettered discretion, there is always the risk that they will impose requirements which local authorities have neither the facilities nor the resources to meet' (DHSS, 1985a, p.131). Hence the Children Act requires only that 'the responsible person is to comply with any directions given by the supervisor requiring him to attend, with or without the child, at a specified place for the purpose of taking part in specified activities (the responsible person has to consent to this requirement)' (Allen, 1990, p.139). The only specified activities the Child Care Law Review (DHSS, 1985a) mentioned were child care classes and mother and toddler groups. The failure to give wider discretion to social workers is unfortunate as it was the flexibility and specificity of the 'voluntary measures' (like where a child slept and the treatment arrangements for the parents) that were so helpful in the management of the cases by the Quebec social workers. The flexibility of the interpretations of the requirements that will be allowed remains to be seen and will determine how valuable the new provisions will be.

Treatment

The most acclaimed treatment model of incestuous families involves individual and/or group treatment of the father, daughter and mother, marital therapy and family therapy, with family therapy only occurring after the other interventions have been made. (See, in particular, Giaretto, 1981.) Very few of the cases in either sample received this type of treatment programme; most received one or more (but not all) of these types of interventions. However, it is clear that overall, the Canadian professionals provided more therapeutic contact to the cases than the British professionals. This was particularly true in regards to the victim; approximately double the number of interventions were made with Canadian than British victims (individual, group and family therapy). Monitoring and family intervention were more common in the British sample.

It is interesting, given the emphasis on the fact that the perpetrator is the one responsible for the abuse (see, for example, Conte, 1990; Howarth, 1994; Sgroi, 1982b; Herman, 1977), that in both samples he receives much less treatment than the victim. The social worker probably finds it less painful to speak with the victim and less difficult to persuade him/her to accept to be seen. In fact, it may not always be necessary to treat the victim. Cooper and Cormier (1990), who described how a number of victims, once they feel safe, resist treatment, suggest that coercing them into treatment may amount to further victimisation. It may be preferable, therefore, to keep the door open and offer treatment only at the victim's request.

Clinical authors stress the importance of the mother-daughter relationship in the resolution of the incest (Giaretto, 1981; Herman, 1981; Meiselman, 1978). The present data confirmed the tendency of some mothers to turn against the victim as a result of disclosure. In a number of cases in both samples the child was not allowed to return home because of the mother's hostility. In both samples the social workers seemed to find it easier to separate mother and victim than to try to modify their hostile relationship - another instance, perhaps, of their attempts to avoid pain. British studies have observed social workers' frequent reluctance to work with difficult emotional situations like removing a child from home and placing him/her in care and concluded that 'it is not clear whether the pain and grief goes unrecognised or whether it is recognised but social workers shut their eyes to it because, lacking support themselves, they cannot tolerate the pain of getting involved and working with feelings' (DHSS, 1985b, pp.21, 22). It seemed that social workers in the English sample often actively encouraged the hostility. In many cases they told the mother to choose between the father-perpetrator and victim; in one cases where a mother struck her daughter upon learning of the sexual abuse, the social worker recommended that the mother be charged (which was consequently done). Charging the offender (which created great stress for both mother and father as they had to wait months for the court outcome) and incarcerating him was also likely to exacerbate the hostility between mother and victim.

Adult criminal proceedings

Because many more of the British cases were investigated by the police (89 versus 16), many more of the English victims were subjected to medical examinations and to one or more police interviews (some as long as three hours) and many more of the perpetrators were charged (40 versus 11) [18] and sentenced to prison (20 versus 2). The impact on the victim, perpetrator, victim's mother and other children in the family cannot be overestimated. Since the discovery of child abuse in the 1960s, there has been a growing concern about the serious iatrogenic effects of the criminal justice system. (In particular, see Gibbens & Prince, 1965; Schultz, 1980 and Walters, 1975). At disclosure, each family member must deal not only with their extremely powerful feelings about the fact that incest has occurred (Paulsen, 1978), but with the intrusion of the different systems as well.

Various consequences have been noted for the victim. For example, multiple interviews can be harmful, particularly as they may reinforce guilt feelings (Sgroi, 1982a). Furthermore, because of the anxieties commonly associated with approaches from the police, it must be unpleasant when interviews are done by a police officer, no matter how gently or skillfully. Medical examinations were much more common in the British sample where it was usually part of the police investigation. Their value has been questioned (Gentry, 1978; Goodwin, 1982a) and victims may associate them with the sexual abuse and thus feel further assaulted or punished (Schetky, 1988a). West (1987) observes that 'genital examination carried out in a clinical setting by unfamiliar personnel, using instruments and swabs, can be frightening and embarrassing and create in the child's mind an unfortunate link between sex and sickness, so they should not be done without good reason' (p.227). As both samples showed, the main purpose, to obtain corroborative evidence, is rarely successful (Finkelhor, 1978; Sgroi, 1982a). It is interesting that the lack of medical examination in the Canadian sample (only 19 had examinations) did not prevent the social workers from concluding that abuse had occurred or from registering the case and working with the family. It would seem more sensible to reserve medical examinations for relevant situations, such as when there has been physical trauma (Gentry), when the last incident of penetration was very recent [19] and corroborative evidence is required, when the child is very young, when the victim would appear to be reassured by an examination (Sgroi, 1982a) [20] or when there is suspicion that the victim might have a sexually transmitted disease.

Prosecution of the perpetrators probably also affected the victims by exacerbating their guilt about disclosure (Cormier et al., 1962). Incest victims may only want the incest to stop, not to break up the family (MacFarlane, Jones & Jenstrom, 1980) nor to punish the perpetrator to whom they are often lovingly attached and with whom they would like to have an appropriate nurturing relationship (Cooper & Cormier, 1990; Gentry, 1978; Meiselman, 1978). Acquittal of a family perpetrator, which occurred in a few British cases, may make the victim feel disbelieved and betrayed (Libai, 1969).

Paulsen (1968) succinctly described the impact on the family and the victim's place in the family when he wrote that:

> a criminal proceeding may punish an offender who deserves punishment, but it may also divide rather than unite a family. The criminal law can destroy a child's family relationship; it cannot preserve or rebuild it... the beginning of a prosecution is likely to be the end of a chance to improve a child's home situation (p.176).

Besharov (1975) elaborated further by saying that:

> criminal prosecution is likely to do more harm than good for the family. The criminal court process may embitter the parents, making them resent their children even more and reinforcing their lack of trust in people, particularly in authority figures (p.31).

The exacerbation of conflict between family members as a result of criminal prosecution (DeFrancis, 1969; MacFarlane & Bulkley, cited in Finkelhor et al., 1984; Paulsen, 1968) was well illustrated in the British sample where more parent figures separated and more victims had a change in their living situation at follow-up. In fact the majority of parental separation occurred in cases when the father/perpetrator was prosecuted. The frequent hostility of the mother towards the victim following disclosure was evident in both samples. However, the British social workers, who often literally told the mothers they had to choose between the perpetrator (who was either their mate or child) and the victim, actually promoted the family polarisation which was often further exacerbated by his prosecution.

Prosecution had four possible outcomes, with the first three occurring more frequently: (1) the father/perpetrator and wife, in spite of charges, resumed living together and excluded the victim from the home (2) the father/perpetrator and mother separated permanently and the victim stayed with the mother (3) charges against the father resulted in the victim and his/her siblings being placed in care either because the father was the only parent in the home, or the mother rejected the victim or was unable to take care of the children on her own and (4) the father, mother and victim managed to resume family living. With the exception of one case followed extensively by the NSPCC, this always took place against the social workers' wishes and efforts.

The lengthy time delays that occur in the criminal court process aggravates the stress on the family (Cooper & Cormier, 1990; Paulsen, 1968; Porter, 1984). In both samples it took from three months to a year before the final sentence was given. The family, as well as the professionals, probably lived in a stressful state of emotional limbo, not knowing what was to happen to the family perpetrator. This clearly prolongs the family's disequilibrium brought about by the crisis of disclosure, a time when, given the appropriate treatment, the family could begin to resolve some of its problems. The turmoil caused by prosecution and the threat of a care order works against this process and the victim's status as a potential prosecution witness impedes therapeutic discussion of the abuse.

The additional stress on the family of financial hardship brought about by job loss, caused by arrest and incarceration (Chamberlain *et al.*, 1976; Cooper, 1978; Paulsen, 1978; Tyler & Brassard, 1984) occurred in some of the English sample. The impact of news publicity, another source of stress observed by some authors (Tyler & Brassard; West, 1987), was also experienced by a number of British families who felt humiliated, some to the point of moving away. Some perpetrators were physically threatened by their neighbours.

Apart from the need to register society's disapproval in the hope of deterring others, a prime purpose of imprisoning the offender is said to be to protect victims from further abuse, but it is not always effective in doing so. The offender may reoffend against others. Also, the victim who is sent into care is vulnerable to further sexual abuse. Two Canadian victims were sexually abused after disclosure while in the care of social services – one by foster parents and one by a staff member in a residential treatment centre. [21]

Besharov (1975) described the adverse impact of the criminal process on the rehabilitation of the abuser (see also, Cooper & Cormier, 1990 and DeFrancis, 1969) as follows:

> When parents are acquitted, they may regard the acquittal as approval of their parenting behaviour. When they are convicted, their behaviour is seldom altered by a prison term or a suspended sentence. Criminal prosecution rarely results in rehabilitative treatment for the parents' underlying problems. Nothing prevents them from continuing to maltreat their children or bearing other children whom they may abuse of neglect. Rehabilitative work, at this point, becomes more difficult if not impossible (pp.31, 32).

It was not clear exactly how criminal prosecution of the perpetrator affected his rehabilitation. It appeared that the goal of criminal prosecution in the English sample was primarily punitive; probation was used in only a minority of cases and in these, with one exception, the opportunity to attach a requirement to undergo treatment was not taken. This was in contrast to the Canadian sample where those sentenced to probation had a condition of treatment at a psychiatric clinic. Fewer English perpetrators received treatment, and unlike in the Canadian sample where a good proportion were treated by a psychiatric service, most were followed by a probation officer who, in many cases, did not appear to focus on the sexual abuse. Treatment was not offered in prison and it is likely that incarceration worked against the perpetrator gaining insight into his problem (Cormier & Cooper, 1982; Pollock & Steele, 1972). [22] It was clear in at least one British case incarceration of the perpetrator (a father) contributed to his recidivism. [23]

In England a high proportion of imprisoned sex offenders against children, forced by the animosity of fellow inmates, ask for protection under Rule 43 (Williams & Avis, 1988), and although data on this were not available for the present sample there was no reason to suppose the exceptional in this regard. The necessity for doing this segregation, which, in local prisons, involves long periods of solitary confinement and in other prisons, close association with other sex offenders, can only make rehabilitation more difficult. Although reforms have been suggested (Prison Department Working Group, 1989), those who remain on Rule 43 long enough to be transferred to special segregation units in the company of fellow outcasts still do not usually receive any specialist treatment and conditions in which they live are so bad that the Prison Reform Trust (1990) recommended eliminating Rule 43 altogether in spite of the risk of very serious violence if there is any breakdown in disciplinary control, such as occurred in the Strangeways riot (1990).

There is considerable injustice in the application of criminal law to incest cases. Only a minority of known perpetrators are ultimately convicted. The sentence tariff for sexual abuse of children has always been high in Britain and particularly so for offences against the perpetrator's own children (West, 1987). The Howard League working party (Howard League, 1985) recommended that all cases of assault on or indecency with a minor be dealt with under the same laws, regardless of the relationship between perpetrator and victim. There were gross variations in the penalties applied to the perpetrators who were charged in this study. Furthermore, it is unjust that those who confess to their acts are prosecuted, while those resolute enough to resist confessing are not. The policy of the new Crown Prosecution Service (1986) suggests that there will be little discretion in the prosecution of these cases.

> Sexual assaults upon children should always be regarded seriously... in such cases, where the Crown Prosecution is satisfied as to the sufficiency of the evidence there will seldom be any doubt that prosecution will be in the public interest (p.6).

Factors contributing to the different professional responses in the two samples

History of child welfare philosophy and practice

Explanations for the marked differences in the professionals' responses in the two samples are complex. However, one very evident factor was the influence on the Canadian professionals of the policy of family rehabilitation entrenched in the 1977 Act. An examination of current child welfare practice in the United States suggests that American and Canadian policies are similar in that they have essentially therapeutic goals. A national survey of child protection services in the United States in 1980 clearly showed that therapeutic intervention was the most common intervention and had increased from 48% in 1976 to 73% in 1980. Court action (apparently child welfare court) constituted only 14%

of the services provided (Brown, 1983). Brown described the current policy as geared at a 'helping, non-punitive intervention aimed at protecting children by helping their parent whenever possible' (p.152).

In contrast, British child welfare practice is seen as 'still child- rather than family-oriented and focused on child rescue and case control' (Millham et al., 1986, p. 199), therefore not fulfilling the changes envisioned by the 1968 Seebohm report (Home Office, Ministry of Education and Science, Ministry of Housing and Local Government). The Millham group argue that 'much of our present welfare approach is based on the Poor Law and social work practice is still influenced by ideas of less eligibility, of parental inadequacy and contamination' (1986, p.36). While the notion about the importance of natural families to children has been better appreciated since World War II, there are still elements in practice which treat parents as failures who cannot participate in the care of their children.

There is a paucity of literature on the history of child welfare services in Canada but it would appear that it has been strongly influenced by the United States which has had a primarily therapeutic approach to the problem since the early part of this century. Prior to that the focus was on 'the rescue of children from "bad homes", prosecution of parents, and the placement of "cruelly treated" children in institutions' (Brown, 1983, p.152). A major force in the development of child welfare services and policies was the Society for the Prevention of Cruelty to Children (SPCC) founded in 1874 (Giovannoni & Beccerra, 1979). At first it had primarily a law enforcement function but eventually defined protective work as a social-work endeavour. The importance of preserving the family, if possible, using the least coercive means, was identified as early as 1910 in a policy statement.

Child protective services became a specialisation within the profession of social work practice and while bringing cases to court was seen as part of the work 'it was viewed as a virtual admission of failure of the work attempted through the relationship between the professional social worker and the voluntary client' (Giovannoni & Beccerra, 1979, p.69). In 1955 this view was reinforced by the American Humane Association (AHA) who defined the focus of child protective services as 'preventive and non-punitive... geared towards rehabilitation through identification and treatment of the motivating factors which underlie the problems' (AHA, 1955, cited in Giovannoni & Beccerra, 1979, p.69). Giovannoni and Beccerra observed that this orientation of the association is completely representative of the American social work profession in its child protection services and also is entirely compatible with the perspective of Kempe and his colleagues on solutions for the problem of child maltreatment which had at its core the provision of a therapeutic relationship with the parents (Steele & Pollock, 1974). The policy of the 1977 Canadian Youth Protection Act of attempting to keep families together, if possible, reflects this American perspective.

Professional self-image of the social workers

Underlying the more intrusive interventions by British child welfare workers is the issue of professional self-image and power. These are linked to two factors - the level of skill development and the relationship of social workers to the police.

Development of skills The rarity of creative and therapeutic work with abusive families by British social workers, as well as their avoidance of risk taking has been observed before (Dale, Davies, Morrison, Noyes & Roberts, 1983). Reflecting on their failure to work with the children and families in their care, the DHSS concluded that

> the combined messages from these nine research studies do seem to be that social workers and their seniors are not offered the opportunity to acquire the sophisticated skills, knowledge and qualitative experiences to equip them to deal confidently with the complex and extremely emotive issues raised by work with children and families (1985b, p.21).

Researchers showed a lack of knowledge of child development, family dynamics and theories of social work practice, as well as a lack of good supervision. Packman (1975) succinctly commented that 'so much attention has been paid to improving communications between professionals about families that the crucial issue of communicating with families may have been neglected' (p.180). Furthermore, in contrast to the two year training requirement for British social workers, identified as essentially inadequate (DHSS), Canadian social workers have a minimum of three years university based training.

The present research was not able to show that the Canadian social workers were more skilled than their British counterparts; in fact there was evidence of less than adequate skill in some of the cases. However, it is possible that the Quebec social workers, because of their longer training and the fact that they were forced by their rehabilitative policy to engage the families and children in treatment, were able to develop a higher level of skill. Without a clear policy to avoid compulsory measures whenever possible, and with less opportunity to develop skill and knowledge, the British workers in this study may have found it easier to resort to statutory interventions. This has been suggested by others (Aber, 1980: DHSS, 1985b).

Relationship of police and social workers   An examination of the two professional groups revealed two things: (a) British social workers were in a much more precarious position than the Canadian ones due to the tendency in Britain to pillory those involved in child abuse deaths (Freeman, 1983; Greenland, 1987; 1990; Packman, 1975) or in mismanaged sex abuse cases as in Cleveland (Bell, 1988; Home Office, 1988): This has not happened in Canada. (b) British social workers made decisions with police officers. American studies have pointed out the contrasting views of different professionals about issues like prosecuting the sexual abusers. One study found criminal justice personnel strongly favouring prosecution and giving attempts to try to keep the family together as a low priority; social service workers had completely opposite views (Finkelhor et al., 1984). A second study reported similar findings about the desirability of prosecuting the offender (Saunders, 1988).

Given the strongly divergent views of criminal justice personnel and child welfare workers, the conflict about interventions probably becomes more pronounced when both sets of professionals are involved in a face to face discussion about a case, as occurred in the British sample where they met in the case conference. In principle, decisions about police investigation and prosecution could be influenced by clinical considerations. This sometimes happens in programmes of deferred prosecution as, for example, in Devon and Cornwall (Porter, 1984) and Colorado (Topper & Aldridge, 1981). In fact, in cases of physical abuse, police officers apparently were less often involved in the investigation and prosecution was less frequent. However, in this study, decisions to prosecute were made on purely legal grounds - that is, based on the probability of successful conviction. Effects on the victim or family were not considered. This is in line with the current official policy of the Crown Prosecution Service (CPS, 1986). 'In such cases (sexual assaults upon children), where the Crown Prosecutor is satisfied as to the sufficiency of the evidence there will seldom be any doubt that prosecution will be in the public interest' (p.6).

Whether British social workers concurred was not clear, although they would appear to have since there was no evidence of disagreement in the minutes. If their views were at all similar to those reported of other social workers (Finkelhor et al., 1984; Saunders, 1988), it is possible that they did not feel sufficiently powerful to voice their objections.

Packman's observations on social work decision-making about care proceedings may be helpful in examining the apparently superior power of the police in the case conference and social workers' reaction to it (Packman, 1975). She argues that in their work in child abuse, social workers have more power than they often realise, power 'to ignore or challenge departmental policy and to fill in its broad outlines with their own detailed interpretations: a power that was sanctioned by the department's stated reliance on "professional judgment"' (p.149). She further argues that what social workers do becomes policy if it is done with any consistency and starts to establish a trend. Although they often feel powerless because of inadequate resources, the frequent criticism from the public and the confining structures and procedures, paradoxically they are in a unique position where they can and do practice a good deal of discretion *'so long as no other powerful agency becomes involved'* (emphasis added, p.150).

Thus it would appear that even if they have reservations about prosecution, when faced with the police whom they apparently view as more powerful, the British social workers do not voice any disagreement. Social workers, however, deal with the victims and family remnants and are the professionals who are confronted with the impact of legal interventions on the family members and who struggle to help them deal with it. If child welfare professionals in Britain decide that a therapeutic, non-legal approach (with the perpetrator), with an emphasis on family rehabilitation, is appropriate, they should deploy the powers and knowledge they have and challenge opposing views from the police.

Implications of study for social responses to incest

Advocates of the criminal justice system should consider the issue of its impact on the victim and other children in the family. Dickens (1984) argues that, 'To contend that relief of secondary victims is of no concern to the law, or at most a responsibility of civil welfare authorities, diminishes compassion and sensitivity in the practice of criminal law enforcement, and offends against the qualities retribution is directed to promote' (p.86). He sees a paradox or incongruity 'in a court punishing a parent for ignoring a child's welfare while itself ignoring the child's welfare' (p.85). If rehabilitation of the family is seen as an essential goal of helping the victims (rescuing 'the home for the child' rather than rescuing the child from the home, Mondiale, 1978), then the issue of the rehabilitation and/or punishment of the perpetrator must be addressed. The pioneers in clinical work with physically abusive parents were adamantly opposed to the idea of punishment, since they saw it as working against the noncritical, accepting attitude of the therapist, considered essential for changing the abusive behaviour (Pollock & Steele, 1972; Steele & Pollock, 1974). An analagous perspective has been expressed by Chapman and his colleagues (1985) who succinctly described the situation facing professionals in child sex abuse cases as one where 'the crucial decision to be made is whether (and, if so, when) to allow the child to return to its parents... this decision depends entirely on whether the parents can be effectively helped with their problems' (p.4). Opposed to using the criminal justice system, they concluded that 'an adult who is not fit to care for children will not become so as a result of punishment or the passage of time, but only through receiving adequate help for his or her own personality disorder' (p.11).

While this view of abusive parents has gained wide acceptance in the programmes for child protection in America and Canada, there seems to have been more reluctance to apply it to incestuous family perpetrators, probably because of irrational fears rather than any clinical evidence. Meiselman (1978), for example, wrote:

A horrified attitude prevents recognition of the true scope of the problem and causes incest to be relegated to the realm of events that are so bizarre that they occur only among the scum of society or in the context of extreme psychopathology. We need to adopt the attitude, as professionals, that incest is an unfortunate event that is preventable, detectable, and treatable. The image of Oedipus with his eyes gouged out may be good theater, but the incest horror it expresses can only impede the search for realistic solutions (p. 332).

The idea of society's response to child physical abuse as a 'moral panic', marked by labelling, hysteria and over-reaction (Forbes & Thomas, 1990; Freeman, 1983; Greenland, 1990) is even more applicable to the problem of child sexual abuse. This reaction poses serious barriers to the development of a rational, helpful response to incestuous families. Labelling families (or persons) as 'dangerous' results in excluding them from treatment (Forbes & Thomas). The medicalisation and legalisation of child abuse is a way for individual professionals to distance themselves from the problem (Newberger & Bourne, 1978). Such an approach only alienates, rather than helps. Walters (1975), warning against playing detective in incest cases, advises that 'participants are not "suspects" or "subjects"'; they are people. If the approach is police-like or investigative in tone, there is every reason to believe that the participants will behave like impersonal "suspects" or "subjects"' (p.136). (He further argues strongly against the social worker helping the police gather data for a prosecution.) This suggestion corresponds to actual practice in the Canadian sample where the perpetrator's immediate admission of his acts was not vital to continuing with the case. The 'medical-legal' approach adopted by the British professionals caused cases to be dropped or continued with alienated families.

It has been observed that recidivism of incest is highly unlikely as long as there has been full disclosure of the incest and appropriate interventions taken (Cormier *et al.*, 1962; Cooper & Cormier, 1990). This means that the family can be reunited with no risk of abuse (Cormier *et al.*; Giaretto, 1981). A period of separation of the perpetrator from the family is usually needed, at least until the assessment is completed, or longer, if there has not been sufficient resolution of the problems (Sgroi, 1982a; Cooper & Cormier). The perpetrator will probably be more inclined to co-operate with such a separation, if he is assured it is not necessarily permanent and that the eventual goal is to reunite the family.

Clearly the perpetrator poses the major problem for social workers. If a non-punitive, treatment oriented approach to incestuous perpetrators, similar to that operating in child physical abuse, is to be developed, then attitudes towards the abuser will have to change. Giaretto (1981) asserts that he [the counsellor] cannot claim to be working for the best interests of the child-victim if he destroys her father... The hateful reactions of the counsellor towards abusive parents must be replaced with productive interventions based on understanding of the complex psychological dynamics that led to the abusive acts' (p.189).

Unfortunately, changing attitudes towards the incest perpetrator is difficult, as a 1989 British publication on child sexual abuse demonstrates (Blagg, Hughes & Wattam). Unlike the professionals in the current study who viewed the perpetrator as untreatable, they see him as 'treatable' but 'incurable'. For them, child sexual abuse is 'an addictive cycle of deviant and compulsive behaviour... the risk of re-offending is very high, and treatment is aimed at controlling, rather than curing, behaviour *with the risk of recidivism being life-long*' (emphasis added, p.74). While this position represents some progress from the one revealed by the British professionals in this sample, it is clear that much more is needed.

However, professional training which includes the experience of working with the incestuous abuser in a clinical setting, can eliminate much of these misconceptions which are based on fear and revulsion (Giaretto, 1981). Understanding the intentions of perpetrators facilitates a therapeutic approach. Zigler (1979) has criticised the general lack of concern 'with the actor's intentions' (p.176) in approaches which focus only on observable behaviour. Schultz and Jones (1983) have criticised the legal processes that neglect 'the act's intended nature' (p.105). The intentions of the incestuous perpetrator are rarely to harm the victim or even primarily to satisfy sexual needs. 'They [fathers] use sex with their young daughters as a vain attempt to satisfy a variety of emotional needs, needs they are not able to understand and have no way of knowing how to meet appropriately' (Ayalon, 1984, p.135).

A number of treatment programmes for incest perpetrators have been developed but the majority have been in collaboration with the criminal justice system, for example, deferred prosecution (Topper & Aldridge, 1981) or treatment either as an alternative to imprisonment or post imprisonment (Giaretto, 1981). In England, Bentovin and his colleagues have worked with imprisoned incestuous abusers (Bentovin, Elton, Hidelbrand, Trantor, 1988). The current study indicated that the use of the criminal justice system was often unnecessary and even counter indicated. While the criminal court clearly punishes the perpetrator, it also harms other family members who are emotionally and financially attached to him. In addition, it only protects the victim for a short period of time (and essentially, only if he is incarcerated). There has been some support for this contention from other studies. Cooper and Cormier (1990), on the basis of thirty years of clinical work with incest perpetrators and their families, strongly advocate a therapeutic approach centered in the child protection system with criminal proceedings only used as a last resort and in exceptional situations. (See also Alström, 1977; Kennedy and Cormier, 1966; Kutchinsky, 1986 and West, 1987). This approach rests on the principle that if the abusive parent proves, after a reasonable period of treatment, unable to alter the abusive behaviour, then legal action should be taken to separate (or maintain the separation) of the child from his/her parents. 'It goes without saying that this should be viewed as a drastic step, to be taken only after failure of all efforts to induce the parents to accept help and refrain from prematurely demanding the child's return' (Chapman *et al.*, 1985, p.5).

A programme operating in the Netherlands, the 'confidential doctor system', uses a similar though even less intrusive approach (Christopherson, 1981; Doek, 1978; Baneke, 1983). Set up in 1972, the system is based on the principle that compulsory intervention (usually removing the child) is a 'last resort, which should not be used, and which is incompatible with the basic idea of help, voluntary cooperation based on mutual trust' (Baneke, p.310). One advantage of such an approach is that it allows more people to disclose and to be helped. It has been observed that a punishment approach deters discovery of child abuse (Chapman *et al.*, 1985). A comparison of reports in Holland and England showed a much greater increase in the number of disclosures in Holland (Christopherson). [24]

The voluntary measures used by the Quebec professionals which allowed a minimum amount of coercion to be used initially, also worked well. In the few cases where they did not succeed, the professionals had the option to take a more intrusive step and 'seize the court'. (Approximately half of those that did not work out were because of inadequate interventions by the social workers.) British professionals have the option of using voluntary care orders as a first option, a choice Packman (1986) recommends over compulsory care orders whenever possible because it avoids the negative impact on the child and family. Supervision orders are also an option, particularly with the changes in the new Children Act (1989), which allows some requirements to be expected of the parents in terms of their active co-operation. [25]

It has been suggested that as therapeutic expertise with the problem increases in Britain, the legal system may become more flexible (Will, 1983). This would seem unlikely considering the policy of the Crown Prosecution Service described earlier (CPS, 1986) and the recent influential decision in the court of appeal by the Chief Justice whose first use of the new power to increase the severity of a sentence on appeal was to lengthen a sentence for incest, thereby setting a precedent (Court of Appeal, 1989). [26] While there are no readily available statistics in Quebec, it has been observed that in the last few years it has become much more difficult to obtain a sentence of probation for incestuous offences. [27] The late 1980s and early 1990s in England saw the rapid emergence of a number of therapeutic efforts with the perpetrator, as advocated by various reports in England (Home Office, 1988; Blagg et al., 1989). These were mainly group work treatment programmes aimed primarily at intrafamily child sex abusers. While such advances are positive, a troubling aspect of these and other programmes is the overtly confrontational style of interviewing that has emerged (Morrison, 1998). 'A new discipline of sexual aggression intervention has developed over the last decade utilising a very interventionist philosophy' (Ross, 1990). This frequently borders on humiliating, psychological assault that can be viewed as unethical (Thompson-Cooper, 1992). As Morrison has observed:

> Whatever an offender has done, this does not permit systems or individual practitioners to treat him as if he had forfeited his basic civil liberties (p.51).

There is a practical problem in that, faced with a steady increase in disclosures (NSPCC, 1989) the courts may be unable to handle the numbers of cases produced. The overburdened child protection system already identifies more cases than it can follow through adequately (Besharov, 1985; Solnit, 1980) and the system has been described as near to collapse (Fraser, 1976), particularly since sex abuse concerns were added to those for physical abuse (Krugman, 1988; Wynne, 1989). The criminal courts, whose procedures are more complex and time consuming than those of the juvenile justice system, are even more vulnerable to becoming clogged.

Developments in child welfare services post research

Interestingly, there have been some major changes in each of the research areas after the period of the study, 1979 - 1985. Essentially, with the adoption of a new 'incest protocol' in 1985 requiring youth protection workers to refer cases to the police, Quebec moved closer to the practices in place in England at the time of the research; England, with the new 1989 Children Act, moved closer to the philosophy and some of the practices of the Quebec youth protection system.

England

The Cleveland Inquiry in 1987 was a major catalyst to the Children Act 1989 which brought about fundamental changes in the philosophy of child welfare work and represented a major shift away from paternalistic state intervention towards an emphasis on family support and partnership, similar to the Quebec's Youth Protection Act (Morrison, 1997). Some of the concerns raised in the present research have been addressed. For example three years after the Act's implementation, there was a dramatic reduction in the numbers of emergency applications for the removal of children from home and fewer applications for care orders. Overall, there was a slight fall in the numbers of children 'looked after' by local authorities and the number under voluntary arrangement rose (Department of Health, 1994). While these changes are clearly in line with the intentions of the Act, the number of child protection investigations and the number placed on child protection registers continue to rise (Jack, 1997). In fact, in one research, the period of study 1991 - 1993 showed an increase of 23% in registrations for the specific criteria of physical and sexual abuse and neglect (Department of Health, 1994).

The core principle in the Children Act of involving the parents in the decision making is similar to the 'voluntary measures' applied with apparent success by the child welfare workers in the Quebec sample. However the notion of partnership has apparently been difficult to define and some recent studies of the impact of the policy of involving parents show that many still feel alienated and not helped (Corby & Millar, 1997; Corby, Millar & Young, 1995; Farmer & Owen, 1995; Rochdale Area Child Protection Committee, 1993). For example, the Corby and Millar research of 29 families reported that most felt confused about what was required of them in terms of good parenting and disappointed about the general lack of help and support that they had expected of the social workers (1997). A 1994 study of the operation of the Children Act noted that the implementation of the family support provisions in the Act has been slow (Department of Health, 1994). (One study showed that in only three out of 220 child protection cases had there been a true partnership with the families [Thoburn & Lewis, 1992]).

Several areas of practice which showed a need for improvement in the British sample in this study have recently received attention in England. Research has shown that there has been an improvement in social workers' ability to collect information in child abuse cases (Munro, 1998). However this has not been matched by an improvement in assessments or better record keeping. The general lack of treatment services and follow-up for the incest victims and their families was evident in the study. This issue appears to be of wider concern now in England where the Social Services Inspectorate has noted that:

> post-initial child protection conference work appear(s) to be marked by a lack of inter-agency intervention and often only monitoring visits by social workers (Social Services Inspectorate, 1994, p.32).

The need for more training is voiced by many, (see, for example, Birchall & Hallett, 1995, Horwath & Calder, 1998 and Munro), as well as the importance of good supervision (Morrison, 1997).

In summary, while the new Act represents a major breakthrough in child welfare practice in England, there has been increasing concern that the basic principles of the Children Act which emphasize family support and partnership are being undermined; too many cases are being brought into the child protection net and the few who are in need of interventions are often missed (Parton, 1996). The potential of the Act has not been realized largely because of cutbacks in resources, most of which go towards investigation and surveillance rather than support for families (Morrison, 1997; Jack & Stepney, 1995).

Quebec

In 1985, the youth protection agencies in Quebec adopted a policy of referring all cases of child sexual abuse that were referred to them to the police. This represented a major shift in the ethos of social work practice since, except for very serious physical abuse cases, Canadian social workers had never referred cases to the police (Cooper & Cormier, 1985; Thompson-Cooper, Cormier & Fugere, 1993). As a result many more cases are now investigated and charged by the police, with all of the family disruption that entails. For example, one study of disclosed cases of intrafamily child sexual abuse in two Quebec areas in 1995 showed a 22% rate of criminal charges, compared to the 11% in the current study (Oxman-Martinez, Rowe & Straka, 1998). (It was actually only 9% of cases where criminal charges were laid as three of the 11 perpetrators were charged in Juvenile Court, a disposition no longer available). In addition, it appears that social workers themselves are now taking more coercive types of interventions, i.e. 'seizing the court' rather than applying 'voluntary measures'. Only 27% of the cases in the 1995 study had 'voluntary measures', compared to the 65% in the current study. Furthermore, shortly after referral, 47% underwent legal proceedings in Juvenile Court and an additional 11% had legal measures later on in the process, with a total of 58% compared to the 23% in the current study.

It appears that there has been a sharp decrease in the number of disclosures of child sexual abuse to the youth protection authorities in Quebec (37% decrease from 1992-93 to 1995-96 [Felix, 1997; Wright, Boucher, Frappier, Lebeau & Sabourin, 1997]). One suggestion for the drop in referrals is a loss of confidence by professionals and the community in the agencies' abilities to respond appropriately (Oxman-Martinez et al., 1998). Major financial cutbacks has resulted in staff cuts, higher caseloads, delayed responses, fewer resources and a general malaise in the whole Quebec youth protection system (Tzintzis, 1998;

Oxman-Martinez et al; Zacharias, 1998). Another possible reason for the lack of confidence in the system's ability to respond helpfully to a disclosure of child sexual abuse is the fact that now the consequences are much more drastic than previously, given that the youth protection agency now refers the cases to the police.

Apparently there has also been a marked reduction in the number of confirmed cases of child sexual abuse that are retained for follow-up and treatment. (In the 1995 Quebec study of two regions, only 18% and 14% of cases were followed). This is felt to be due to the loss of workers with the expertise necessary for a proper assessment of child sexual abuse with the result that they close the case prematurely (Oxman-Martinez et al, 1998).

In summary, it appears that subsequent to the period of the research, the advantages apparent in the Canadian sample, in particular the lack of police involvement and the amount of treatment available to the incest family, has been altered. The Children Act in England has brought their system more in line with the Quebec youth protection system with its emphasis on working collaboratively with families whenever possible. Both systems are suffering from a lack of resources which is curtailing their potential to help families in trouble. This, however, can be altered with a careful re-thinking of priorities and a political will.

The issue of whether or not to use the criminal justice system in cases of child sexual abuse has yet to be resolved. The current Quebec policy of referring sexual abuse cases to the police (and rarely cases of child physical abuse), is not based on empirical data. This study showed that positive outcomes could (and, in the Canadian sample, did) result from working collaboratively with a family including the abuser, without recourse to the criminal justice system. The current policy in both England and Canada is one which deserves to be re-examined. Others are now advocating for an avoidance of criminal court whenever possible (Platt, 1996a; Wattam, 1992) and suggesting alternative models such as the Dutch 'confidential doctor system' (Jack, 1997) and family group conferences (Morrison, 1997).

Summary and conclusions

This research was able to compare two child protection systems - one where the criminal justice system was an integral part and the other which primarily used therapeutic measures. The former, represented by the British sample, resulted in more family disruption including parental separation and an alteration in the living situation for the victim. In spite of the higher level of legal intervention in the British sample (both criminal and civil), the recidivism rate was similar to that of the Canadian. This would indicate that victims of intrafamilial child sexual abuse can be protected, and with less trauma, by using therapeutic and non-punitive measures.

This conclusion is a comment about a system of service delivery and not about the level of clinical skills of the social workers in the two countries. In fact, there was evidence that in some cases workers in the Canadian sample provided less than adequate assessment and/or treatment. However, it appeared that the system which placed the responsibility for assessment on one worker, supervised by another, as Howells (1974) has suggested, may have allowed the Canadian social workers, in general, to develop expertise and feel more comfortable dealing with their cases. The policy of rehabilitation obliged them to work therapeutically with the family members, including the perpetrator, and this must have contributed to skill development.

Intrafamilial child sexual abuse is a complex phenomenon rooted in individual and family pathology which poses considerable problems for child welfare professionals, particularly because of its tabooed nature. The incest victim is frequently prevented from disclosing by fear of breaking up the family (de Young, 1982; Goodwin, 1982a). What the victim often wants is simply to have the sexual abuse stopped, not lose her family (or even the perpetrator) (Will, 1983). An appropriate goal would be to use the minimum amount of intervention necessary to secure the safety of the child, while at the same time attempting to preserve the family relationships. This is usually how child physical abuse is managed and it is logical that child sexual abuse, which is often less of an emergency situation, can be handled in a similar way. Not all families can be 'saved' (Kempe & Kempe, 1978; Server & Janzen, 1982), but it is an end professionals should work towards. The sensitive balancing of therapeutic and control interventions necessary to achieve this requires much more effort and skill than an automatic reliance on court proceeding (civil or criminal).

To achieve such a balance and minimise the sort of victimisation by professionals described in the Cleveland Report (Home Office, 1988) requires two things - first, an adequate and well resourced psycho-social-legal structure which maximises the opportunities for therapeutic interventions, but allows for control measures to be taken when these efforts are not sufficient to protect the child; secondly, the availability of professionals who have overcome their hostility towards the perpetrator and developed the therapeutic skills to respond to the complex needs of the different family members.

Two principles that may be helpful to professionals in their descision-making role are

i) The concept of *primium non nocere*; first do no harm. This is a stronger moral imperative than to do good and requires the intervener to show justification for any actions which upset the status quo (Somerville, 1984). This implies that the professional needs to have knowledge about the phenomenon of incest and the necessary skills to intervene helpfully with all members of the family.

ii) The imperative, enunciated by Justice Butler-Sloss 'to listen to the children' (Home Office, 1988, p.245). This means not only giving credence to children when they disclose sexual abuse (and also, of course, believing them when they say they were not abused) but it also means that children's expressed wishes about interventions need to be carefully attended to by the professionals wanting to help and protect them. In this way the needs of the victims, perpetrators and other family members should be met and iatrogenic trauma avoided.

Notes

---

1   For descriptions of the multi-problem incest family, see Chaneles (1967) and Nakashima and Zakus (1977).

2   Finkelhor and Baron (1986) observed that 'although (physical child) abuse is certainly not limited to the lower classes, as the stereotype might suggest, to most researchers it makes sense that the frustrations of poverty, joblessness, lack of education, and inadequate housing contribute to the conditions that increase violence towards children' (p.67).

3   While more English victims were penetrated vaginally and anally, more Canadian victims had a younger age of onset and a lengthier abusive relationship.

4   This is suggested by Browne and Finkelhor (1986) in a review of the research. They wrote that 'Given that the relationship between duration and impact is widely endorsed by clinicians as well, there is strong, if not conclusive, evidence to establish the connection' (p.167). Commenting on the research on the impact of penetration, they concluded that '... it is premature to concludes that molestation involving more intimate contact is necessarily more traumatic' (p.169).

5   It is likely, however, that the number of cases where the abuser was prosecuted was low, as in the current sample.

6   These findings generally correspond to a study of all of the cases of father-daughter incest reported to and treated by the youth protection authorities in

the province of Quebec from January 1981 to June 1981, where 22% were placed and parental rights were applied for in 14% of the cases (Messier, 1987).

[7] It was not possible to determine precisely whether the British professionals were intervening more in cases of sexual abuse than physical abuse. However it was clear from informal discussions with NSPCC staff that there was certainly more police involvement.

[8] In these 29 cases the family as well as the perpetrator was assessed, thus providing a comprehensive view of the incest dynamics in the family.

[9] There were only two cases where case conference members disagreed strongly with the decisions. In both situations, however, the professionals concerned (in one, a medical doctor, and in the other, a social worker) objected outside the actual meeting (although they communicated their objections to case conference members).

[10] This was not articulated in a policy but was evident from their discussions.

[11] The term 'social worker' refers to either a social worker employed by the social service department or to a NSPCC worker who sometimes took the responsibility of seeing the families.

[12] Some have gone as far as severely criticising any view that would see child sex abusers as warranting clinical intervention. For example, Berliner and Barbieri have implied that it is wrong that '... many mental health professionals believe that such offenders have psychological disorders, that, in some sense, *excuse their behaviour and make them candidates for mental health intervention..*'. (Berliner & Barbieri, cited in Saunders, 1988, p.86, emphasis added).

[13] It is interesting to note the reported poor success of child welfare professionals in engaging males in therapy. For example, the NSPCC Devon House study of physical abuse reported a low contact rate with the fathers, not necessarily the abusers, who were referred to as 'shadowy figures' (Baker et al., 1976). However they acknowledged that they had focused most of their efforts on the mothers. A survey of studies of physically abusive parents between 1976 and 1980 revealed a lack of information about abusive men and the lack of treatment resources for them (Martin, 1984). A factor that may contribute to the difficulty of social workers engaging male abusers is that the majority of social workers and their clients are women; thus social workers do not have as much expertise with male clients. A Quebec study noted a higher level of comfort by male workers with incest fathers (Messier, 1987); (not surprisingly, they also reported a higher estimation of the progress the fathers had made than their female colleagues). Also, it is less socially acceptable for men to ask for psychological help (Goldberg, 1977). It may be that difficulties in working with male incestuous abusers is part of a larger issue.

[14] One-half in the British sample also admitted their offences to a non-legal authority; however most of these had already been interviewed by the police.

15   Abel and his colleagues (Abel, Becker, Murphy & Flanagan, 1979) questioned this. Their study of six incest offenders' penile responses to descriptions of erotic interaction with children and adult females showed that all the men reacted more to stimuli involving children, suggesting that they were pedophiles. Other studies, however, have shown that in general incest offenders are not pedophilic (Gebhard *et al.*, 1965; Paitich, Langevin, Freeman, Mann & Handy, 1977; Quinsey, Chaplin & Carrigan, 1979).

16   Rosenfeld & Newberger, 1979. Rosenfeld & Newberger, 1979.

17   The 1989 Children Act makes sweeping changes in the place of safety order which was subjected to major criticism in the Cleveland Inquiry (Home Office, 1988). The new emergency protection order corrects the problems contained in the POSO which have been described as follows: Its name (POSO) is said to conceal the fact that it is, or should be, only aimed at emergencies; it can last for 28 days, an excessively long period; the legal position of the various parties during the place of safety period is unclear; and there is no effective right of challenge available to the child's family (Allen, 1990, p.86).

18   Three of the adults in the Canadian sample were charged in juvenile court where the maximum penalty was two years imprisonment; only one of these was given a custodial sentence (of one year).

19   Sperm is detectable for approximately 24 hours following penetration (West, 1987).

20   Sgroi maintains this is adequate reason to always do a medical examination. It would seem, however, that not all children would require this and for some, the examination would have the opposite effect. Sgroi maintains this is adequate reason to always do a medical examination. It would seem, however, that not all children would require this and for some, the examination would have the opposite effect.

21   There were no reported cases in the British sample; however, because of the higher number of cases where information was missing (82 compared to 60 Canadian), it is possible that such reabuse occurred.

22   Cormier and Cooper (1982) have described how incarceration frequently reinforces the perpetrator's denial of his incestuous acts, even when he had admitted them to the police.

23   In this case [#60], a father, convicted and imprisoned for incestuous behaviour with his eldest daughter, while in prison, actually planned how he would have an incestuous relationship with his next daughter. However, the sexual acts he planned (and later carried out) were accompanied by considerable violence and sadism. These plans, which became more detailed as time passed, were contained in a diary which was confiscated by the prison authorities.

24   The rate of referrals in Holland rose from 430 in 1972 to 899 in 1976 and to 3,000 in 1979. In England registrations at NSPCC special units rose from

778 in 1975 to 1,070 in 1978-79 and to 1,143 in 1979-80 (Christopherson, 1981).

[25] See p. 215 for a further discussion of this aspect of the 1989 Children Act.

[26] Lord Lane increased from three years to six the prison term imposed on an offender who had pleaded guilty to three counts of incest on one daughter and one count of indecent assault on another daughter. He also gave suggestions about the level of sentences for various categories of incest. For example. for a girl aged from 13 to 16, he recommended between three years custody to five; for a girl just under 13 when there are no adverse or favourable features on a not guilty plea, six years (Court of Appeal, 1989).

[27] Personal communication, Dr. R. Fugere, Director of the McGill Clinic in Forensic Psychiatry, Montreal, Canada, February, 1998.

Appendix 1

Annex to
LASSL(76)26
BC(76)50
Home Office Circular 179/76

Roles of the Organisations Chiefly Concerned in Cases of Non-accidental Injury to Children {LASSL)76)26}

1. The Police

The involvement of the police in cases of non-accidental injury to children arises from their general responsibilities for the protection of life, and the prevention, investigation and prosecution of offences; and from their position as one of the recognised emergency services. Police officers have a number of statutory responsibilities for the protection of children and young persons. In particular they share with the local authority Social Services Department and the NSPCC the power to initiate care proceedings; and under section 28 of the Children and Young Persons Act 1969 they have power in certain circumstances to detain a child and to make arrangements for the child's detention in a place of safety without prior application to a court. The responsibilities of the police require them to examine each case individually, though they are no doubt aware of the implications which their actions may have for the family as a whole.

2. The Personal Social Services

The social services department has a statutory responsibility for the provision of social services to children and their families. The social workers, who may be based in hospital or area teams, provide advice, guidance and assistance to prevent the need for children to be received into care or brought before a court. Where necessary the department has a statutory duty to initiate care proceedings. The social services department has a duty to give first consideration to the need to promote the welfare of the child throughout his childhood.

3. The Health Services

a. *Primary health care*

Primary health care services are provided by general practitioners, district nurses, health visitors, midwives and their supporting staff. The general practitioner normally has knowledge of a family's background and medical history from which he can contribute to a case conference. The midwife is involved during the particularly vulnerable period of the mother's pregnancy, delivery and early post-natal care. The Health Visitor visits all families with children under 5, which gives her an opportunity to observe and assess family health and relationships in the home. Preventive and advisory services for parents and their pre-school children are also provided by child health clinics, staffed by child health doctors, health visitors and nurses who have a knowledge of the child and the family, developed from surveillance at the clinic and visits to the home. The School Health Service provides similar surveillance of school children and support and advice to teachers and parents. School doctors and school nurses are able to contribute a knowledge of the child in the education environment.

b. *Hospital and specialist services*

Cases of non-accidental injury may be referred to a specialist by a GP or by admission through the Accident and Emergency Department of a hospital. The specialist will make a diagnosis and will be concerned to identify a child's medical needs and ensure these are met. In all cases the paediatrician has a central coordinating role. Psychiatrists help to evaluate the significance of the complex feelings which exist within families and deal with any mental disturbance in the parents or children. Others who may be involved include orthopaedic, ophtalmic, neurological and dental specialists. Nurses play an important part in the initial identification of cases, and provide observation of and support for the child and his parents in the ward.

4. The Education Services

School staff, especially in nursery and primary schools, and education welfare officers may be among the first to observe and draw attention to the early warning signs of non-accidental injury in children of school age and will be involved in the care and oversight of the children at school. In consequence, previous circulars have advised that ARCs should include representatives of Directors of Education; and that wherever appropriate teachers and education welfare officers should take part in case conferences.

5. NSPCC

The NSPCC is a voluntary organisation concerned to identify and prevent cruelty to children and to help and advise parents, many of whom approach it voluntarily for its assistance. It undertakes its work primarily through its country-wide inspectorate, who may in appropriate cases, on instruction from Headquarters, take legal proceedings in Magistrates' Courts. An important role is also discharged by its playgroups, its Special Units set up specifically to identify, prevent and treat cases of non-accidental injury, and its National Advisory Centre on the Battered Child in London. The Society is authorised (as are the social service departments and police) to bring court proceedings for the care of children. Work in conjunction with the police and social work agencies in the interests of children has always been a part of its policy.

6. The Probation Service

The involvement of probation officers in cases of non-accidental injury to children can arise directly from their statutory supervisory duties with respect to persons convicted of offences against children. But officers may also to a substantial extent encounter cases of children at risk in the course of their various other duties.   These include the statutory supervision of adult offenders generally and of children involved in care, domestic and divorce proceedings; acting as guardians *ad litem* in certain adoption proceedings; providing voluntary marriage guidance counselling, supervising offenders released from custody under statutory or voluntary after-care; and the preparation of reports on persons appearing before the courts.

Appendix 2

Guidelines for Workers re Voluntary Measures - Quebec, Canada - Article 54

The director may recommend the following as voluntary measures:

a) that the child remain in his family environment and that his parents present a report periodically on the measures they apply in their own or in their child's regard to correct a previous situation;

b) that certain persons refrain from coming into contact with the child;

c) that the child be entrusted to other persons;

d) that a person working for an establishment or body provide aid, counsel or assistance to the child and his family;

e) refer the child to a hospital centre, a local community service centre, or to a body in order that he may there receive the care and assistance he may need;

f) that the child or his parents report in person, at regular intervals, to the director and inform him on the progress of the situation;

g) that the child receive certain health services;

h) that the child be entrusted for a fixed period to a reception centre or foster family chosen by the social service centre;

i) that the child execute minor tasks or render an appropriate service to the community.

Voluntary Measures Contract

Ville-Marie Social Service Centre

Director of Youth Protection

Service Point

Consent to Voluntary Measures

First Agreement?   Renewal?

I/We understand that under the provisions of the Youth Protection Act (Chapter 20), the Director of Youth Protection, named above, is taking charge of my/our child/me

_____
(Name of child)

In accordance with Section 54 of the Youth Protection Act, I/We agree voluntarily to the measures listed below in regard to the above-named child/myself.

I/We understand that this agreement is binding from _____
                                                                              (date)

Until _____ . On or before the date of expiration, the agreement
           (date)

will be reviewed by me/us and by the Director of Youth Protection to determine if the situation of my/our child/myself warrant these or different measures at that time (Section 57).

I/We are aware that I/We have the right to refuse to agree to these measures, in which case the matter may be referred to the Youth Court upon my/our request or upon the request of the Director of Youth Protection (Sections 74 and 60).

List of Abbreviations - Appendix 3 and 4

att. bug'y	=	attempted buggery
accept.	=	accepted
art.33	=	article 33
conc.	=	concurrent
cust.	=	custody
dir.	=	direction
dur.	=	duration
f'nd	=	found
freq.	=	frequency
ind.ass.	=	indecent assault
ind'y^w child	=	indecency with child
invest.	=	investigation
involvem't	=	involvement
matrim'l	=	matrimonial
mths.	=	months
no.	=	number
perp.	=	perpetrator
rel.	=	relationship
sex'l	=	sexual
super.	=	supervision
susp.	=	suspended
USI$\underline{u}$13	=	unlawful sexual intercourse under 13
vict.	=	victim
$\underline{w}$	=	with
wk.	=	week
yrs.	=	years

Appendix 3

Cases in English Sample

Note: Cases refer to victims. The following pairs and triads of victims were involved with the same perpetrators: [#82] and [#83]; [#84] and [#87]; [#86] and [#91]; [#89] and [#90] [#96] and [#38]; [#44], [#45] and [#95]; [#22] and [#64]; [#8] and [#21]; [#53] and [#54]; [#24] and [#25] and [#95]; [#9] and [#40]; [#31] and [#32] and [#32]; [#12] and [#39]; [#23], [#33] and [#34].

Please see footnote #3 in chapter 4, pp. 79 - 80, for an explanation of Appendices 3 and 4.

Appendix 3 - English Sample

Case no.	Sex of vict.	Rel. of perp. and vict.	Age at onset of sex'l contact	Freq./ dur. of sex'l contact	Age of onset of inter-course	Freq./ dur. of inter-course/ buggery*	Age at re-ferral	Initial charges
1	F	step-father	10	100+	-	-	12/06	USI<u>u</u>13(1) ind.ass.(3)
2	F	step-father	10	100+	-	-	13/11	indecency^w child(1) ind. assault(1)
3	F	father	15	100+	-	-	15/07	no charges
4	F	step-father	7	61-100	-	-	11/10	indecent assault(1)
5	F	father	11/09	31-60	-	-	13/09	no charges
6	F	uncle	3/08	21-30	-	-	5/01	ind. ass.(1)
7	F	step-father	12	21-30	-	-	12/06	no charges
8	M	step-father	9	21-30	-	-	12/04	ind'y^w child under 14(1)
9	F	step-father	13	1 yr.	-	-	14	no charges
10	F	father	13/06	11-20	-	-	14/05	ind. ass.(2)
11	F	half-sibling	7/06	11-20	-	-	7/10	ind. ass.(1)
12	F	father	7/06	6-10	-	-	8/10	indeceny^w child (2) ind. ass.(1)
13	F	half-sibling	7	2¹ᐟ² mths.-	-	-	7/05	no charges
14	F	father	13/06	6-10	-	-	15/11	no charges
15	F	father	13/04	2	-	-	13/04	indecent exposure(1)
16	F	father	5	2- 5	-	-	5/05	ind'y^w child under 14(1) ind. ass.(1)
17	F	father	10	2- 5	-	-	10/10	ind. ass.(1)
18	F	father	12/06	2- 5	-	-	13/02	ind. ass.(2)
19	F	father	13	2- 5	-	-	15/03	no charges

Appendix 3 - English Sample

Case no.	Final Result	Victim removed from home	Length of time out of home	POSO applied for/ granted	Care order applied for/ granted	Other
1	18 mths. imprisonment	no	-	no/no	no/no	super. order
2	6 mths. custody suspended for 2 yrs.	yes	2 mths.	no/no	yes/yes	
3	police caution	yes	9 mths.+	no/no	no/no	
4	6 mths. cust. susp. for 2 yrs.	yes	20 mths.	no/no	yes/yes	
5	-	yes	6 mths.+	yes/yes	no/no	
6	2 yrs. probation	no	-	no/no	no/no	
7	-	yes	6 mths.+	yes/yes	yes/yes	
8	charge dropped	no	-	no/no	no/no	
9	-	no	-	no/no	no/no	
10	2 yrs. probation	no	-	no/no	no/no	
11	charge dropped police caution	no	-	no/no	no/no	
12	18 mths. cust . susp. 2yrs. super.order 2 yrs. conc.	no	-	no/no	yes/yes	
13	-	no	-	no/no	no/no	
14	-	yes	2 yrs.+	yes/yes	yes/yes	
15	3 mths. custody	no	-	no/no	no/no	
16	found not guilty 6 mths cust. susp. 2yrs + £50.00 fine	no	-	no/no	no/no	
17	probation dropped/no	yes	10 mths.	no/no	initially but	
18	found not guilty by direction of judge(1) 1yr. cust.(1)	yes	12 mths.	yes/yes	no/no	
19	-	yes	10 mths.+	yes/yes	yes/yes	

Appendix 3 - English Sample (continued)

Case no	Sex of vict.	Rel. of perp. and vict.	Age at onset of sex'l contact	Freq./ dur. of sex'l contact	Age of onset of inter-course	Freq./ dur. of inter-course/ buggery*	Age at re-ferral	Initial charges
20	F	sibling	4	2- 5	-	-	5/08	no charges
21	F	step-father	9	2- 5	-	-	9/10	no charges
22	F	male co-habitee	16	2- 5	-	-	16/02	no charges
23	F	grand-father	7	2- 5	-	-	7/02	ind. ass.(1)
24	F	father	12	2- 5	-	-	12/04	no charges
25	F	father	12	2- 5	-	-	12/04	no charges
26	F	male co-habitee	12	2- 5	-	-	12/04	no charges
27	F	father	13	1	-	-	13	no charges
28	F	step-father	13/09	1	-	-	13/09	no charges
29	F	sibling	14	1	-	-	14/04	no charges
30	F	male co-habitee	10/05	1	-	-	10/05	incitement to commit gross indec'y(1)
31	F	male co-habitee	7/06	1	-	-	7/10	ind. ass.(1)
32	F	male co-habitee	6/08	1	-	-	6/08	ind. ass.(1)
33	F	father	5/06	8 yrs.	-	-	13/06	gross indec'y(1) ind. ass.(2)
34	F	father	5/06	5$^{1/2}$ yrs.	-	-	12/06	gross ind'y(2) ind. ass.(1)
35	F	father	10	4$^{1/2}$ yrs.	-	-	14/07	no charges
36	F	step-father	8	3$^{1/2}$ yrs.	-	-	11/10	no charges
37	F	sibling	8	3 yrs.	-	-	11	no charges
38	F	father	10/06	2 yrs.	-	-	12/06	attempted incest(1) attempted USIu13(1) ind. ass.(5)

Appendix 3 - English Sample (continued)

Case no.	Final Result	Victim removed from home	Length of time out of home	POSO applied for/ granted	Care order applied for/ granted	Other
20	-	yes	10 mths.+	no/no	yes/other reasons/yes previously	
21	-	no	-	no/no	no/no	
22	-	yes	2 yrs. +	yes/yes	no/no	
23	2 yrs. custody	no	-	no/no	no/no	
24	police caution	no	-	no/no	no/no	3 yr. sup. order
25	police caution	no	-	no/no	no/no	
26	-	no	-	no/no	no/no	
27	-	no	-	no/no	no/no	
28	police caution	no	-	no/no	no/no	
29	police caution	no	-	no/no	no/no	
30	2 yrs. probation	yes	5 mths.+	no/no	no/no	
31	found not guilty by dir. of judge	no	-	no/no	no/no	
32	found not guilty by dir/ of judge	no	-	no/no	no/no	
33	2 yrs. custody concurrent	yes	12 mths.+	no/no	yes/yes	
34	2 yrs. custody concurrent	yes	12 mths.+	no/no	yes/yes	
35	-	yes	15 mths.	yes/yes	yes/yes	
36	-	yes	2 mths.	no/no	no/no	
37	-	no	-	no/no	no/no	
38	not guilty/accept to lie on file 3 yrs. cust.	yes	4 yrs.+	no/no	vol. care order yes/yes	

Appendix 3 - English Sample (continued)

Case no	Sex of vict.	Rel. of perp. and vict.	Age at onset of sex'l contact	Freq./ dur. of sex'l contact	Age of onset of inter-course	Freq./ dur. of inter-course/ buggery*	Age at re-ferral	Initial charges
39	F	father	6	1 yr.	–	–	7	indecency[w] child(2) ind. ass.(1)
40	M	step-father	11	1 yr.	–	–	12	no charges
41	F	grand-father	5/06	1 yr.	–	–	6/05	ind. ass.(4)
42	F	step-father	1	6-12 mths.	–	–	2	no charges
43	F	father	11	6-12 mths.	–	–	12/11	incest(1) ind. ass.(1)
44	M	b-in-law	12	5 mths.	–	–	12/05	no charges
45	F	b-in-law	10/02	9 mths.	–	–	11	no charges
46	F	step-father	8/06	3 mths.	–	–	9/05	ind. ass.([u])
47	F	grand-father	7/10	2 mths.	–	–	8	no charges
48	F	father	5	N.K.	–	–	5/03	no charges
49	M	mother	N.K.	N.K.	–	–	1/08	no police involvem't
50	F	father	N.K.	N.K.	–	–	10/05	no charges
51	M	uncle	10/06	N.K.	–	–	10/06	no charges
52	F	grand-father	N.K.	N.K.	–	–	7/08	no charges
53	F	step-father	N.K.	N.K.	–	–	15/06	no police involvem't
54	F	step-father	N.K.	N.K.	–	–	13/07	no police involvem't
55	F	male co-habitee	N.K.	N.K.	–	–	7/05	no police involvem't
56	F	father	N.K.	N.K.	–	–	13/09	no charges
57	F	father	5	4 yrs.	–	–	9/02	no police involvem't
58	F	father	N.K.	N.K.	–	–	4/10	no police involvem't
59	F	step-father	N.K.	N.K.	–	–	8/06	no police involvem't

Appendix 3 - English Sample (continued)

Case no.	Final Result	Victim removed from home	Length of time out of home	POSO applied for/ granted	Care order applied for/ granted	Other
39	18 mths. custody susp. for 2 yrs. super.order 2 yrs. conc.	no	-	no/no	yes/yes	
40	-	no	-	no/no	no/no	
41	18 mths. cust. susp. 12 mths. conc.	no	-	no/no	no/no	
42	-	yes	14 mths.	no/no	yes/yes	
43	charges dropped	no	-	no/no	no/no	
44	-	no	-	no/no	no/no	
45	-	no	-	no/no	no/no	
46	1 yr. probation	no	-	no/no	no/no	
47	police caution	no	-	no/no	no/no	
48	-	no	-	no/no	no/no	
49	-	no	-	no/no	no/no	
50	-	yes	1 wk.	yes/yes	no/no	
51	-	no	-	no/no	no/no	
52	-	no	-	no/no	no/no	
53	-	no	-	no/no	no/no	
54	-	no	-	no/no	no/no	
55	-	yes	2 yrs.+	yes/yes	yes/yes	
56	-	no	-	no/no	no/no	
57	-	already removed 3 yrs. prior	2 yrs.+	no/no	yes/for other reasons	
58	-	already 1 yr. prior	16 mths.+	no/no	yes/for other reasons	
59	-	no	-	no/no	no/no	

Appendix 3 - English Sample (continued)

Case no	Sex of vict.	Rel. of perp. and vict.	Age at onset of sex'l contact	Freq./ dur. of sex'l contact	Age of onset of inter-course	Freq./ dur. of inter-course/ buggery*	Age at re-ferral	Initial charges
60	F	father	13	100+	13	100+/ 2- 5 buggery	15/11	incest(7) ind. ass.(6) buggery(1)
61	F	father	14	100+	14	100+/ 2- 5 buggery	16/07	incest(2) buggery(1)
62	F	step-father	11	100+	11	100+	14/07	USIu13(6)
63	F	step-father	7	100+	12/06	100+	16/01	no charges
64	F	male co-habitee	11	100+	13	100+	20/10	no charges
65	F	father	12/06	100+	13	100+	14/01	incest (1or2)
66	F	step-father	12	61-100	12/06	61-100	14/07	USIu13(3) USIu16(1)
67	F	father	12	2 yrs.	14	31- 60	14/04	incest(2)
68	F	step-father	13	21-30	13	11- 20	15	no charges
69	F	father	8/06	5 yrs.	11/06	11- 20	13/05	incest(1)
70	F	father	12/06	11-20	12/06	6- 10	13/08	ind. ass.(2)
71	F	father	10/06	31-60	11	6- 10	12/07	incest(2)
72	F	father	15	6-10	15	6-10	17/01	incest(1)
73	F	father	14	31-60	14	6-10/ 1 buggery	16/05	incest(4)
74	M	uncle	9	4 mths.	-	6-10 buggery	9/04	attempted buggery(2) ind. ass.(2)
75	F	male co-habitee	N.K.	N.K.	14	2- 5	14/10	USIu16(1)
76	F	uncle	13	7 mths.	13	2- 5	13/07	USIu16(1) USIu13(1)
77	F	sibling	12/06	2- 5	16	2- 5	16/01	incest(2)
78	F	step-father	14	11-20	14	2- 5	15/05	USIu16(2)

Appendix 3 - English Sample (continued)

Case no.	Final Result	Victim removed from home	Length of time out of home	POSO applied for/ granted	Care order applied for/ granted	Other
60	5 yrs. cust. charge dropped	no	-	no/no	no/no	
61	15 mths. cust. concurrent	no	-	no/no	no/no	
62	12 mths. cust. concurrent	yes	13 mths.	yes/yes	yes/yes	
63	caution	no	-	no/no	no/no	
64	-	yes	14 mths.+	no/no	no/no	
65	2 yrs. cust. susp. for 2 yrs.^{w} super. order	yes	5 mths.+	yes/yes	yes/no	super. order
66	6 mths. cust. 2 yrs. cust. conc.	yes	3 yrs.+	no/no	yes/yes	
67	$2^{1/2}$ yrs. cust. concurrent	yes	4 mths.	no/no	no/no	
68	-	yes	10 mths.+	no/no	yes/N.K.	
69	21 mths. cust.	yes	13 mths.+	no/no	yes/yes	
70	2 yrs. probation	yes	15mths.	no/no	yes/yes	
71	5 yrs. 3 mths. cust. concurrent	no	-	no/no	no/no	
72	9 mths. cust./ 2 yrs. susp.^{w} super.	yes	3 yrs.+	no/no	no/no	
73	15 mths. custody suspended for 2 yrs.	no	-	no/no	no/no	
74	found not guilty $2^{1/2}$ yrs. custody concurrent	no	-	no/no	no/no	
75	3 mths. cust.	yes	7 mths.+	yes/yes	no/no	
76	2 yrs. probation	yes	18 mths.+	yes/yes	yes/yes	
77	f'nd not guilty(1) charge dropped(1)	no	-	no/no	already in care	
78	6 mths. cust. conc. susp. 2 yrs. (each)	yes	15 mths.+	no/no	yes/yes	

Appendix 3 - English Sample (continued)

Case no	Sex of vict.	Rel. of perp. and vict.	Age at onset of sex'l contact	Freq./ dur. of sex'l contact	Age of onset of inter- course	Freq./ dur. of inter- course/ buggery*	Age at re- ferral	Initial charges
79	F	father	14	1 yr.	15	2- 5	15	incest
80	F	father	10	100+	13	2- 5	16/03	incest(2) indec'yʷ childu14(1) ind. ass.(2)
81	F	male co-habitee	16/06	2- 5	16/06	2- 5	16/09	no charges
82	F	sibling	13	21-30	13	2- 5	15/07	incest(2) attempted incest(1) ind. ass.(1)
83	F	sibling	12	21-30	$13^{1/2}$	2- 5	13/09	incest(2) attempted incest(1)
84	F	father	12	N.K.	13	2- 5	13/07	incest(1)
85	F	step-father	9	21-30	-	2- 5 buggery	10/09	buggery(2) indec'yʷ child
86	F	father	N.K.	-	-	2- 5 buggery	4/02	buggery(4)
87	F	father	6/06	N.K.	N.K.	1	7/10	ind. ass.(1)
88	F	father	12/06	2- 5	12/06	1	12/11	incest(1) USIu13(1) ind. ass.(1)
89	M	male co-habitee	N.K	1	-	1 buggery	2/03	no charges
90	M	male co-habitee	N.K	1	-	1 buggery	1/01	no charges
91	M	uncle	11	2- 5	-	1 buggery	11/03	buggery(1) ind. ass. on male (1or2)
92	F	sibling	13	N.K.	13	1	13/01	ind. ass.(1)
93	M	sibling	8	100+	-	2 yrs. buggery	10/04	att.bug'y(2) buggery(1) indec'yʷ childu14(2) ind.ass.(2)

Appendix 3 - English Sample (continued)

Case no.	Final Result	Victim removed from home	Length of time out of home	POSO applied for/ granted	Care order applied for/ granted	Other
79	charges dropped	yes	15 mths.+	yes/yes	initially/ but dropped	
80	9 mths. custody concurrent	yes	5 mths.+	yes/yes	no/no	
81	-	yes	1 yr.+	no/no	no/no	
82	charges dropped charge dropped supervision order	no	-	no/no	no/no	
83	charges dropped charge dropped	no	-	no/no	no/no	
84	9 mths. cust.	already	4 yrs.+	no/no	already in care	
85	4 yrs. custody 18 mths cust. concurrent	no	-	no/no	no/no	
86	5 yrs. custody	no	-	no/no	no/no	
87	9 mths. cust. in care	already	4 yrs.+	no/no	already	
88	$2^{1/2}$ yrs. custody charge dropped 2 yrs. cust. conc.	no	-	no/no	matrim'l superv. order	
89	-	no	-	no/no	no/no	
90	-	no	-	no/no	no/no	
91	2 yrs. custody	no	-	no/no	no/no	
92	caution	yes	1 yr+	no/no	no/no	
93	charges dropped 3 yr. super. order	no	-	no/no	no/no	

Appendix 3 - English Sample (continued)

Case no	Sex of vict.	Rel. of perp. and vict.	Age at onset of sex'l contact	Freq./ dur. of sex'l contact	Age of onset of inter-course	Freq./ dur. of inter-course/ buggery*	Age at re-ferral	Initial charges
94	F	step-father	N.K.	N.K.	12	3 mths.	12/03	no charges
95	F	b-in-law	N.K.	N.K.	13/06	N.K.	14/10	USIu16(1) ind. ass.(1)
96	F	father	N.K.	N.K.	N.K.	N.K.	14/09	no charges

* If buggery occurred, it is indicated

Appendix 3 - English Sample (continued)

Case no.	Final Result	Victim removed from home	Length of time out of home	POSO applied for/ granted	Care order applied for/ granted	Other
94	-	no	-	no/no	no/no	
95	9 mths. custody	no	-	no/no	no/no	
96	-	yes	4 yrs.+	no/no	voluntary care order yes/yes	

Appendix 4

Cases in Canadian Sample

Note: Cases refer to victims. The following pairs and triads of victims were involved with the same perpetrators: [#3] and [#73]; [#4] and [#35]; [#7] and [#22]; [#10] and [#33]; [#16] and [#43]; [#17] and [#55]; [#36] and [#68]; [#37] and [#38]; [#50] and [#69]; [#51] and [#72]; [#64] and [#65]; [#67] and [#92]; [#70] and [#71]; [#13] and [#19] and [#34]; [#39] and [#40] and [#66]; [#74] and [#75] and [#82].

Appendix 4 - Canadian Sample

Case no.	Sex of vict.	Rel. of perp. & victim	Age of onset of sexual contact	Freq./ dur'n of sex'l contact	Age of onset of inter- course	Freq./ dur'n of inter- course/ buggery*	Age at re- ferral	Initial charges
1	M	grand-father	6	100+	-	-	16/04	charged but type N.K.
2	F	father	4	100+	-	-	16	no police invest
3	F	father	7	100+	-	-	14/11	no police invest.
4	F	father	9	100+	-	-	15/08	no charges
5	F	father	5	100+	-	-	12/11	art.33(1)
6	F	sibling	6	100+	-	-	13/09	no police invest.
7	F	father	9	100+	-	-	15/03	no police invest.
8	F	father	11	100+	-	-	15/02	no police invest.
9	M	mother	< 1yr.	100+	-	-	14/09	no police invest.
10	F	father	8/06	100+	-	-	12/06	no police invest.
11	F	father	13/06	100+	-	-	15/08	no police invest.
12	F	step-father	15	100+	-	-	16/11	no police invest.
13	M	step-father	7/06	100+	-	-	9/08	no police invest.
14	F	father father	8	61-100	-	-	15/07	no police invest.
15	F	father	10	61-100	-	-	17	no police invest.
16	F	step-father	6	61-100	-	-	12	no police invest.
17	F	father	9/06	61-100	-	-	11/09	no police invest.
18	F	father	13	31-60	-	-	14/03	indec. ass.(1)
19	M	step-father	5	31-60	-	-	5/05	no police invest.
20	M	father	5	11-20	-	-	6	no police invest.

Appendix 4 - Canadian Sample

Case no.	Final result	Placem't of victim out of home	Length of time out of home	Urgent Measures applied for/ granted	'Seize' the court applied for/ granted	Volunt'y measures	Other
1	N.K.	yes	20 mths.	no/no	yes/yes	no	
2	-	yes	2 yrs.+	yes/yes	yes/yes	no	
3	-	yes	15 mths.	no/no	yes/yes	yes	
4	-	no	-	no/no	no/no	no	
5	2 yrs. probation	yes	4 yrs.+	yes/yes	no/no	yes	
6	-	yes	16 mths.+	yes/yes	yes/yes	yes	
7	-	no	-	no/no	no/no	yes	
8	-	no	-	no/no	no/no	yes	
9	-	no	-	no/no	no/no	no	
10	-	no	-	no/no	no/no	yes	
11	-	yes	2 days	yes/yes	no/no	yes	
12	-	no	-	no/no	no/no	yes	
13	-	no	-	no/no	no/no	yes	
14	-	no	-	no/no	no/no	yes	
15	-	no	-	no/no	no/no	no	
16	-	no	-	no/no	no/no	yes	
17	-	no	-	no/no	no/no	yes	
18	2 yrs. probation	no	-	no/no	no/no	yes	
19	-	no	-	no/no	no/no	yes	
20	-	no	-	no/no	no/no	yes	

Appendix 4 - Canadian Sample (continued)

Case no.	Sex of vict.	Rel. of perp. & victim	Age of onset of sexual contact	Freq./ dur'n of sex'l contact	Age of onset of inter-course	Freq./ dur'n of inter-course/ buggery*	Age at re-ferral	Initial charges
21	M	step-father	10	6-10	-	-	14/01	no police invest.
22	F	father	12	6-10	-	-	13/01	no police invest.
23	F	grand-father	8/06	2	-	-	9/03	no police invest.
24	F	father	13/06	3	-	-	14	no police invest.
25	F	father	6/06	1	-	-	6/11	no police invest.
26	F	father	13	2	-	-	13/04	article 33(1)
27	F	father	14/06	2-5	-	-	15/01	no police invest.
28	F	father	13	1	-	-	14/06	no police invest.
29	F	uncle	10/04	1	-	-	10/04	no charges
30	F	step-father	11	3	-	-	13/11	no police invest.
31	F	father	14/06	2-5	-	-	14/06	no police invest.
32	F	uncle	16/06	2-5	-	-	16/08	no police invest.
33	M	father	10	2-5	-	-	14/03	no police invest.
34	F	step-father	14/06	2-5	-	-	14/11	no police invest.
35	F	uncle	8/06	2	-	-	10/02	no charges
36	F	mother	6	7 yrs.	-	-	14	no police invest.
37	F	father	11	4 yrs. 9 mths.	-	-	15/09	no charges
38	F	father	7	4 yrs. 11 mths.	-	-	11/11	no charges
39	F	male co-habitee	7	4 yrs. 10 mths.	-	-	11/10	no police invest.
40	F	male co-habitee	7	4 yrs. 10 mths.	-	-	11/10	no police invest.

Appendix 4 - Canadian Sample (continued)

Case no.	Final result	Placem't of victim out of home	Length of time out of home	Urgent Measures applied for/ granted	'Seize' the court applied for/ granted	Volunt'y measures	Other
21	-	no	-	no/no	no/no	no	
22	-	no	-	no/no	no/no	yes	
23	-	no	-	no/no	no/no	no	
24	-	no	-	no/no	no/no	no	
25	-	no	-	no/no	no/no	no	
26	1 yr. custody	no	-	no/no	yes/yes	yes	
27	-	yes	7 mths.	yes/yes	yes/yes	no	
28	-	no	-	no/no	no/no	yes	
29	-	no	-	no/no	no/no	no	
30	-	already	already 3yrs.+	no/no	no/no	yes	
31	-	yes	10 days	no/no	no/no	yes	
32	-	yes	2 mths.+	yes/yes	no/no	no	
33	-	no	-	no/no	yes/yes	yes	
34	-	yes	1 mth.	no/no	no/no	yes	
35	-	no	-	no/no	no/no	no	
36	-	yes	29 mths.	no/no	yes/yes	yes	
37	-	no	-	no/no	no/no	yes	
38	-	no	-	no/no	no/no	yes	
39	-	no	-	no/no	no/no	yes	
40	-	no	-	no/no	no/no	yes	

Appendix 4 - Canadian Sample (continued)

Case no.	Sex of vict.	Rel. of perp. & victim	Age of onset of sexual contact	Freq./ dur'n of sex'l contact	Age of onset of inter- course	Freq./ dur'n of inter- course/ buggery*	Age at re- ferral	Initial charges
41	F	father	6	4 yrs.	-	-	15/03	no police invest.
42	M	father	2 yrs. or less	4 yrs.	-	-	5/11	no police invest.
43	F	father	3-4	3-4	-	-	7	no police invest.
44	F	step-father	13	3 yrs.	-	-	16/01	no police invest.
45	F	male co-habitee	9	2 yrs.	-	-	15	no police invest.
46	M	cousin	8/06	3 yrs.	-	-	12	no police invest.
47	F	father	10/06	2 yrs.	-	-	12/06	no police invest.
48	M	male co-habitee	4/06	15 mths.	-	-	5/09	no police invest.
49	F	step-father	14	16 mths.	-	-	15/04	no police invest.
50	F	father	6/06	1 yr.	-	-	8/08	no police invest.
51	F	father	3/06	15 mths.	-	-	4/09	no police invest.
52	F	step-father	8	1 yr.	-	-	9	article 133 article 453
53	F	sibling	13	6 mths.	-	-	13/06	no police invest.
54	M	father	5/06	5 mths.	-	-	5/11	no police invest.
55	F	father	9	4 mths.	-	-	9/04	no police invest.
56	F	father	9/06	3 mths.	-	-	9/09	no police invest.
57	F	father	8	1 mth.	-	-	8/10	no police invest.
58	F	father	N.K.	3 wks.	-	-	11/05	charged initially but type N.K.

Appendix 4 - Canadian Sample (continued)

Case no.	Final result	Placem't of victim out of home	Length of time out of home	Urgent Measures applied for/ granted	'Seize' the court applied for/ granted	Volunt'y measures	Other
41	-	no	-	no/no	no/no	no	
42	-	no	-	no/no	no/no	no	
43	-	no	-	no/no	no/no	yes	
44	-	no	-	no/no	no/no	yes	
45	-	yes	7 mths.+	no/no	no/no	yes	
46	-	no	-	no/no	no/no	no	
47	-	yes	3 yrs.+	no/no	no/no	yes	
48	-	yes	20 mths.	no/no	no/no	yes	
49	-	no	-	no/no	initially but dropped	yes	
50	-	already out	N.K.	no/no	no/no	yes	
51	-	no	-	no/no	no/no	no	
52	N.K.	no	-	no/no	no/no	yes	
53	-	no	-	no/no	no/no	yes	
54	-	yes	16 mths.	no/no	no/no	yes	
55	-	no	-	no/no	yes/yes	yes	
56	-	yes	9 mths.	no/no	no/no	yes	
57	-	no	-	no/no	no/no	no	
58	N.K.	yes	27 mths.+	no/no	no/no	no	

Appendix 4 - Canadian Sample (continued)

Case no.	Sex of vict.	Rel. of perp. & victim	Age of onset of sexual contact	Freq./ dur'n of sex'l contact	Age of onset of inter- course	Freq./ dur'n of inter- course/ buggery*	Age at re- ferral	Initial charges
59	F	father	N.K.	N.K.	-	-	11	no police invest.
60	F	step-father	3	N.K.	-	-	10/08	no police invest.
61	F	father	N.K.	N.K.	-	-	7/08	no charges
62	F	sibling	N.K.	N.K.	-	-	5/00	no police invest.
63	F	father	N.K.	N.K.	-	-	14/11	no police invest.
64	F	father	N.K.	N.K.	-	-	15	no police invest.
65	F	father	N.K.	N.K.	-	-	12	no police invest.
66	F	father	N.K.	N.K.	-	-	9/03	no police invest.
67	F	sibling	N.K.	N.K.	-	-	13/10	no police invest.
68	F	mother	N.K.	N.K.	-	-	12/11	no police invest.
69	F	father	6	N.K.	-	-	6/09	no police invest.
70	F	step-father	N.K.	N.K.	-	-	7/03	no police invest.
71	F	step-father	N.K.	N.K.	-	-	2/05	no police invest.
72	F	father	N.K.	N.K.	-	-	3/02	no police invest.
73	F	father	N.K.	N.K.	-	-	13/04	no police invest.
74	F	uncle	N.K.	N.K.	-	-	17	no police invest.
76	F	father	8	100+ 2 yrs. buggery	8	100+	14/09	article 33
77	F	step-father	9	100+	11	61-100	14	no police invest.
78	F	step-father	10/06	100+	12/06	61-100	14/10	USIu16

Appendix 4 - Canadian Sample (continued)

Case no.	Final result	Placem't of victim out of home	Length of time out of home	Urgent Measures applied for/ granted	'Seize' the court applied for/ granted	Volunt'y measures	Other
59	-	yes	1 wk.	yes/yes	yes/yes	yes	
60	-	no	-	no/no	no/no	yes	
61	-	no	-	no/no	no/no	no	
62	-	no	-	no/no	no/no	yes	
63	-	no	-	no/no	N.K.	no	
64	-	no	-	no/no	yes/yes	no	
65	-	no	-	no/no	yes/yes	no	
66	-	no	-	no/no	no/no	no	
67	-	yes	6 mths.+	no/no	no/no	yes	
68	-	yes	1-2 wks.	no/no	no/no	yes	
69	-	no	-	no/no	no/no	yes	
70	-	no	-	no/no	no/no	no	
71	-	no	-	no/no	no/no	no	
72	-	no	-	no/no	no/no	no	
73	-	yes	15 mths.	no/no	yes/yes	yes	
74	-	no	-	no/no	no/no	no	
75	-	no	-	no/no	yes/N.K.	no	
76	2 yrs. probation	no	-	no/no	no/no	no	
77	-	no	-	no/no	no/no	yes	
78	N.K.	no	-	no/no	no/no	no	

Appendix 4 - Canadian Sample (continued)

Case no.	Sex of vict.	Rel. of perp. & victim	Age of onset of sexual contact	Freq./ dur'n of sex'l contact	Age of onset of inter- course	Freq./ dur'n of inter- course/ buggery*	Age at re- ferral	Initial charges
79	F	step-father	9/06	31-60	9/06	31-60	10/04	no police invest.
80	F	sibling	11	100+	15	21-30	16/06	no police invest.
81	F	father	8/06	11-20	8/06	11-20	11/07	incest(1)
82	F	uncle	14	2 yrs.	14	6	15/11	no police invest.
83	F	father	10	2	10	2	10/08	no police invest.
84	F	father	14/06	2-5	14/06	1	14/08	no charges
85	F	step-father	16	6-10	11/06	1	16/02	no police invest.
86	F	father	11	100+	13	2-3	15	no police invest.
87	F	father	5	2 yrs.	5	N.K.	7/02	no police invest.
88	M	father	1/06-2	2-3 yrs.	N.K.	buggery N.K.	4/08	no police invest.
89	F	step-father	13	16 mths.	13	16 mths.	14/04	charged but type N.K.
90	F	sibling	14/06	14 mths.	14/06	14 mths.	15/08	no police invest.
91	F	father	13	7 mths.	13	7 mths.	13/07	no police invest.
92	F	sibling	N.K.	N.K.	N.K.	buggery N.K.	15/11	no police invest.
93	F	father	N.K.	N.K.	N.K.	N.K.	12/11	no police invest.
94	F	father	N.K.	N.K.	N.K.	N.K.	16	no police invest.
95	F	father	11/06	3	N.K.	N.K.	13/05	no police invest.

*   If buggery occurred, it is indicated

Appendix 4 - Canadian Sample (continued)

Case no.	Final result	Placem't of victim out of home	Length of time out of home	Urgent Measures applied for/ granted	'Seize' the court applied for/ granted	Volunt'y measures	Other
79	-	yes	6 mths.	no/no	no/no	no	
80	-	yes	7 mths.+	yes/yes	yes/yes	yes	
81	2 yrs. custody	no	-	no/no	no/no	no	
82	-	no	-	no/no	no/no	no	
83	-	already	3 yrs+	no/no	already for other reasons/yes	no	
84	-	yes	4 mths.+	no/no	no/no	no	
85	-	yes	21 mths.+	no/no	no/no	yes	
86	-	yes	3 yrs.+	yes/yes	yes/yes	yes	
87	-	yes	4 mths.+	yes/yes	yes/yes	no	
88	-	no	-	no/no	no/no	no	
89	N.K.	yes	7 mths.	no/no	yes/yes	yes	
90	-	yes	11 mths.	no/no	no/no	no	
91	-	yes	2 mths.	yes/yes	no/no	no	
92	-	no	-	no/no	no/no	yes	
93	-	no	-	no/no	no/no	no	
94	-	no	-	no/no	no/no	no	
95	-	yes	43 mths.+	no/no	no/no	no	

Bibliography

Aarens, M., Cameron, T., Roizen, J., Room, R., Schnerberk, D., Wingard, D. (1978), *Alcohol, Casualties and Crime*, Berkely, CA: Social Research Group.

Abel, G., Becker, J.A., Murphy, N.D., & Flanagan, B. (1979, March), 'Identifying Dangerous Child Molesters', *Paper presented at the International Conference on Behaviour Modification*, Banff, Canada.

Aber, J.L. (1980), 'The Involuntary Child Placement Decision: Solomon's Dilemma Revisited', in Gerbner, G., Ross, C.J., & Zigler, E.Z. (eds.), *Child Abuse: An Agenda for Action*, New York: Oxford University Press.

Adams-Tucker, C. (1981), 'A Socioclinical Overview of 28 Sex-abused Children', *Child Abuse and Neglect*, 5, pp. 361-367.

Allen, N. (1990), *Making Sense of the Children Act 1989: A Guide for the Social and Welfare Services*, Harlow: Longman.

Alström, C.H. (1977), 'A Study of Incest with Special Regard to the Swedish Penal Code', *Acta Psychiatrica Scandinavica*, 56, pp. 357-372.

American Humane Association (1981), *National Study on Child Neglect and Abuse Reporting*, Denver, CO: Author.

Amphlett, S. (1987, December 14). *Statement To the Cleveland Inquiry*, Bishop's Stortford, Herts: Parents Against Injustice.

Anderson, S.C., Bach, C.M., & Griffith, S. (1981, April), 'Psychosocial Sequelae in Intrafamilial Victims of Sexual Assault and Abuse', *Paper presented at the Third International Conference on Child Abuse and Neglect*, Amsterdam, The Netherlands.

Askew, H. (1976), *Causal Modelling*, London: Sage.

Avery-Clark, C., O'Neil, J.A., & Laws, D.R. (1981), 'A Comparison of Intrafamilial Sexual and Physical Child Abuse', in Cook, M. & Howells, K. (eds.), *Adult Sexual Interest in Children*, London: Academic Press.

Ayalon, O. (1984), 'The Daughter as a Sexual Victim in the Family', in Carmi, A. & Zimrin, H. (eds.), *Child Abuse*, Berlin: Springer-Verlag.

Baher, E., Hyman, L., Jones, L., Jones, R., Kerr, A., & Mitchell, R. (1976), *At Risk: An Account of the Work of the Battered Child Research Department*, NSPCC, London: Routledge & Kegan Paul.

Bailey, V. & Blackburn, S. (1979), The Punishment of Incest Act 1908: A Case Study of Law Creation, *The Criminal Law Review*, pp. 708-719.

Bailey, V. & McCabe, S. (1979), 'Reforming the Law of Incest', *Criminal Law Review*, pp. 749-764.

Baker, A.W. & Duncan, S.P. (1985), 'Child Sexual Abuse: A Study of Prevalence in Great Britain', *Child Abuse and Neglect*, 9, pp. 457-467.

Ballantyne, A. (1988, July 13), 'Cleveland Chief Claims 83 Cases Vindicate Action', *The Guardian*, p. 20.

Baneke, J.W. (1983), 'The Dutch Approach to Child Abuse', in Leavitt, J.E. (ed.), *Child Abuse and Neglect*, The Hague: Martinus Nijhoff.

Barry, M. & Johnson, A. (1958), 'The Incest Barrier', *Psychoanalytic Quarterly*, 27, p. 485.

Batshaw Committee (1976), *Report of the Study Committee on Socially Disturbed Children in Juvenile Institutions*, Quebec: Ministry of Social Affairs.

Bedford, A. (1987), *Child Abuse and Risk*, (Occasional Paper Series No.2), London: National Society for the Prevention of Cruelty to Children.

Bell, L. & Pennington, D. (1990, January 18), 'Strategies for Management', *Community Care*, pp. 24-25.

Bell, S. (1988), *When Salem Came to the Boro*, London: Pan.

Belson, W.A. & Hood, R. (1967), *The Research Potential of Case Records of Approved School Boys*, London: The Survey Research Centre.

Bender, L. & Blau, A. (1937), 'The Reaction of Children to Sexual Relations with Adults', *American Journal of Orthopsychiatry*, 7, pp. 500-518.

Bentovin, A., Elton, A., Hidelbrand, J., & Trantor, M. (1988), *Sexual Abuse in the Family*, Bristol: Wright.

Berliner, L. (1977), 'Child Sexual Abuse: What Happens Next?' *Victimology, An International Journal*, 22, pp. 327-331.

Berliner, L. & Stevens, D. (1982), 'Clinical Issues in Child Sexual Abuse', in Conte, J.R., & Shore, D. (eds.), *Social Work and Child Sexual Abuse*, New York: Haworth.

Besharov, D.J. (1975), 'Case Management', in *Child Abuse and Neglect: The Problem and its Management*, (pp. 29-53). (DHEW Publication No.OHD 75-30073), Washington, DC: U.S. Government Printing Office.

Besharov, D.J. (1981), 'The Third International Congress on Child Abuse and Neglect: Conference Highlights', *Children Today*, 10, pp. 12-15, 36.

Besharov, D.J. (1985), 'Right Versus Rights: The Dilemma of Child Protection', *Public Welfare* (Spring), pp. 19-27.

Birchall, E. & Hallett, C. (1995), *Working Together in Child Protection*, London: HMSO.

Blagg, H., Hughes, J.A., & Wattam, C. (1989), *Child Sexual Abuse: Listening, Hearing and Validating the Experiences of Children*, Harlow: Longman.

Blalock, H.M. (1961), *Causal Inferences in Nonexperimental Research*, Toronto: University of North Carolina Press.

Blumberg, M. (1977), 'Treatment of the Abused Child and the Child Abuser', *American Journal of Psychotherapy*, pp. 204-215.

Bohmer, C. (1974), 'Judicial Attitudes Toward Rape Victims', *Judicature*, 57, pp. 303-307.

Booth, M. (1979), 'The Abused Child in the Courts', *Child Abuse and Neglect*, 3, pp. 45-49.

Brandon, S., Boakes, J., Glaser, D. & Green, R. (1998), 'Recovered Memories of Childhood Sexual Abuse: Implication for Clinical Practice', *British Journal of Psychiatry*, 172, pp. 296-307.

Brant, R.S.T. & Tisza, V. (1977), 'The Sexually Misused Child', *American Journal of Orthopsychiatry*, 47, pp. 80-90.

Brewer, (1977), *Report of the Review Panel Appointed by the Somerset Area Review Committee to Consider the Case of Wayne Brewer*, Somerset County Council.

Briere, J. (1984, April), 'The Long-term Effects of Childhood Sexual Abuse: Defining a Post-Sexual-Abuse Syndrome', *Paper presented at the Third National Conference on Sexual Victimization of Children*, Washington, D.C.

British Association for the Study and Prevention of Child Abuse and Neglect (BASPCAN) (1981), *Child Sexual Abuse*, London: Author.

Brown, L. (1983), Status of Child Protective Services in the United States: An Analysis of Issues and Practice, in Leavitt, J.E. (ed.), *Child Abuse and Neglect*, The Hague: Martinus Nijhoff.

Browne, A. & Finkelhor, D. (1986), 'Initial and Long-term Effects: A Review of the Research', in Finkelkor, D. (ed.), *A Sourcebook on Child Sexual Abuse*, Beverly Hills, CA: Sage.

Browning, D.H. & Boatman, B. (1977), 'Incest: Children at Risk', *American Journal of Psychiatry*, 134, pp. 69-72.

Brunhold, H. (1964), 'Observations After Sexual Traumata Suffered in Childhood', *Excepta Criminologica*, 4, pp. 5-8.

Burgess, A. W., Holmstrom, L.L., & McCausland, M.P. (1977), Child Abuse Assault by a Family Member: Decisions Following Disclosure, *Victimology: An International Journal*, 11, pp. 236-250.

Burgess, A., W., Holmstrom, L.L., & McCausland, M.P. (1978), 'Counseling Young Victims and Their Families', in Burgess, A.W., Groth, A.N., Holmstrom, L.L. & Sgroi, S. (eds.), *Sexual Assault of Children and Adolescents*, Lexington, MA: Lexington Books.

Burgess, A.W. & Laszlo, A.T. (1976), 'When the Prosecutrix is a Child: The Victim Consultant in Cases of Sexual Assault', in Viano, E.C. (ed.), *Victims and Society*, Washington, DC: Visage.

Burton, L. (1968), *Vulnerable Children*, London: Routlege.

Canada (1984), *Sexual Offences Against Children* (Vols.1 & 2), Ottawa: Canadian Government Publishing.

Carter, J. (1977), 'Is Child Abuse a Crime?', in Franklin, A.W. (ed.), *The Challenge of Child Abuse*, London: Academic Press.

Cavallin, H. (1966), 'Incestuous Fathers: A Clinical Report', *American Journal of Psychiatry*, 122, pp. 1132-1138.

Cervi, B. (1991), "Obsessed with Satanic Abuse, Says Judge', *Community Care*, January 3, p. 3.

Chamberlain, M., Krell, W., & Pries, K. (1976), 'Legal Aspects of Child Abuse and Neglect', *American Journal of Forensic Psychiatry*, pp. 151-158.

Chaneles, S. (1967), 'Child Victims of Sexual Offences', *Federal Probation*, 31, pp. 52-56.

Chapman, M.G.T., Woodmansey, A.C., & Garwood, A. (1985), 'The Society of Clinical Psychiatrists' Policy on Child Abuse' (SCP Report No.13). *Supplement to British Journal of Clinical and Social Psychiatry*, 3(2).

'Child Sexual Abuse Scandal', (1988, July 7), *Daily Mail*, p. 2.

Christopherson, R.J. (1981), 'Two Approaches to the Handling of Child Abuse. A Comparison of the English and Dutch Systems', *Child Abuse and Neglect*, 5(4), pp. 369-373.

Clarke, K., Barnhorst, R., & Barnhorst, S. (1977), *Criminal Law and the Canadian Criminal Code*, Toronto: McGraw-Hill Ryerson.

Cleaver, H. & Freeman, P. (1996), 'Suspected Child Abuse and Neglect: Are Parents' Views Important?' in Platt, D. & Shemmings, D. (eds.), *Making Enquiries into Alleged Child Abuse and Neglect: Partnership with Families*, Brighton: Pennant.

Collie, J. (1975), 'The Police Role' , in Franklin, A.W. (ed.), *Concerning Child Abuse*, Edinburgh: Churchill Livingstone.

Colwell, M. (1974), *Report of the Committee of Inquiry Into the Care and Supervision Provided in Relation to Maria Colwell*, London: HMSO.

Comité de la Protection de la Jeunesse (1981), *Procedure Manual*, Montreal: Department of Youth Protection.

Comité de la Protection de la Jeunesse (1984), 'Social Work with Maltreated Children: A Time for Re-evaluation?', Quebec: *Gouvernement du Quebec*.

Constantine, L. & Martinson, F. (1981), *Children and Sex: New Findings and New Perspectives*, Boston: Little Brown.

Constantine, L.L. (1981), 'The Sexual Rights of Children: Implications of a Radical Perspective', in Constantine, L.L., & Martinson, J.M. (eds.), *Children and Sex: New Findings New Perspectives*, Boston: Little Brown.

Conte, J.R. (1984), 'The Justice System and Sexual Abuse of Children', *Social Service Review* , pp. 556-568.

Cooper, I. (1978), 'Decriminalization of Incest: New Legal-clinical Responses', in J.M. Eekelaar & S.M. Katz (eds.), *Family Violence*, Toronto: Butterworths.

Cooper, I. (1984, September), 'Professional Response to Intrafamily Child Sexual Abuse: Abuse, Misuse or Help?', *Paper presented at the IV International Conference on Child Abuse and Neglect*, Montreal, Canada.

Cooper, I. & Cormier, B.M. (1982), 'Intergenerational Transmission of Incest', *Canadian Journal of Psychiatry*, 27, pp. 231-235.

Cooper, I. & Cormier, B.M. (1985, September), 'The New Incest Protocol: Professional Avoidance of an Ancient Taboo', *Paper presented at the Annual Meeting of the Canadian Psychiatric Association*, Toronto, Canada.

Cooper, I. & Cormier, B. (1990), 'Incest', in Bluglass, R. & Bowden, P. (eds.), *Principles and Practice of Forensic Psychiatry*, Edinburgh: Churchill Livingstone.

Corby, B. & Millar, M. (1997), 'A Parents' View of Partnership', in Bates, J., Pugh, R. & Thompson, N. (eds.), *Protecting Children: Challenges and Change*, Aldershot: Ashgate.

Corby, B., Millar, M. & Young, L. (1995), 'Parental Participation at child Protection Conferences'; *Journal of Health and Social Care*, 3(3), pp. 197-200.

Cormier, B.M. & Cooper, I. (1982), *Incest in Contemporary Society: Legal and Clinical Management*, in Children's Psychiatric Research Institute 20th Anniversary Symposium, London, Ontario, Canada.

Cormier, B.M., Kennedy, M., & Sangowicz, J. (1962), 'Psychodynamics of Father-daughter Incest', *Canadian Journal of Psychiatry*, 7, pp. 203-217.

Corsini-Munt, L.A. (1982), 'A Canadian Study: Sexual Abuse of Children and Adolescents', in Schlesinger, B. (ed.), *Sexual Abuse of Children: A Resource Guide and Annotated Bibliography*, Toronto: University of Toronto.

Court of Appeal (1989), *Attorney General's Reference* (No.1 of 1989), Lord Lane C.J.

Creighton, S.J. (1985), 'An Epidemiological Study of Abused Children and Their Families in the United Kingdom Between 1977 and 1982', *Child Abuse and Neglect*, 9, pp. 441-448.

Creighton, S.J. & Noyes, P. (July, 1989), *Child Abuse Trends in England and Wales 1983-1987*, London: National Society for the Prevention of Cruelty to Children.

Criminal Law Review Committee (1980), *Working Paper on Sexual Offences*, London: HMSO.

Criminal Law Review Committee (1984), *Sexual Offences: Fifteenth Report*, (Cmnd. 9213), London: HMSO.

Crine, A. (1983, February 14), 'Behind the Figures', *Community Care*, pp. 15-17.

Crown Prosecution Service (1986), *Code for Crown Prosecutors,* London: Author.

Dale, P. & Davies, M. (1984, September 24), 'Child Abuse: Three-act Tragedies', *Community Care*, pp. 12-14.

Dale, P., Davies, M., Morrison, T., Noyes, P., & Roberts, W. (1983), 'A Family Therapy Approach to Child Abuse: Countering Resistence', *Journal of Family Therapy*, 5, pp. 117-145.

Davies, R. (1979), 'Some Neuropsychiatric Findings', *The International Journal of Psychiatry in Medicine*, 9, pp. 115-121.

Davis, L. (1981), 'Without Prejudice', *Social Work Today*, 13, pp. 8-10.

Davoren, E. (1975), 'Working with Abusive Parents: A Social Worker's View', *Children Today*, 4, pp. 38-43.

Deer, B. (1988, July 10), 'Why We Must Look', *The Sunday Times*, p. 12.

DeFrancis, V. (1969), *Protecting the Child Victim of Sex Crimes Committed by Adults*, Denver, CO: American Humane Association.

DeFrancis, V. (1970), *Child Abuse Legislation in the 1970's*, Denver, CO: American Humane Association.

Delaney, J.J. (1972), 'The Battered Child and the Law', in Kempe, C.H. & Helfer, R.E. (eds.), *Helping the Battered Child and his Family*, Philadelphia: Lippincott.

Department of Health (1994), *Children Act Report 1993*, London: HMSO.

Department of Health and Social Security (1976), *Non-accidental Injury to Children: Area Review Committees*, Letter LASSL(76)2.

Department of Health and Social Security (1978), *Violence to Children: A Response to the First Report from the Select Committee on Violence in the Family* (Cmnd.7123), London: HMSO.

Department of Health and Social Security (1980), *Child Abuse: Central Register Systems Circular*, LASSL(80)4 HN(80)20.

Department of Health and Social Security (1985a), *Review of Child Care Law*, London: HMSO.

Department of Health and Social Security (1985b), *Social Work Decisions in Child Care: Recent Research Findings and Their Implications*, London: HMSO.

Department of Health and Social Security and Home Office (1976), *Non-accidental Injury to Children: The Police and Case Conferences*, Letter LASSl(76)26.

Department of Health and Social Security and Welsh Office (1988), Working Together: *A Guide to Arrangements for Inter-agency Co-operation for the Protection of Children from Abuse*, London: HMSO.

De Young, M. (1981), 'Promises, Threats and Lies: Keeping Incest Secret', *Journal of Humanics*, 9(1), pp. 61-71.

De Young, M. (1982), *The Sexual Victimization of Children*, Jefferson, NC: McFarland.

Dickens, B.M. (1984), 'Child Abuse and Criminal Process: Dilemmas in Punishment and Protection', in Carmi, A. & Zimrin, H. (eds.), *Child Abuse*, Berlin: Springer-Verlag.

Dingwall, R. & Eekelaar, J. (1982), *Care Proceedings: A Practical Guide for Social Workers, Health Visitors and Others*, Oxford: Basil Blackwell.

Dingwall, R., Eekelaar, J., & Murray, T. (1983), *The Protection of Children: State Intervention and Family Life*, Oxford: Basil Blackwell.

Doek, J.E. (1978), 'Child Abuse in the Netherlands: The Medical Referee', *Chicago-Kent Law Review*, 54, pp. 785-826.

Doek, J.E. (1981), 'Sexual Abuse of Children: An Examination of European Criminal Law', in Mrazek, P.B. & Kempe, C.H. (eds.), *Sexually Abused Children and their Families*, Oxford: Pergamon.

Drapkin, I. (1975), 'Introduction', in Drapkin, I. & Viano, E. (eds.), *Victimology: A New Focus (Vol.IV) Violence and its Victims*, Toronto: Lexington.

Duncan, C. (1979), 'They Beat Children Don't They?', in Gill, D. (ed.), *Child Abuse and Violence*, New York: AMS Press.

Eaton, L. (1991), 'Ritual Abuse: Fantasy or Reality?', *Social Work Today*, 9, September 6, pp. 8-12.

Eleveel, M.E. & Ephross, P.H. (1987), 'Initial Reactions of Sexually Abused Children', *Social Casework: The Journal of Contemporary Social Work*, Feb., pp. 109-124.

Farmer, E. & Owen, M. (eds.) (1995), *Child Protection Practice: Private Risks and Public Remedies.* London: HMSO.

Featherstone, B & Lancaster, E., (1997), "Contemplating the Unthinkable: Men Who Sexually Abuse Children' in *Critical Social Policy*, London: Sage.

Finkelhor, D. (1978), 'Psychological, Cultural and Family Factors in Incest and Family Sexual Abuse', *Journal of Marriage and Family Counsellors*, 4, pp. 41-49.

Finkelhor, D. (1979), *Sexually Victimized Children*, New York: Free Press.

Finkelhor, D. (1980), 'Risk Factors in the Sexual Victimization of Children', *Child Abuse & Neglect*, 4, pp. 265-273.

Finkelhor, D. (1983a), 'Common Features of Family Abuse', in Finkelhor, D., Gelles, R.J., Hotaling, G.T. & Straus, M.A. (eds.), *The Dark Side of Families*, Beverly Hills, CA: Sage.

Finkelhor, D. (1983b), 'Removing the Child-Prosecuting the Offender in Cases of Sexual Abuse: Evidence from the National Reporting System for Child Abuse and Neglect', *Child Abuse & Neglect*, 1, pp. 195-205.

Finkelhor, D. (1984a), *Child Sexual Abuse: New Theory and Research*, New York: The Free Press.

Finkelhor, D. (1984b), 'How Widespread is Child Sexual Abuse?', *Children Today*, 13, pp. 18-20.

Finkelhor, D. (1984c), 'Implications for Theory, Research, and Practice', in Finkelhor, D. (ed.), *Child Sexual Abuse: New Theory and Research*, New York: Free Press.

Finkelhor, D. (1988), 'The Trauma of Child Sexual Abuse: Two models', in Wyatt, G.E.W. & Powell, G.J. (eds.), *Lasting Effects of Child Sexual Abuse*, London: Sage.

Finkelhor, D. & Baron, L. (1986), 'High Risk Children', in Finkelhor, D.(ed.), *A Sourcebook on Child Sexual Abuse*, Beverley Hills, CA: Sage.

Finkelhor, D., Gomes-Schwartz B., & Horowitz, J. (1984), 'Professionals' Responses', in Finkelhor, D. (ed.), *Child Sexual Abuse: New Theory and Research*, New York: Free Press.

Finkelhor, D. & Hotaling, G.T. (1984), 'Sexual Abuse in the National Incidence Study of Child Abuse and Neglect', *Child Abuse and Neglect*, 8, pp. 22-33.

Finkelhor, D & Russell, D. (1984), 'Women as Perpetraters: Review of the Evidence', in Finkelhor, D. (ed.), *New Theory and Research*, New York: Free Press.

Fisher, S.M. (1979), 'Life in a Children's Detention Centre: Strategies of Survival', in Gill, D. (ed.), *Child Abuse and Violence*, New York: AMS Press.

Flanzer, J.P. & Sturkie, D.K. (1983), *Arkansaw Alcohol/child Abuse Demonstration Project (Final Report)*, Little Rock, AR: Graduate School of Social Work, University of Arkansas at Little Rock.

Forbes, J. & Thomas, T. (1990, January 11), 'Dangerous Classifications', *Community Care*, pp. 19-21.

Franklin, A.W. (1977), 'Child Abuse as a Challenge', in Franklin, A.W. (ed.), *The Challenge of Child Abuse*, London: Academic Press.

Fraser, B. (1974), 'A Pragmatic Alternative to Current Legislative Approaches to Child Abuse', *American Criminal Law Review*, 12 (1), pp. 103-124.

Fraser, B. (1979), 'Child Abuse in America: A De Facto Legislative System', *Child Abuse and Neglect*, 3, pp. 35-43.

Fraser, B. (1981), 'Sexual Child Abuse: The Legislation and the Law in the United States', in Mrazek, P.B. & Kempe, C.H. (eds.), *Sexually Abused Children and their Families*, Oxford: Pergamon.

Freeman, M.D.A. (1983), *The Rights and Wrongs of Children*, London: Frances Pinter.

Freud, S. (1918, 1950), *Totem and Taboo*, London: Routledge & Kegan Paul.

Fromuth, M.E. (1983), *The Long Term Psychological Impact of Childhood Sexual Abuse*, unpublished doctoral dissertation, Auburn University.

Frude, N. (1982), 'The Sexual Nature of Sexual Abuse: A Review of the Literature', *Child Abuse and Neglect*, 6, pp. 211-223.

Furniss, T. (1983), 'Mutual Influence and Interlocking Professional Family Process in the Treatment of Child Sexual Abuse and Incest', *Child Abuse and Neglect*, 7, pp. 207-223.

Garfinkel, H. (1967), *Studies in Ethnomethodology*, Englewood Cliffs, NJ: Prentice Hall.

Geach, H. (1981, August 27), 'Case Conferences-Time for a Change?' *Community Care*, pp. 16-17.

Geach, H. & Szwed, E. (1983), 'Introduction', in Geach, H. & Szwed, E. (eds.), *Providing Civil Justice for Children*, London: Edward Arnold.

Gebhard, P., Gagnon, J., Pomeroy, W., & Christenson, C. (1965), *Sex Offenders: An Analysis of Types*, New York: Harper & Row.

Gelles, R.J. & Cornell, C.P. (1983), 'International Perspectives on Child Abuse', *Child Abuse and Neglect*, 7, pp. 375-386.

Gentry, C.E. (1978), 'Incestuous Abuse of Children: The Need for an Objective View', *Child Welfare*, 57, pp. 355-364.

Giaretto, H. (1976), 'Humanistic Treatment of Father-daughter Incest', *Child Abuse and Neglect*, 1 (2-4), pp. 411-426.

Giaretto, H. (1981), 'A Comprehensive Child Sexual Abuse Treatment Program', in Mrazek, P.B. & Kempe, C.H. (eds.), *Sexually Abused Children and their Families*, Oxford: Pergamon.

Gibbens, T.C.N. & Prince, J. (1963), *Child Victims of Sex Offences*, London: Nell.

Gil, D. (1970), *Violence Against Children: Physical Abuse in the United States*, Cambridge, MA: Harvard University.

Gil, D. (1975), 'Unravelling Child Abuse', *American Journal of Orthopsychiatry*, 45(3), pp. 346-356.

Gil, D. (1981), 'The United States Versus Child Abuse', in Pelton, L. (ed.), *The Social Context of Child Abuse*, New York: Human Sciences Press.

Giovannoni, J.M. & Beccerra, R.M. (1979), *Defining Child Abuse*, New York: Free Press.

Gligor, A.M. (1966), *Incest and Sexual Delinquency: A Comparative Analysis of Two Forms of Sexual Behaviour in Minor Females*, unpublished doctoral dissertation, Case Western Reserve University.

Goldberg, H. (1977), *The Hazards of Being Male: Surviving the Myth of Masculine Privilege*, New York: New American Library.

Goodwin, J. (1982a), 'Helping the Child Who Reports Incest: A Case Review', in Goodwin, J. (ed.), *Sexual Abuse: Incest Victims and their Families*, Littleton, MA: John Wright PSG.

Goodwin, J. (1982b), 'Suicide Attempts: A Preventable Complication of Incest', in Goodwin, J. (ed.), *Sexual Abuse: Incest Victims and their Families*, Littleton, MA: John Wright PSG.

Goodwin, J., McCarthy, T., & DiVasto, P. (1982), 'Prior Incest in Mothers of Abused Children', *Child Abuse and Neglect*, 5, pp. 87-95.

Gordon, L. & O'Keefe, P. (1984), 'Incest as a Form of Family Violence: Evidence from Historical Records', *Journal of Marriage and the Family*, 46, pp. 27-34.

Gorry, P.J. (1986), *Incest: The Offence and Police Investigation*, unpublished master's thesis, University of Cambridge, England.

Graves, P.A. & Sgroi, S.M. (1982), 'Law Enforcement and Child Sexual Abuse', in Sgroi, S. (ed.), *Handbook of Clinical Intervention in Child Sexual Abuse*, Lexington, MA: Lexington Books.

Green, A.H. (1975), 'The Child Abuse Syndrome and the Treatment of Abusing Parents', in Pasternack, S.A. (ed.), *Violence and Victims*, New York: Spectrum.

Green, A.H. (1988a), 'Overview of the Literature on Child Sexual Abuse', in Schetky, D. & Green, A.H. (eds.), *Child Sexual Abuse: A Handbook for Health Care and Legal Professionals*, New York: Brunner/Mazel.

Green, A.H. (1988b), 'Special Issues in Child Abuse', in Schetky, D. & Green, A.H. (eds.), *Child Sexual Abuse: A Handbook for Health Case and Legal Professionals*, New York: Brunner/Mazel.

Greenland, C. (1987), *Preventing CAN Deaths*, London: Tavistock.

Greenland, C. (1990), 'Family Violence: Review of the Literature', in Bluglass, R. & Bowden, P. (eds.), *Principles and Practice of Forensic Psychiatry*, Edinburgh: Churchill Livingstone.

Gruber, K. & Jones, R. (1983), 'Identifying Determinants of Risk of Several Victimization of Youth', *Child Abuse and Neglect*, 7, pp. 17-24.

Guttmacher, M.S. (1951), *Sex Offences*, New York: Norton.

Hall, M.H. (1978), The Team Approach, in Carver, V. (ed.), *Child Abuse: A Study Text*, Milton Keynes: Open University Press.

Hall, J.G. & Mitchell, B.H. (1979), 'The Endangered Child in the U.S.A. and in England: A Comparative Study of Juvenile Justice Standards', *Child Abuse and Neglect*, 3, pp. 725-731.

Hallett, C. & Stevenson, O. (1980), *Child Abuse: Aspects of Interprofessional Co-operation*, London: George Allen & Unwin.

Hallet, S. (1991), 'Criminal Prosecutions for Abuse and Neglect', in Bala, N., Hornick, J.P. & Vogl, R. (eds.), *Canadian Child Welfare Law*, Toronto: Thompson Educational Publishing.

Hansard (1908, June 26), *House of Lords Debates, Punishment of Incest Act 1908*, Vol.191, cols.285-288, London: HMSO.

Henderson, D.J. (1972), 'Incest: A Synthesis of Data', *Canadian Psychiatric Association Journal*, 17, pp. 299-313.

Herman, J. (1981), *Father-daughter Incest*, Cambridge, MA: Harvard University Press.

Herman, J. & Hirschman, L. (1977), 'Father-daughter Incest', *Signs: Journal of Women in Culture and Society*, 2, pp. 735-756.

Herman, J. & Hirschman, L. (1981), 'Families at Risk for Father-daughter Incest', *American Journal of Psychiatry*, 138, pp. 967-970.

Hobbs, C.J. & Wynne, J.M. (1986, October 4), 'Buggery in Childhood - a Common Syndrome of Child Abuse', *The Lancet*, pp. 792-796.

'Holy War Over Repressed Memory', (1995, April 1), *The Globe and Mail*.

Holt, J. (1974), *Escape From Childhood: The Needs and Rights of Children*, New York: Ballantine Books.
Home Office (1977), *Criminal Statistics England and Wales*, 1976, London: HMSO.
Home Office (1978), *Criminal Statistics England and Wales*, 1977, London: HMSO.
Home Office (1981a), *Criminal Statistics England and Wales*, 1980, London: HMSO.
Home Office (1981b), *Report of the Royal Commission on Criminal Procedure*, (Cmnd.8092), London: HMSO.
Home Office (1984), *Criminal Statistics England and Wales*, London: HMSO.
Home Office (1988), *Report of the Inquiry into Child Abuse in Cleveland 1987*, (Cmnd.412), London: HMSO.
Home Office, Ministry of Education and Science, Ministry of Housing and Local Government (1968), *Seebohm Committee, Committee on Local Authority and Allied Personal Social Services*, (Cmnd 3703), London: HMSO.
Horton, A., Johnson, B., Roundy, L.M. & Williams, D. (eds.), (1990), *The Incest Perpetrator: A Family Member No One Wants To Treat*, London: Sage.
Horvath, J & Calder, M.C. (1998), 'Working Together to Protect Children on the Child Protection Register: Myth or Reality', *British Journal of Social Work*, 28, pp. 879-895.
House of Commons Select Committee on Violence in the Family (1977), First Report, London: HMSO.
Howard League (1985), *Unlawful Sex: Offences, Victims and Offenders in the Criminal Justice System of England and Wales*, London: Waterlow.
Howells, J.G. (1974), *Remember Maria*, London: Butterworths.
Howitt, D. (1992), *Child Abuse Errors: When Good Intentions Go Wrong*, Harvester Wheatsheaf.
Ingram, M. (1979), 'Participating Victims: A Study of Sexual Offences with Boys', *British Journal of Sexual Medicine*, 6(44), Jan., pp. 22-25, 6(44), Feb., pp. 24-26.
'Is Society's Child Nobody's Child?' (1998, June 27), *The Gazette*, pp.1, 8.
Jack, G. (1997), 'Discourses of Child Protection and Child Welfare', *British Journal of Social Work*, 27, pp. 659-678.
Jack, G. & Stepney, P. (1995), 'The Children Act 1989 – Protection or Persecution? Family support and Child Protection in the 1990s', *Critical Social Policy*, 43, pp. 26-39.

Jacobs, J. (1978), 'Child Abuse, Neglect and Deprivation and the Family: A Perspective from Canada', in Smith, S. (ed.), *The Maltreatment of Children*, Lancaster, England: MTP Press.

Janeway, E. (1981), 'Incest: A Rational Look at the Oldest Taboo', *Ms Magazine*, November.

Jones, D.N., McClean, R., & Vobe, R. (1979), 'Case Conferences on Child Abuse: The Nottinghamshire Approach', *Child Abuse and Neglect*, 3, pp. 583-590.

Jordan, B. (1975), 'Is the Client a Fellow Citizen?', *Social Work Today*, 6(15), pp. 471-475.

Julian, V. & Mohr, C. (1979), 'Father-daughter Incest: Profile of the Offender', *Victimology: An International Journal*, 4, pp. 348-360.

Julian, V., Mohr, C., & Lapp, J. (1980), 'Father-daughter Incest: A Descriptive Analysis', in Holden, W. (ed.), *Sexual Abuse of Children: Implications for Treatment*, Denver: American Humane Association.

Justice, B. & Justice, R. (1979), *The Broken Taboo: Sex in the Family*, New York: Human Sciences.

Katz, S. & Mzur, M. (1979), *Understanding the Rape Victim: A Hypothesis of Research Finding*, New York: John Wiley & Sons.

Kaufman I., Peck, A., & Tagiuri, C. (1954), 'The Family Constellation and Overt Incestuous Relations Between Father and Daughter', *American Journal of Orthopsychiatry*, 24, pp. 266-279.

Kempe, C.H. (1978), 'Recent Developments in the Field of Child Abuse', *Child Abuse and Neglect*, 2, pp. 261-267.

Kempe, C.H., Silverman, F.N., Branot, F., Droegemueller, W., & Silver, H.K. (1962), 'The Battered Child Syndrome', *Journal of the American Medical Association*, 18, pp. 17-24.

Kempe, R.S. & Kempe, C.H. (1978), *Child Abuse*, London: Fontana/Open Books.

Kempe, R.S. & Kempe, C.H. (1984), *The Common Secret: Sexual Abuse of Children and Adolsescents*, New York: W.H. Freeman.

Kennedy, M. & Cormier, B.M. (1969), 'Father-daughter Incest: Treatment of the Family', *Laval Medical*, 40, pp. 946-950.

Kerlinger, Fred N., (1986), *Foundations of Behavioural Research*, (3rd. ed.), New York: Holt, Rinehart & Winston.

King, M. (1981), 'Welfare and Justice', in King, M. (ed.), *Childhood, Welfare and Justice*, London: Billing & Son.

Krell, H.L. & Okin, R.L. (1984), 'Countertransference Issues in Child Abuse and Neglect Cases', *American Journal of Forensic Psychiatry*, 5(1), pp. 6-16.

Kubo, S. (1959), 'Researches and Studies on Incest in Japan', *Hiroshima Journal of Medical Sciences*, 8, pp. 99-159.

Kutchinsky, B. (1986), *Consultation on Child Sexual Abuse*, (Copenhagen, December, 1985), World Health Organization.

LaBarbesa, J.D., Martin J.C., Dozier, J.C. (1980), 'Child Psychiatrist's View of Father-daughter Incest', *Child Abuse and Neglect*, 4, pp. 147-151.

Landis, J.T., (1956), 'Experiences of 500 Children with Adult Sexual Deviation', *Psychiatric Quarterly Supplement*, 30, pp. 91-109.

Langevin, R., Day, D., Handy, L., & Russon, A. (1985), 'Are Incestuous Fathers Pedophilic and Agressive?' in Langevin, R. (ed.), *Erotic Preference Gender Identity and Agression*, Hillsdale, NJ: Erlbaum.

Law Reform Commission of Canada (1978), *Sexual Offences*, Ottawa: Canadian Government Publishing Center.

Lea, J. (1985), 'The Criminal Prosecution of Parents', in Besharov, D. (ed.), *Child Abuse Neglect Law: A Canadian Perspective*, Washington: Child Welfare League of America.

Lempp, R. (1978), 'Psychological Damage to Children as a Result of Sexual Offences', *Child Abuse and Neglect*, 2, pp. 243-245.

Lesnik-Oberstein, M. (1982), 'Iatrogenic Rape of a Fourteen-year-old Girl: A Note', *Child Abuse and Neglect*, 6, pp. 103-104.

Levi-Strauss, C. (1969), *The Elementary Structure of Kinship*, Boston: Beacon Press.

Libai, D. (1969), 'The Protection of the Child Victim of a Sexual Offense in the Criminal Justice System', *Wayne Law Review*, 14, pp. 977-1009.

Lukianowicz, N. (1972), 'Incest', *British Journal of Psychiatry*, 120, pp. 301-313.

Lusk, R. & Waterman, J. (1986), 'Effects of Sexual Abuse on Children', in Macfarlane, K. & Waterman, J. (eds.), *Sexual Abuse of Young Children*, London: Holt, Rinehart and Winston.

MacFarlane, K., Jones, B., & Jenstrom, L. (1980), *Sexual Abuse of Children: Selected Readings*, Washington: DHHS.

MacFarlane, K. & Krebs, S. (1986), 'Videotaping of Interviews and Court Testimony', in MacFarlane, K. & Waterman, J. (eds.), *Sexual Abuse of Young Children*, London: Holt, Rinehart & Winston.

Machotka, P., Pittman, F.S., & Flomenhaft, K. (1967), Incest as a Family Affair, *Family Process*, 6, pp. 98-116.

Madge, J. (1965), *The Tools of Social Science*, London: Longmans, Green & Co.

Maisch, H. (1972), *Incest*, New York: Stein & Day.

Malcolm Page (1981), *Report of Panel Appointed by Essex A.R.C. to Consider the Case of Malcolm Page*, Chelmsford, Essex C.C.

Manchester, A.H. (1978), 'Incest and the Law', in Eekelaar, J.M. & Katz, S.N. (eds.), *Family Violence*, Toronto: Butterworths.

Mannarino, A.P. & Cohen, J.A. (1986), 'A Clinical-demographic Study of Sexually Abused Children', *Child Abuse and Neglect*, 10, pp. 17-23.

Martin, J.A. (1984), 'Neglected Fathers: Limitations in Diagnostic and Teatment Resources for Violent Men', *Child Abuse and Neglect*, 8, pp. 387-392.

Martz, H.E. (1979), 'Indiana's Approach to Child Abuse and Neglect: A Frustration of Family Integrity', *Valpariso University Law Review*, 14, pp. 69-121.

Marvasti, J. (1985), 'Fathers Who Commit Incest: Jail or Treatment? Need for a Victim Oriented Law', *American Journal of Forensic Psychiatry*, 6, pp. 8-13.

Masters, R.E.L. (1963), *Patterns of Incest*, New York: Basic Books.

McKenna, J.J. (1974), 'Case Study of Child Abuse: A Former Prosecutor's View', *American Criminal Law Review*, 12, pp. 165-178.

Mehmedagi, A. (1981), *Report of an Independent Inquiry Established by the London Borough of Southwark, the Lambeth, Southwark and Lewisham Area Health Authority (Teaching) and the Inner London Probation and After-care Service.*

Meiselman, K.C. (1978), *Incest*, San Francisco: Jersey Bass.

Messier, C. (1987), *Treatment of Father-Daughter Incest Cases: A Difficult Task*, Comité de la Protection de la Jeunesse, Quebec: Gouvernement du Quebec.

Miller, P. (1976), *Blaming the Victim of Child Molestation: An Empirical Analysis* (doctoral dissertation, Northwestern University), Dissertation Abstracts International, University Microfilms No.77-10069.

Millham, S., Bullock, R., Hosie, K., & Haak, M. (1986), *Lost in Care: The Problems of Maintaining Links Between Children in Care and their Families*, Aldershot: Gower.

Mnookin, R. & Szwed, E. (1983), 'The Best Interests Syndrome and the Allocation of Power in Child Care', in Geach, H. & Szwed, E. (eds.), *Providing Civil Justice for Children*, London: Edward Arnold.

Morgan, J. & Zedner, L. (1992), *Child Victims: Crime, Impact, and Criminal Justice*, Oxford: Clarendon Press.

Mondiale, W.F. (1978), 'Introductory Comments', *Chicago-Kent Law Review*, 54(3), pp. 635-639.

Morgan, J. & Aedner, L. (1992), *Child Victims: Crime Impact, and Criminal Justice*, Oxford: Clarendon Press.

Morgan, P. (1982), 'Alcohol and Family Violence: A Review of the Literature', in *National institute of Alcoholism and Alcohol Abuse, Alcohol Consumption and Related Problems*, (Alcohol and Health Monograph 1) Washington, DC: Department of Health and Human Services.

Morris, P. (1988, July 21), 'Why was DHSS Not Called... Nor Provide Proper Guidance?' *Community Care*, 5.

Morrison, J.L. (1988), 'Perpetrator Suicide Following Incest Reporting: Two Case Studies', *Child Abuse and Neglect*, 12, pp. 115-117.

Morrison, T. (1994), 'Contexts, Constraints and Considerations for Practice', in Morrison, T. Erooga, M. & Beckett, C. (eds.), *Sexual Offending Against Children: Assessment and Treatment of Male Abusers*, New York: Routledge.

Morrison, T. (1997), 'Emotionally Competent Child Protection Organizations: Fallacy, Fiction or Necessity?' in Bates, J., Pugh, R. & Thompson, N. (eds.), *Protecting Children: Challenges and Change*, Aldershot: Ashgate.

Mounsey, J. (1975), 'Offences of Criminal Violence, Cruelty and Neglect Against Children in Lancashire', in Franklin, A.W. (ed.), *Concerning Child Abuse*, Edinburgh: Churchill Livingstone.

Mrazek, P.B., Lynch, M., & Bentovin, A. (1981), 'Recognition of Child Sexual Abuse in the United Kingdom', in Mrazek, P.B. & Kempe, C.H. (eds.), *Sexually Abused Children and their Families*, Oxford: Pergamon Press.

Mrazek, P.B., Lynch, M., & Bentovin, A. (1983), 'Sexual Abuse of Children in the United Kingdom', *Child Abuse and Neglect*, 7, pp. 147-153.

Mrazek, P.B. & Mrazek, D.A. (1981), 'The Effects of Child Sexual Abuse: Methodological Considerations', in Mrazek, P.B. & Kempe, C.N. (eds.), *Sexually Abused Children and their Families*, Oxford: Pergamon Press.

Munro, E. (1998), 'Improving Social Workers' Knowledge Base in Child Protection Work', *British Journal of Social Work*, 28, pp. 89-105.

Nakashima, I. & Zakus, G.E. (1977), 'Incest: Review and Clinical Experience', *Pediatrics*, 60(5), pp. 696-701.

Nash, C.L. & West, D.J. (1985), 'Sexual Molestation of Young Girls', in West, D.J. (ed.), *Sexual Victimisation*, Aldershot: Gower.

National Centre on Child Abuse and Neglect (NCCAN). (1981), *Study Findings: National Study of Incidence and Severity of Child Abuse and Neglect*, Washington, DC: Department of Health, Education and Welfare.

National Council for Civil Liberties (1976), *Sexual Offences: Evidence to the Criminal Law Reform Committee* (Report No.12), London: Author.

National Council of Welfare (1979), *In the Best Interests of the Child: A Report by the National Council of Welfare on the Child Welfare System in Canada*, Ottawa: Canadian Government Publishing Center.

National Society for the Prevention of Cruelty to Children, *Annual Report for 1892-93*, PRO, HO 45/A57406/1.

Nelson, B.J. (1979), 'The Politics of Child Abuse and Neglect: New Governmental Recognition for an Old Problem', *Child Abuse and Neglect*, pp. 99-105.

Newberger, E.H. & Bourne, R. (1978), 'Medicalization and Legalization of Child Abuse', in Eekelaar, J.M. & Katz, S.M. (eds.), *Family Violence*, Toronto: Butterworths.

Ortiz y Pino, J. & Goodwin, J. (1982), 'What Families Say: The Dialogue of Incest', in Goodwin, J. (ed.), *Sexual Abuse: Incest Victims and their Families*, Littleton, MA: PSG.

Oxman-Martinez, J., Rowe, W. & Straka, S. (1998), 'Dichotomy Between Disclosure of Sexual Abuse and the Child Welfare System's Response', *The Social Worker*, (Winter), pp. 56-65.

Packman, J. (1975), *The Child's Generation: Child Care Policy From Curtis to Houghton*, Oxford: Basil Blackwell.

Packman, J. (1986), *Who Needs Care? Social Work Decisions About Children*, Oxford: Basil Blackwell.

Packman, J & Jordan, B. (1991), 'The Children Act: Looking Forward, Looking Back', *British Journal of Social Work*, 21, pp. 315-327.

Pagelow, M.D. (1984). *Family Violence*, New York: Praeger.

Paitich, D., Langevin, R., Freeman, R., Mann, K., & Handy, L. (1977), 'A Clinical Sex History Questionnaire for Males', *Archives of Sexual Behaviour*, 6, pp. 421-435.

Palmer, S. (1989). 'Mediation in Child Protection Cases: An Alternative to the Adversary System', *Child Welfare*, 68(1), pp. 21-31.

Parker, J. (1976), 'The Precultural Basis of the Incest Taboo: Toward a Biosocial Theory', *American Anthropologist*, 87, pp. 285-305.

Parker, J. (1982), 'The Rights of Child Witnesses: Is the Court a Protector or a Perpetrator?' *New England Law Review*, 17, pp. 643-713.

Parsons, T. (1951), *The Social System*, Glencoe, Ill: Free Press.

Parsons, T. (1954), 'The Incest Taboo in Relation to Social Structure and the Socialization of the Child', *British Journal of Sociology*, 5, pp. 101-117.

Parsons, T. (1964), *Social Structure and Personality*, New York: The Free Press.

Parsons, T. & Bales, R. (1955), *Family, Socialization and Interaction*, Glencoe: The Free Press.

Parton, N. (1996), 'Child Protection, Family Support and Social Work; A Critical Appraisal of the Department of Health Research Studies in Child Protection', *Child and Family Social Work*, 1(1), pp. 3-11.

Paulsen, M.G. (1968), 'The Law and Abused Children', in Helfer, R.E. & Kempe, C.H. (eds.), *The Battered Child*, Chicago: University of Chicago Press.

Paulsen, M.G. (1978), 'Incest and Sexual Molestation: Clinical and Legal Issues', *Journal of Clinical Child Psychology* , (Fall), pp. 177-180.

Pelton, L.H. (1981), *The Social Context of Child Abuse and Neglect*, New York: Human Sciences Press.

Peters, J.J. (1976), 'Children Who are Victims of Sexual Assault and the Psychology of Offenders', *American Journal of Psychotherapy*, 30, pp. 398-421.

Peters, S.D. (1984), *The Relationship Between Childhood Sexual Victimization and Adult Depression Among Afro-American and White Women*, unpublished doctoral dissertation, University of California at Los Angeles. (University Microfilms No: 84-28, 555).

Peters, S.D., Wyatt, G.W., & Finkelhor, D. (1986), 'Prevalence', in Finkelhor, D. (ed.), *A Sourcebook on Child Sexual Abuse*, Beverley Hills, CA: Sage.

Pfohl, S. (1977), 'The "Discovery" of Child Abuse', *Social Problems*, 24(3), pp. 310-323.

Pickett, J. & Maton, A. (1977), 'Protective Casework and Child Abuse: Practice and Problems', in Franklin, A.W. (ed.), *The Challenge of Child Abuse*, London: Academic Press.

Pickett, J. & Maton, A. (1979), 'The Multi-disciplinary Team in an Urban Setting: The Special Unit Concept'. *Child Abuse and Neglect*, 3, pp. 115-121.

Pierce, R.L. & Pierce, L.H. (1985), 'Analysis of Sexual Hotline Reports', *Child Abuse and Neglect*, 9, pp. 37-45.

Platt, D. (1996a), 'Conclusion: Does It Ever End?', in Platt, D. & Shemmings, D. (eds.), *Making Enquiries into Alleged Child Abuse and Neglect: Partnership with Families*, Brighton: Pennant.

Platt, D. (1996b), 'Enquiries and Investigations: the Policy Context', in Platt, D. & Shemmings, D. (eds.), *Making Enquiries into Alleged Child Abuse and Neglect: Partnership with Families*, Brighton: Pennant.

Poitrast, P. (1976), 'The Judicial Dilemma in Child Abuse Cases', *Psychiatric Opinion*, 13(2), pp. 23-25.

Pollock, C & Steele, B. (1972), 'A Therapeutic Approach to the Parents', in Kempe, C.H. & Helfer, R.E. (eds.), *Helping the Battered Child and his Family*, Philadelphia: Lippincott.

Porter, R. (ed.), (1984), *Child Sexual Abuse Within the Family*, London: Tavistock Books.

Prison Reform Trust (1990), *Sex Offenders in Prison*, London: Author.

Prison Department Working Group (1989), *The Management of Vulnerable Prisoners,* (Report No.157/22/2), London: Author.

Quebec (1980a), *Department of Youth Protection: History,* Quebec: Government of Quebec.

Quebec (1980b), *Department of Youth Protection: The System of Protection,* Quebec: Government of Quebec.

Quinsey, V.L., Chaplin, T., & Carrington, W. (1979), 'Sexual Preference Among Incestuous and Nonincestuous Child Molesters', *Behaviour Therapy,* 10, pp. 562-565.

Rabb, J. & Rindfleisch, N. (1985), 'A Study to Define and Assess Severity of Institutional Abuse/neglect', *Child Abuse and Neglect,* 9, pp. 285-294.

Rada, R.T. (1976), 'Alcoholism and the Child Molester', *Annals of New York Academy of Science,* 273, pp. 492-496.

Reich, J.W. & Gutierres, S.E. (1979), 'Escape/aggression Incidence in Sexually Abused Juvenile Delinquents', *Criminal Justice and Behaviour,* 6, pp. 239-243.

Rindfleisch, N. & Rabb, J. (1984), 'How Much of a Problem is Resident Mistreatment in Child Welfare Institutions?' *Child Abuse and Neglect,* 8, pp. 33-40.

Roberts, J.C. & Hawton, K. (1980), 'Child Abuse and Attempted Suicide', *British Journal of Psychiatry,* 137, pp. 319-323.

Rochdale Area Child Protection Committee (1993), *Parental Participation in Child Protection Conferences,* Rochdale, Rochdale ACPC.

Rosen, S., Newsom, S., & Boneh, C. (1979), *Protective Service Reports in May 1978: A Preliminary Analysis,* Boston: Commonwealth of Massachusetts, Department of Public Welfare.

Rosenfeld, A., Nadelson, C., Krieger, M., & Backman, J. (1979), 'Incest and Sexual Abuse of Children', *Journal of the American Academy of Child Psychiatry,* 16, pp. 327-339.

Rosenfeld, A.A. & Newberger, E.H. (1979), 'Compassion vs. Control: Conceptual and Practical Pitfalls in the Broadened Definition of Child Abuse', in Bourne, R. & Newberger, E.H. (eds.), *Critical Perspectives on Child Abuse,* Lexington, MA: Lexington Books.

Rosenthal, M.P. (1979), 'Physical Abuse of Children by Parents: The Criminalization Decision', *American Journal of Criminal Law,* 7, pp. 141-169.

Roybal, L & Goodwin, J. (1982), 'The Incest Pregnancy', in Goodwin, J. (ed.), *Sexual Abuse: Incest Victims and Their Families,* Littleton, MA: PSG.

Rush, F. (1980), *The Best Kept Secret: Sexual Abuse of Children*, New York: McGraw-Hill.

Russell, D. (1983), 'The Incidence and Prevalence of Intrafamilial and Extrafamilial Sexual Abuse of Female Children', *Child Abuse and Neglect*, 7, pp. 133-146.

Russell, D. (1984), 'The Prevalence and Seriousness of Incestuous Abuse: Stepfathers vs. biological Fathers', *Child Abuse and Neglect*, 8, pp. 15-22.

Russell, D.E.H. (1986), *The Secret Trauma: Incest in the Lives of Girls and Women*, New York: Basic Books.

Sakheim, D.K. & Devine, S.E. (1992) (eds.), *Out of Darkness: Exploring Satanism and Ritual Abuse*, New York, Lexington.

Santiago, L. (1973), *The Children of Oedipus*, New York: Libra.

Sarafino, E. (1979), 'Estimates of Sexual Offences Against Children', *Child Welfare*, 58, pp. 127-133.

Saunders, E.J. (1988), 'A Comparative Study of Attitudes Towards Child Sexual Abuse Among Social Work and Judicial System Professionals', *Child Abuse and Neglect*, 12, pp. 83-90.

Schetky, D.H. (1988a), 'The Clinical Evaluation of Child Sexual Abuse', in Schetky, D & Green, A. (eds.), in *Child Sexual Abuse: A Handbook for Health Care and Legal Professionals* , New York: Brunner/Mazel.

Schetky, D.H. (1988b), 'Prevention of Child Sexual Abuse', in Schetky, D. & Green, A. (eds.), *Child Sexual Abuse: A Handbook for Health Care and Legal Professionals* , New York: Brunner/Mazel.

Schetky, D.H. (1988c), 'Treatment of the Sexually Abused Child', in Schetky, D. & Green,A. (eds.), *Child Sexual Abuse: A Handbook for Health Care and Legal Professionals*, New York: Brunner/Mazel.

Schultz, L.G. (1975), 'The Child as a Sex Victim: Socio-legal Perspectives', in Drapkin, I. & Viano, E. (eds.), *Victimology: A New Focus, (Vol.IV), Violence and its Victims*, Toronto: Lexington Books.

Schultz, L.G. (1980a), 'Diagnosis and Treatment-Introduction', in Schultz, L.G. (ed.), *The Sexual Victimology of Youth*, Springfield, Ill: Charles C. Thomas.

Schultz, L.G. (1980b), 'Incest: Introduction', in Schultz, L.G. (ed.), *The Sexual Victimology of Youth*, Springfield, Ill: Charles C. Thomas.

Schultz, L.G. (1981), 'Child Sexual Abuse in Historical Perspective', *Journal of Social Welfare and Human Sexuality*, 1, pp. 21-35.

Schultz, L.G. & Jones, P. (1983), 'Sexual Abuse of Children: Issues for Social Service and Health Professionals', *Child Welfare*, 62, pp. 99-108.

Schur, E.M. (1965), *Crimes Without Victims: Deviant Behaviour and Public Policy: Abortion, Homosexuality, Drug Addiction*, NJ: Englewood Cliffs.

Seligman, B.Z. (1950), 'The Problem of Incest and Exogamy: A Restatement', *American Anthropologist*, 52, pp. 305-316.

Server, J.C. & Janzen, C. (1982), 'Contraindications to Reconstitution of Sexually Abusive Families', *Child Welfare*, 61, pp. 279-288.

Sgroi, S. (1975), 'Sexual Molestation of Children: The Last Frontier in Child Abuse', *Children Today*, 4, pp. 18-21.

Sgroi, S. (1982a), 'An Approach to Case Management', in Sgroi, S. (ed.), *Handbook of Clinical Intervention in Child Sexual Abuse*, Lexington, MA: Lexinton Books.

Sgroi, S. (1982b), 'Family Treatment', in Sgroi, (ed.), *Handbook of Clinical Intervention in Child Sexual Abuse*, Lexington, MA: Lexington Books.

Sgroi, S.M., Blick, L.C., & Porter, F.S. (1982), 'A Conceptual Framework for Child Sexual Abuse', in Sgroi, S. (ed.), *Handbook of Clinical Intervention in Child Sexual Abuse*, Lexington, MA: Lexington Books.

Sgroi, S., Porter, F., & Blick, L. (1982), 'Validation of Child Sexual Abuse', in Sgroi, S. (ed.), *Handbook of Clinical Intervention in Child Sexual Abuse*, Lexington, MA: Lexington Books.

Shaughnessy, M.F. (1984), 'Institutional Child Abuse', *Children and Youth Services Review*, 6, pp. 67-74.

Shelton, W.R. (1975), 'A Study of Incest', *International Journal of Offender Therapy and Comparative Criminology*, 19, pp. 139-153.

Shemmings, D. (1996), 'Introduction', in P.att, D. & Shemmings, D. (eds.), *Making Enquiries into Alleged Child Abuse and Neglect: Partnership with Families*, Brighton: Pennant.

Shireman, J., Miller, B., & Brown, H.F. (1981), 'Child Welfare Workers, Police, and Child Placement', *Child Welfare*, 60, pp. 413-422.

Silver, L.B. (1968), 'Child Abuse Syndrome: A Review', *Medical Times*, 96, pp. 803-820.

Silverberg, N.E. & Silverberg, M.C. (1982), 'Meta-abuse: A Pitfall for Child Protection: Abusing Poor Children by Trying to Protect Them', *Child and Youth Services*, 4(½), pp. 133-137.

Simmons, T. (1986), *Child Sexual Abuse: An Assessment Process*, (Occasional Paper Series No.1), London: National Society for the Prevention of Cruelty to Children.

Skinner, A.E. & Castle, R.L. (1969), 78, *Battered Children: A Retrospective Study*, London: National Society for the Prevention of Cruelty to Children'.

Sklar, R.B. (1979), 'The Criminal Law and the Incest Offender: A Case for Decriminalization', *Bulletin of American Academy of Psychiatry and Law*, 7, pp. 69-77.

Skolnick, J.H. & Woodworth, R. (1967), 'Bureaucracy, Information and Social Control', in Bordua, D. (ed.), *The Police: Six Sociological Essays*, New York: Wiley.

Slater, M.K. (1959), 'Ecological Factors in the Origin of Incest', *American Anthropologist*, 61, pp. 1042-1059.

Sloan, Irving, J. (1983), *Child Abuse: Governing Law and Legislation*, London: Oceana Publications.

Smith, P. (1987, August 21), 'A Place of Safety', *New Society*, 81, (No.1286), pp. 18-19.

Smith, R. (1979), *Social Work and Law: Children and the Courts*, London: Sweet & Maxwell.

Smith, S.M. (1975), *The Battered Child Syndrome*, London: Butterworths.

Smith, S. & Noble, S. (1973, November 15), 'Battered Children and their Parents', *New Society*, 26, pp. 393-395.

Snowden, R. (1982), 'Working with Offenders: Excuses, Excuses, Excuses', *Aegis* (Summer), pp. 56-63.

Social Security Inspectorate (1994), *Evaluation Child Protection Services: Findings and Issues. Inspections of Six Local Authority Child Care Services 1993, Overview Report*, London: HMSO.

Solnit, A.J. (1980), 'Too Much Reporting, Too Little Service: Roots and Prevention of Child Abuse', in Gerbner, G., Ross, C.J., Zigler, E. (eds.), *Child Abuse: An Agenda for Action*, New York: Oxford University Press.

Somerville, M.A. (1984), 'Professional Intervention in the Family', in Carmi, A. & Zimrin, H. (eds.), *Child Abuse*, Berlin: Springer-Verlag.

Soothill, K.L. (1980), 'Incest: Changing Patterns of Social Response', in Armytage, W.H., Chester, R.H. & Peel, J. (eds.), *Changing Patterns of Sexual Behaviour*, London: Academic Press.

Spencer, J.R. (1987), 'Child Witnesses,Video-technology and the Law of Evidence', *The Criminal Law Review*, 73 (152), pp. 76-83.

Spencer, J. & Flin, R. (1989), *The Evidence of Children*, London: Blackstone.

Steele, B.F. (1976), *Working with Abusive Parents from a Psychiatric Point of View*, Washington, DC; Office of Human Development/Office of Child Development, Children's Bureau/ National Centre on Child Abuse and Neglect. (DHEW NO. OHD 75-70).

Steele, B.F. & Alexander, H. (1981), 'Long-term Effects of Sexual Abuse in Childhood', in Mrazek, P.B. & Kempe, C.H. (eds.), *Sexually Abused Children and their Families*, Oxford: Pergamon.

Steele, B.F. & Pollock, C.B. (1974), 'A Psychiatric Study of Parents Who Abuse Infants and Small Children', in Helfer, R.E. & Kempe, C.H. (eds.), *The Battered Child* (2nd ed.), Chicago: University of Chicago Press.

Stevenson, O. (1975), *The Social Worker's Responsibility to the Child*, Paper Presented at the Meeting of the British Association of Social Workers, Manchester.

Straus, M.A., Gelles, R., & Steinmetz, S. (1980), *Behind Closed Doors: Violence in the American Family*, Garden City, NY: Doubleday.

Sudnow, D. (1973), 'Normal Crimes', in Rubington, E. & Weinber, M.S. (eds.), *Deviance: The Interactionist Perspective*, New York: Macmillan.

Summit, R. (1986), 'Foreward', in MacFarlane, K. & Waterman, J.W. (eds.), *Sexual Abuse of Young Children: Evaluation and Treatment*, London: Holt, Rinehart & Winston.

Swanson, L. & Biaggio, M.K. (1985), 'Therapeutic Perspectives on Father-daughter Incest', *American Jounal of Psychiatry*, 142, pp. 667-674.

Swift, C. (1977), 'Sexual Victimization of Children: An Urban Mental Health Centre Survey', *Victimology: An International Journal*, pp. 322-327.

Szabo, D. (1958), 'L'inceste en Milieu Urbain', *L'Année Sociologigue, Troisième Série*, 1957-8.

Tamm, K.P. (1965), *Die Unzucht Mit Abhangigen* (174 No.1 st GB), unpublished legal dissertation, Hamburg.

Teebay, P. (1983, May 12), 'Necessary for the Best Outcome', *Community Care*, 27.

Thoburn, J. & Lewis, A. (1992), 'Partnership with Parents of Children in Need of Protection' in Gibbons, J. (ed.), *The Children Act 1989 and Family Support: Principles into Practice,* London: HMSO.

Thomas, B.R. (1982), 'Protecting Abused Children: Helping Until it Hurts', *Child and Youth Services*, 4, pp. 139-154.

Thomas, D.A. (1970), *Principles of Sentencing*, London: Heineman.

Thomas, E.K. (1974), 'Child Neglect Proceedings: A New Focus', *Indiana Law Journal*, 50, pp. 60-81.

Thompson-Cooper, I. (1992), 'Current Trends in the Treatment of Incest Fathers - A Study in Professional Misconceptions', *Paper presented at the annual meeting of the Canadian Psychiatric Association*, Montreal, Quebec.

Thompson-Cooper, I., Fugere, R. & Cormier, B. (1993), 'The Child Abuse Reporting Laws: An Ethical Dilemma for Professionals', *Canadian Journal of Psychiatry*, 38, pp. 557-562.

Tibbits, J. (1977), 'Punishment, Retribution, and Rehabilitation: A View from the Probation Service', in Franklin, A.W. (ed.), *The Challenge of Child Abuse*, London: Academic Press.

Topper, A. & Aldridge, D. (1981). 'Incest: Intake and Investigation', in Mrazek, P.B. & Kempe, C.H. (eds.), *Sexually Abused Children and their Families*, Oxford: Pergamon.

Tormes, Y.M. (1968), *Child Victims of Incest*, Denver: American Humane Association.

Tsai, M., Feldman-Summers, S., & Edgar, M. (1979), 'Childhood Molestation: Variables Related to Differential Impact on Sexual Functioning in Adult Women', *Journal of Abnormal Psychology*, 88, pp. 407-417.

Tufts, New England Medical Centre, Discussion of Child Psychiatry (1984), *Sexually Exploited Children: Service and Research Project*, (Final report for the Office of Juvenile Justice and Delinquency Prevention). Washington, DC: U.S. Department of Justice.

Turbett, J.P. (1979), 'Intervention Strategies and Conceptions of Child Abuse', *Children and Youth Services Review*, 1, pp. 205-213.

Tyler, A.H. & Brassard, M.R. (1984), 'Abuse in the Investigation and Treatment of Intrafamilial Child Sexual Abuse', *Child Abuse and Neglect*, 8, pp. 47-53.

Tzintzis, S (1998), 'Youth Protection Irked by Commission's Study", *The Gazette* (july 18), p. 5.

United Nations (1983), 'Human rights: A Compilation of International Instruments', New York: Author.

'Unjustified Attack on Free Speech', (1993, November 13), *The Gazette*, p. 3.

Uviller, R.K. (1980), 'Save Them From Their Saviours: The Constitutional Rights of the Family', in Gerbner, G., Ross, C.J. & Zigler, E. (eds.), *Child Abuse: An Agenda for Action*, New York: Oxford University Press.

Vander Mey, B.J. & Neff, R.L. (1986), *Incest as Child Abuse: Research and Applications*, New York: Praeger.

Van Ruller, E. (1981), 'The Confidential Doctor in the Netherlands', *Child Abuse and Neglect*, 5, pp. 491-493.

Vernon, J. & Fruin, D. (1985), *In Care: A Study of Social Work Decision Making*, London: National Children's Bureau.

Virkkunen, M. (1974), 'Incest Offences and Alcoholism', *Medicine, Science & the Law*, 14, pp. 124-128.

Walker, N. (1968), *Crime and Punishment in Britain*, (2nd ed), Edinburgh: Edinburgh University Press.

Walmsley, R. & White, K. (1979), *Sexual Offences, Consent and Sentencing*, (Home Office Research Study: 54), London: HMSO.

Walters, D. (1975), *Physical and Sexual Abuse of Children: Causes and Treatment*, Bloomington: Indiana University.

Walter, J.A. (1977), 'A Critique of the Sociological Studies of Approved Schools', *British Journal of Criminology*, 17, pp. 361-369.

Wattam, C. (1992), *Making a Case in Child Protection*, Harlow, Longman.

Weber, E. (1977, April), 'Sexual Abuse Begins at Home' , Ms, pp. 64-76.

Wedlake, M. (1977), 'A Police View of the Present Position', in Franklin, A.W. (ed.), *Child Abuse - Predication, Prevention and Follow-up*, Edinburgh: Churchill Livingstone.

Weinberg, S.H. (1955), 'Incest Behaviour', New York: Citadel.

Weiner, I.B. (1964), 'On Incest: A Survey', *Excerpta Criminologica*, 4, pp. 137-155.

West, D.J. (1987), *Sexual Crimes and Confrontations*, Aldershot: Gower.

Westermeyer, J. (1978), 'Incest in Psychiatric Practice: A Description of Patients and Incestuous Relationships', *Journal of Clinical Psychiatry*, 39, pp. 643-648.

Wheeler, S. (1969), 'Problems and Issues in Record-keeping', in Wheeler, S. (Ed.), *On Record: Files and Dossiers in American Life*, New York: Russell Sage.

Whitehorn, K. (1988, July 10), *Observer*, p. 35.

Wild, N.J. (1988), 'Suicide of Perpetrators after Disclosure of Child Sexual Abuse', *Child Abuse and Neglect*,12, pp. 119-121.

Wilford, M., McBain, P. Angell, N., & Tarlin, S. (1979), 'English Child Protection Legislation and Procedure: An Aid or a Hindrance to the Abused Child and the Family?', *Child Abuse and Neglect*, 3, pp. 315-321.

Will, D. (1983), 'Approaching the Incestuous and Sexually Abusive Family', *Journal of Adolesence*, 6, pp. 229-246.

Williams, M. & Avis, S. (1988), *The Operation of Rule 42 in 1985*, (Draft), London: Author.

Wisconsin Female Juvenile Offender Study (1982), *Sex Abuse Among Juvenile Offenders and Runaways* (Summary Report), Madison, WI: Author.

Wood, S.C. & Dean, K.S. (1984), *Final Report: Sexual Abuse of Males*, Research Project (90 CA/812), Washington, DC: National Centre on Child Abuse and Neglect.

Wright, S. (1991), 'Family Effects of Offender Removal from the Home', in Patton, M.Q. (ed.), *Family Sexual Abuse: Frontline Research and Evaluation*, London: Sage.

Wright, J., Boucher, J., Frappier, J.Y., Lebeau, T. & Sabourin, S. (1997), 'The Incidence of Child Sexual Abuse in Quebec, *paper presented at the 5th International Family Violence Research Conference*, Durham, N.H.

Wyatt, G.E. & Mickey, M.R. (1988), 'The Support by Parents and Others as It Mediates the Effects of Child Sexual Abuse: An Exploratory study', in Wyatt, G.E. & Powell, J.G. (eds.), *Lasting Effects of Child Sexual Abuse*, London: Sage.

Wynne, J. (1989, July 27), 'Have We Yet Learned the Lessons?' *Community Care*, pp. 14-15.

Yorukoglu, A. & Kemph, J.P. (1966), 'Children Not Severely Damaged by Incest With a Parent', *Journal of American Academy of Child Psychiatry*, 5, pp. 11-124.

'Youth Protection Irked by Commission's Study', (1998, July 18), *The Gazette*, p. 5.

Zacharias, Y (1998), 'Is Society's Child Nobody's Child?' *The Gazette,* (June 27), pp. 1, 8.

Zigler, E. (1979), 'Controlling Child Abuse in America: An Effort Doomed to Failure?' in Bourne, R. & Newberger, E.H. (eds.), *Critical Perspectives on Child Abuse*, Lexington, MA: Lexington Books.